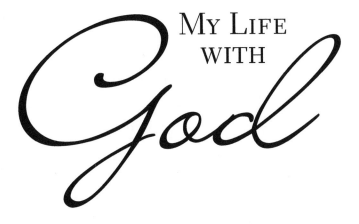

My Life
With
God

A PEDIATRIC SURGEON'S
SUPERNATURAL JOURNEY WHILE
HEALING SICK CHILDREN

JOHN GERARD GALLUCCI, MD

BALBOA.
PRESS
A DIVISION OF HAY HOUSE

Balboa Press books may be ordered through booksellers or by contacting:

Balboa Press
A Division of Hay House
1663 Liberty Drive
Bloomington, IN 47403
www.balboapress.com
1 (877) 407-4847

Because of the dynamic nature of the Internet, any web addresses or links contained in this book may have changed since publication and may no longer be valid. The views expressed in this work are solely those of the author and do not necessarily reflect the views of the publisher, and the publisher hereby disclaims any responsibility for them.

The author of this book does not dispense medical advice or prescribe the use of any technique as a form of treatment for physical, emotional, or medical problems without the advice of a physician, either directly or indirectly. The intent of the author is only to offer information of a general nature to help you in your quest for emotional and spiritual well-being. In the event you use any of the information in this book for yourself, which is your constitutional right, the author and the publisher assume no responsibility for your actions.

Any people depicted in stock imagery provided by Getty Images are models, and such images are being used for illustrative purposes only. Certain stock imagery © Getty Images.

Print information available on the last page.

ISBN: 978-1-9822-2209-3 (sc)
ISBN: 978-1-9822-2211-6 (hc)
ISBN: 978-1-9822-2210-9 (e)

Library of Congress Control Number: 2019902088

Balboa Press rev. date: 03/28/2019

Dedication

My Life with God is dedicated to my nephew Tom Gallucci.

After suffering one terrible medical condition after another for seventeen of your thirty brief years with us, you were finally given your reprieve from pain and suffering. God has taken you home to His world of peace, happiness, and holiness—a world we come from and a world we surely all return to. May God bless you, my dear Nephew. Please pray that we find our lives with God as we each walk our individual paths. May God bless your mother Debbie, father Thomas, and brother Michael Gallucci.

God's love and peace to you!

Love,
Uncle Johnny

Contents

Foreword: In Good Hands

Galaxies are being born and galaxies are dying. This is happening while we live and breathe and move and have our being here on earth. Almost everything in our universe is still a mystery, but Christ's love is real. Life is eternal, and loving one another during our temporary stay here is essential. God is real, and He works in our lives every moment, every millisecond, far beyond time and space. Prayer is tuning into His power and saying, "Thy *will be done.*"

I am an evolutionary biologist by training. My thesis advisor thought it was "sweet" and "quaint" that I believed in God and went to church to praise Him when I studied the lemurs in Madagascar. My best high school teacher, my French teacher and the man who wrote me a letter of recommendation to attend Princeton University in 1992, once walked me to the Princeton chapel after we had shared a breakfast and asked, "You're really going in there now? Like … to pray?" My dissertation advisor at Rutgers University, a man I adore and respect deeply, is a self-described "virulent atheist." My best friend from childhood doesn't believe in God. But my pop did, and my mama does. Pop was a physicist, and my mama is a biologist and artist. For forty years of marriage, they attended Roman Catholic Mass together every Sunday. The other days of the week, they farmed and gardened at home on their sheep farm while they taught science to young minds. It was my father who said, "Work is worship, Kate." And so it goes that I am here today, writing this piece on behalf of the physician who saved my newborn child's life. We live on the remarkable planet we call Earth in a universe where we are each part of a magnificent plan called existence, where time and space are relative, where matter and energy are only partially measurable or explicable, and where God's love is real.

During my sophomore year at Princeton, Professor David Carrasco taught me the Greek word *agape*. It describes the feeling of inexplicable awe one has in confronting the majesty of God. It was at this moment in my life in a lecture hall in 1994 when I realized that the human brain might very well just be a product of biological evolution, completely devoid of any greater meaning, of a Creator, of any life-sustaining loving force, of God. I knew then that it was possible that my love of God might very well just be a product of evolution itself. But I already had twenty years of living behind me, and having since lived twenty more, which is a very brief moment in time in the span of fourteen billion years, I have empirically come to know and love my God, whose love is ever-present, very real, and completely visible and tangible to those who can grow to trust and believe. I thank God every moment of every day that I can embrace this truth.

Our baby boy was born apparently healthy on August 17, 2016. We did not yet know that he had a malrotation and that on August 23, 2016, Dr. John Gallucci would operate to save his life by fixing a volvulus in his intestine while performing a necessary appendectomy that would likely save his life in the future. When Dr. Gallucci told my husband and me that as he had put his hands upon the scalpel, he had asked the Holy Spirit to guide him, I was not surprised. I was grateful but not surprised. I'm never surprised when I hear of God's loving presence working in this world for good. Should I be? I was six years old when I came to really know and love God. This is thanks to my parents, who took me to Catholic Church, and my Waldorf schoolteacher Mrs. Gerry. I was lucky to have been told the story of Jesus. My maternal grandmother Josephine gave me a book that had paintings of Jesus, God, and angels, and I studied it as a little girl. My life has been a wonderful faith journey filled with some legitimate trials and tribulations. However, I am entirely certain that this has all been for a purpose, and that purpose is to grow. I cannot presume to have God's plan all figured out, but I do know that my faith is a gift.

I am not surprised that Dr. Gallucci and I would connect over our faith either. I was overjoyed to meet a physician of such skill who has entrusted his heart to Christ. Love and kindness exude from him as does an air of peace and confidence that defies description. When I looked into my baby boy's eyes at the moment Dr. Gallucci prepared to wheel him away and slice into his abdomen, I knew deep in my soul—inexplicably—that this six-day-old child was in good hands. We use that term lightly, but one's hands can only truly be qualified as *good* if the mind and heart behind them are aligned with love. This doctor's hands were, I knew.

May this book—in *your* hands—serve to deepen your faith to an extent you could never have imagined. May you know fully that your life is in good *hands*, God's hands. May you know God as a living, breathing presence of everlasting love in your life, and may your life be blessed and eternal.

—Katherine Mary Heavers
October 19, 2016

Acknowledgments

A blessing and sincere thank-you to everyone who has ever been a part my life. You are all my teachers, and for that I am profoundly thankful. That being said, I must recognize the following individuals who have played key mentoring and guiding roles in my life and who have directly or indirectly supported my career and/or the writing of this book.

A special thank-you goes out to my early spiritual surgical mentors, Dr. Gus Slotman and Dr. Marc Pello. Gus taught me that praying at work was not only a good idea but that it should be an essential part of every physician's workday … or anyone's for that matter. Dr. Slotman still does outreach work on behalf of those who can't do for themselves. He shares God's love everywhere he goes in Jesus's name.

Dr. Pello had reinforced the importance of prayer and the God connection while at work. I once asked him who he was talking to as we scrubbed for a cancer case. He looked at me and said, "Do you see that man on the table in there? He's somebody's dad, brother, child, husband, or grandfather. We are about to operate on him. I'm praying that God gives us the knowledge, wisdom, and ability to help him the best we possibly can." Drs. Slotman and Pello, you are truly radiating God's light into this world with your good work. God bless you both.

A very special thank-you to Anthony J. Mure, MD FACS. Dr. Mure, you were one of my surgical trauma mentors, but you also showed extraordinary compassion for me when my sister Fran passed during my second year of surgical training. I once asked him that infamous question "Where was God when my sister was suffering and dying?"

Dr. Mure was the very first person in my life who explained to me as he placed his index finger over my heart and said, "John, God is right here, right here in your heart. God may be everywhere, John, but God is in our hearts as well." Your time was too brief with us as you also passed during my surgical training. God bless your soul. I know you watch over us from heaven.

My pediatric surgical mentors—Edward J. Doolin, MD FACS; Thomas V. Whalen, MD FACS; and Michael B. Marchildon, MD FACS— have played a key role in getting me to where I had to be. Thank you for recognizing in me a drive, spirit, and desire that couldn't be quenched. You stood up for me and helped me attain my pediatric surgical fellowship. Thank you all for opening that door for me. It was my destiny *against all odds*, but you made it happen. God bless you for offering an unforgettable and blessed template for my life's path.

A profound thank-you to James B. Alexander, MD FACS. You stood by me through very difficult times as a junior surgical resident. I'm not sure I would have made it through those early days without your mentorship and guidance. God bless you for caring.

With sincere gratitude to the division of cardiothoracic surgery at Cooper University Hospital circa 1988 to 1996. Dr. Anthony J. Del Rossi and Dr. Jon Cilley, your abilities while performing cardiac surgery every day inspired me. When you mentored my performance in your OR, it served to boost my confidence, which was what I needed most. Thank you for your guidance and the confidence you had in me. God bless you for that.

Much gratitude and reverence goes to my pediatric surgical mentors from the Montreal Children's Hospital—Dr. Frank Guttman, MD; Jean-Martin Laberge, MD; Sami Youssef, MD; Luong T. Nguyen, MD; Kenneth S. Shaw, MD; Helene Flageole, MD; and my senior fellowship associate Winston K. Chan, MD. Through your expertise, dedication, and mentorship, you have afforded me a storehouse of knowledge and experience. Thank you for sharing your life's work with me and for reshaping my foibles into fortes.

A very sincere thank-you to my dear friend Rosemary Roche. When I first started at the hospital, I knew nothing about the *system* or the nuts and bolts of the place. You stuck by me and believed in me. You offered countless hours of professional help with committees, presentations, and general how-to issues. Your heartfelt friendship through my good times and difficult times was and still is priceless. God bless you, my dear friend!

Thank you to the families and individuals who gave of themselves by contributing their personal stories to this book through their faith in Jesus. God bless you for your testimony.

Thank you to the family I grew up in—my mom, Catherine Gallucci; my dad, Thomas Charles Gallucci; my brother Tom; my sister Fran; and my cousin Angela DeSimone Slater Esq. Among many other things, Angela got me through the details of properly constructing my endnotes and bibliography as I had no clue. You have all done your part in creating in me a loving and compassionate individual with a ceaseless drive to be the best I can be, know God's truth, and share it with the world.

Thank you to my children—Seth Gerard Gallucci, Arielle Paulina Gallucci, and Gemma Madison Gallucci. I bear witness to your growth and evolution and marvel at how you are all learning from life's challenges. You have all done your part (and still do) in teaching me about life from a father's perspective. May God's peace and love be upon you all the days of your life, and may you always be carried by God's river of love and light.

Thank you to Sandra Johnson—my associate, my living guardian angel, and my Christian spiritual mentor. It was you who urged me to write this book after hearing my stories. Without you, your faith in Jesus, and your faith in me, this book may not have been written.

"A disciple is not above his teacher, nor a servant above his master" (Matthew 10:24 ESV).

May God's love and peace fall afresh on this earth and upon all its inhabitants now and forever.

With much love,
John Gerard Gallucci, MD FACS

Introduction

This book was inspired by God's loving and transformative presence in our lives particularly experienced during times of great human suffering and grief.

The purpose of this book is to *demonstrate* how God does really exist. Not only does God exist, but God will actually live in us and work through us every single day. This book is not a scientific treatise on how God exists. God is beyond science. God is our Holy, metaphysical, supernatural Creator, neither male nor female. God is the magnanimous creative force of pure love energy that imbues life into the universe. Therefore, don't be surprised to know that God is within us all. God's loving Spirit also comes to us from Mother Earth and all her ancient fabrics along with our brothers and sisters of the animal and plant kingdoms that share this planet with us.

To experience God's presence in your life, just allow God's love, light, and energy to live in you. Give God the space and acknowledgment within you that God deserves. Therefore, look within yourselves for the Christ consciousness and nurture it. All you need to do to connect with God is to first allow yourself to see God's work and *remember who you are*, a spark of our divine, loving Creator. In fact, you are a child of God.

God's work is ongoing and will manifest in all of us if we allow it. Once you choose to allow God's love and light to grow in you, then you will radiate love and light back into the world. When you do this, you will change the world you live in. Changing the world from dark to light only requires that you as an individual take on the task. If you are reading this book, then you're well on your way!

The love, light, and energy from God that runs through us, if shared, will in turn run through our brothers and sisters like the Holy Spirit being poured out upon the apostles in the upper room on the very day that is taken to be Pentecost (the birth of the infant church). The same day is also Shavuot on the Hebrew calendar. It commemorates the festival of weeks, which is thought to be the same day God gave the Law to Moses at Mt. Sinai.

Being pure love, God has created us in His image and likeness. Therefore, we are love energy at our core. We are all connected by God's river of love and light. Open your hearts, eyes, and ears to God and see how God works. To best hear the Creator's voice, all you need to do is be silent for a few moments of each day. Sit or meditate in observant silence, and wait on our Lord. Invite the Holy Spirit, God's divine advocate, into your life. You will not be sorry.

Our souls are from God. Therefore, they are perfect! Our souls do not need advancement, growth, or ascension. We come here, however, to do our part in the natural process of advancement, growth, and ascension of humanity. Our physical human form is the lowest expression of our multifaceted being. The agenda is to guide humanity to where it ultimately gets as close as it can spiritually to our highest selves or our God center. There is an initial wide gap between our physical animal nature and our true God center. Through thousands of years of trial and tribulation, humanity will eventually become so spiritually advanced that each of us will directly communicate with God. Remember that God is within us and that we are children of God, so why would it be difficult to imagine direct communication with our Creator?

By my profession I am a pediatric and neonatal general and thoracic surgeon. By the spirit I am a faithful follower of Jesus Christ, a healer, and an empath to my core. I am also a Reiki master and an energy healer. Thus, I approach healing from every angle I can. I in no way believe that being a Reiki master and energy healer is in contradistinction to being a follower of Jesus Christ. Jesus used all the same modalities and much more. Every day and night of my life, I work in service of my brothers and sisters on behalf of our Lord. That's the very purpose of this book—to wake people up to the fact that we are all children of God. God is the Creator of heaven and earth, and we are made in God's image and likeness. Therefore, we are *creators*. Thus, we have created the world we live in. So let's create a much better earth and a much better humanity. God knows we need all the help we can get.

That being said, I am only an imperfect individual who thirsts for heavenly truth and patiently waits on the day of our Lord. Our lives here on earth are truly a gift bringing forth opportunity for tremendous spiritual growth and evolution while in the flesh.

Humanity certainly evolves in a heterogeneous fashion, and we are all at different levels in our advancement. Some of us are at the early stages on these long and challenging roads. Others are here with a bit more evolution under their belts while still others are tremendously advanced. These spiritually advanced individuals may *reincarnate* purely to assist humanity in its evolution and ascension. Many who have been recognized as such through the centuries have been known as saints, sages, and masters.

Certainly, there have been multitudes of good hearts who hold God's love and light yet haven't been recognized for such lofty designations. These people have lived or presently live in obscurity, and yet they still infuse this dark world with their heavenly light. Considering this, I believe we should all want to become saints, but the point of our efforts would be to change the world from darkness to light. In doing so, we will bring the kingdom of God here on earth as it is in heaven by aligning humanity as closely with God as possible.

"No one after lighting a lamp covers it with a basket or puts it under a bed, but puts it on a stand so those who enter can see its light" (Luke 8:16 NAV).

Each of the stories you will read in this book are true accounts of real people and real happenstances. Some of the names have been changed by request in the interest of privacy. Although this book could have very appropriately been titled *Against All Odds*, I believe each story illustrates just what can be accomplished by allowing God's river of love and light to flow through you regardless of how difficult some challenges may seem or how improbable finding a bright silver lining on even the darkest cloud may appear.

After reading this book, you should have a better sense of when and how to let your love shine. Think back to September 11, 2001, and the terrorist attacks in the United States. In the weeks and months following that terrible event, people in many places all over the world acted with love, empathy, and respect toward one another even in places where those feelings weren't typically expressed. It is sad to think that it took such a calamity for people to see one another empathetically. The beautiful feelings that erupted from humanity in the wake of 9/11 sadly didn't last very long.

Just take those wonderful feelings of empathy, respect, and love and use them every day when you walk through your life without any need or expectation of reciprocity. If you allow your heart to lead the way, then you will see the countless opportunities presented to you to go further than you typically do in reaching out to your brothers and sisters. I believe the accounts in this book are examples of exactly that.

Literally, every interaction you have is an opportunity to create a blessing for you and others in your path. Look *within*, and let God's love light shine brightly from you. When you do, watch for the reactions you will get from people. I can remember when I was first getting comfortable with saying to others, "God bless you." At first, I felt like I didn't have the right to say those words. After a while, it began to flow easily and purely. People are often stunned by the gesture. Some turn promptly and say, "Thank you. Thank you so very much!" The next time they see you, the encounter is already on that elevated level, and they also say, "God bless you." Eventually, they also will start saying, "God bless you," to others as you do. It feels good! It's a blessing!

Create blessings every day in your life for others, and you bless yourself in the process. Be that bright lamp shining with God's love on its stand where you are meant to be and for all the world to see! Sharing the love of God becomes addicting and contagious. This is how we change the world one blessed interaction and one loving encounter at a time! God bless you all.

Once on being asked by the Pharisees when the kingdom of God would come, Jesus replied, "The coming of the Kingdom of God is not something that can be observed, nor will the people say, here it is or there it is, because the Kingdom of God is within you" (Luke 17:21 KJV).

May God's grace and peace be within you always.

—John Gerard Gallucci, MD FACS

The next chapter shows how I was given clues all along the way to regard the spirit as my eternal highest self and to think of the physical body as a temple to house that spirit. Sometimes people remind us of this truth, and at other times people may attempt to make us forget this truth in order to weaken us and take advantage of us. When we interact with others, remember to see them as the spirits they truly are and to remember yourself as the same.

Chapter 1

Spiritual Heart and Eyes

For as long as I can remember, I've always seen the world through spiritual eyes. My very first memories are from when I was about six months of age. Most people say they could never remember things that early on, but I believe that many people actually do. They just may not be able to understand and process the memories.

I had many recurring but different visions and lucid dreams as a small child. I used to see myself on a cold table in a hospital. A machine was hanging over me. The walls were light green. There were several people standing around while watching me and what was going on. I can remember a man with a white shirt and rolled-up sleeves and a woman holding me down. I knew that they were caring for me and that what they were doing was desperately needed. I felt safe in their hands. They didn't speak to me, but I could feel their thoughts. They were washing me off with a hose of sorts. They had also inserted a tube into my rectum. I can remember some pain from that tube but nothing else. It was very cold on that table. I can remember my belly feeling full. When they were finished, they cleaned me up, put a dry diaper and blanket on me, and handed me to my mom and dad.

My mom was and still is a strong empath. She didn't say a word, but I could feel her love and her emotions from across the room. I can remember my dad standing at the doorway of this cold room and hiding halfway behind the doorway as if he wasn't supposed to step in. I did see that he was smiling at me and trying to make me smile. Although I was apparently the center of attention and this experience was certainly not pleasant, I could feel the emotions of everyone I was surrounded by. I felt much love. I was not afraid.

I saw this scene over and over again as I went through my childhood. It wasn't until I was in my teens that while we were discussing things like hospital visits, childhood illnesses, and such, my parents told me that I had had intussusception (when the large bowel swallows the small bowel) at six months of age. I needed to go to the hospital, and a radiologist had to insert a tube into my rectum and fill my colon with fluid to fix the intussusception. I never forgot that conversation, and years later after I became a surgery resident, I realized that I indeed had been seeing and reliving the reduction of my intussusception as a six-month-old baby. I could float out of who I was at will and see the scene from a third-party perspective. I never thought anything of this. It's what I always did and often still do.

When I was old enough to understand and learn how to pray, my mom would take the time every night to teach me how to pray and who to pray for. We would start with the Lord's Prayer and then recite the Hail Mary. Then we would bless every single friend and relative we knew by name. God forbid we forgot anyone. We would finish by praying for the whole world to be happy and peaceful. My mom did this with me after she read my brother and me bedtime stories or *Aesop's Fables*. My mom spent lots of time with us. Eventually, I was able to do the whole prayer session by myself. That was probably at about three or four years of age.

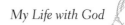

Mom and Dad

My mom and dad lived with their hearts. My dad was the first in his family to go to college. He became a teacher and a coach. My mom went to secretarial school. They both had a profound influence on me in their own ways. Dad was physically very big at six foot three and about 245 pounds. He was a football player. He was well respected in New Jersey scholastic athletics. He instilled in me discipline, duty, responsibility, respect, and love. He also taught me to defend myself when necessary. My mom gave me my sense of empathy. Maybe she was too much an empath and often a doormat for those who were looking to step on others.

I am a natural empath as is my mom, and I've always connected everything to God. My dad was extremely reverent of God, but he didn't express it as emotionally as my mom did. So I always saw people with a spiritual heart and eyes. My parents would naturally reinforce that way of thinking.

Of my own accord, I was keenly aware of the fact that there were good spirits and not-so-good spirits that could be anywhere and at any time. I knew that if I prayed to God and spoke to God, the bad spirits could never get to me. At a very early age, I had refuge in talking to God. There were many times I would look across my bedroom to the curtains and would see large snakes moving along the curtain rod and then down the curtains and onto the floor. They would slowly stalk me as they made their way across the floor and went under my bed. I knew they were evil, and I knew they had a job to do. Their job was to kill me. I would pray myself to sleep often. For sure, everything was better with the morning light.

This was right about the time when I started having dreams and visions of other lifetimes and other dimensions. I saw several of my previous deaths over and over again. There I was—a well-built young man wearing a British Army uniform. It was World War I, and we were in the trenches fighting God knows who. The battle had ended, and the other soldiers and I were talking and assessing what had just occurred. There was a relaxed feeling at that moment. As I stood up, I was hit with an enemy rifle round squarely in the left side of my chest. It knocked me onto my back like a bolt of lightning! I can remember being stunned but having no emotion at all. I collected my wits and sat up. I looked around and realized I had been hit. I didn't know I was dead. I felt no pain and no fear. I looked down at my dark green shirt and saw a hole right over my heart. I pulled my shirt open with my left hand and saw the hole in my chest. I slowly and methodically put my right middle finger into the hole. Blood was on my shirt, chest, and fingers. I looked back at the ground behind me only to see myself lying there dead.

Another very vivid dream I would have was from a completely different time and place. This time I was a skinny male child of about seven years of age. It was somewhere in Southeast Asia or India. I was on a fairly crowded beach with my family and friends. My skin was dark brown as was everyone else's. I could see that I was running around while playing with and chasing other children my age. I wasn't far from my mother at all. We were all having a very good time together.

Then without warning, people started to scream and run frantically away from the ocean. I looked toward the ocean and saw a huge dark wall of water bearing down on us all. I was knocked over by screaming, panicking people running for their lives. I got up and ran for my life while screaming for my mother. I ran as fast as I could, nearing the back edge of the beach when from behind me I was overtaken by the raging, churning water. I was lifted off my feet, tumbled, and was violently rolled repeatedly as I desperately held my breath. I closed my eyes tightly to keep the water out, but my mouth was eventually forced open by the pressure of tons of water crushing the air out of my chest. I started to black out, and soon I was in a silent dream world. No pain. No sound. Just pure white all around me. Done!

Another dream I had many times was of World War II. I was an American airman in a B-17 bomber. I was a side gunner. I remember how cold it was at that altitude and how fast everything would happen once we engaged the enemy ... or rather when the enemy engaged us. I could see the other bombers flying in formation all around us. I could see others being hit and some flipping over and taking out others that weren't hit. Down they would go in fiery, smoky trails. I could feel my machine gun pounding away as I held the handles. The enemy planes we would fire at came by so fast that they were there and gone. It was wild madness. I have no memories of us crashing, just this scene over and over again—complete with the sight, touch, smell, and sounds of the moment. These scenes are forever part of my psyche. I can see them right now as clearly as I did when I had them as a small child. I can smell the dirt in the trenches in WWI, taste the saltwater as it was forced down my throat on that beach, and hear the droning of our engines in that B-17.

My most prevalent vision and lucid dream was of the mountain in the sea. I would transport from my room into a vivid, colorful place that was beautiful, bright, hot, and sunny. I was at the base of a steep, conical mountain surrounded by a beautiful, shimmering blue sea. I was a young adult male who was about nineteen years of age or so. I was with a male friend. We were both very fit and muscular, and we were also very tanned. We had loincloths on and leather sandals that extended up our calves. It was clearly in the Greco-Roman era.

Our quest was to climb this mountain and reach the top. This was no climb for fun; it was a mission of the spirit! The mountain had very large white marble-like blocks for a stairway that went all the way to the top. At about the halfway point, we both stopped to catch our breath and behold the awesome sight afforded us. We were several thousand feet or so up the mountain and thus at the level of the present clouds. We could feel the heat of the sun on our dark skin.

The water was shimmering crystal blue as the bright sun danced off of it. The clouds were white and beautiful as they slowly drifted by us. We would acknowledge our quest and how beautiful it all was. Then we would continue our journey and ascend higher and higher and higher. As we reached the summit, we found a stone altar with a marble floor under it. There was a baptismal pool made of gray granite to the right and a large white columned building about a hundred feet behind it all.

As we approached the altar, we were stunned by a blinding white light that would completely engulf us both. The light was so bright we were lost in it. The vision ends this way every time. The vision is the same over and over again each time I would have it. I would have this recurring vision many times from the age of about two until I was about ten. I wouldn't have that vision again until I was in my fifties.

When I was about five years old, I started having dreams of being in a room with shiny green tiles on the walls. There would be a person lying on a table in the middle of the room. I can remember there being lights that would hang down from the ceiling and shine on the person lying on the table. I was wearing a green cloth gown and had two people with me at the table. I had a small knife in my right hand, and I would slowly and carefully cut the person open from just below the breastbone down to well below the belly button. I can very clearly remember manually wading through and around dilated large-caliber loops of intestines. I could see and feel the fluid and gelatinous debris in the surrounding abdominal cavity. I could feel how sick this person was. I could feel the pain and discomfort although the patient wasn't awake.

I never understood what I was seeing or why. I thought it was just a very weird dream. I was never afraid of what I saw or of what I did. I just didn't understand its significance. I knew what I was doing. I just had no idea why. It wasn't until decades later that I realized I was seeing myself operating on a patient in the operating room. As a five year old, I could see myself performing a perfect laparotomy and running the small and large bowl in this recurring dream. How could I possibly know what this should look like as a five-year-old in 1964?

At about this same age, I had what anyone would consider a very concerning compulsion. My younger sister Franny had several dolls as any two- or three-year-old child would. Some of them had soft rubber heads and limbs, but the bodies were cloth that was stuffed with thick cotton-like material. I would find my mother's sewing kit. I would lay out the scissors, thread, and needles. I would thread the needle with whatever thread I thought would be best. I would then cut open the doll's belly in a perfectly straight line from the top center of the abdomen down to the bottom center just like I did in the dreams. I would pull out all the stuffing, look at it, and put it all back in so that it was a nice fit. Then I would sew the midline incision up with the needle and thread. There! The perfect job!

Tommy, Franny, and me

I did this to several dolls over several weeks as I remember. It was all good as far as I was concerned. Somehow I knew the dolls were better off after rearranging their stuffing than had I not done so. One day I heard my mother screaming like a crazy lady. She was as angry as angry could be, and this was not like my mom at all. I knew this wasn't going to be good, but I was so happy she wasn't angry with me. Then she came running into the room I was in. She screamed at me, "What the hell is this?" as she shook one of the dolls at me!

"What?" I said. Now fear was quickly setting in. She apparently had found my handiwork and didn't like what she saw!

"Who did this? Did *you* do this?"

She was so horribly angry that out of instinctual self-preservation, I blurted out a loud "No, I didn't!"

My older brother Tommy came up behind her, and with a smirk and an accusatory smile, he pointed at me and said, "Yes, he did! He's the one!" My mom looked at me as Caesar would have looked at Brutus just after the stabbing! I let out a yell and started to cry. She slapped me silly, and I ran off to my room, crying bitterly. I didn't know who I was more upset with—my mom for slapping me around or my brother for playing Judas.

Looking back at this bizarre scene, I can only imagine what my mom must have thought. Her sweet little boy was going to grow up to be Jack the Ripper! Who knew back then that from a mostly blue-collar family would come one of New Jersey's top pediatric surgeons? Although I certainly learned my lesson and *never* cut another doll open, I did have that dream of cutting open a patient on an operating table over and over again until I was about thirteen.

By the time I had gotten to mid-grammar school, I was thoroughly into sports. Some sports I excelled in, but I certainly didn't in others. I wasn't very large like the rest of the males in my family, but I had good athletic ability. However, I did lack the confidence that others seemed to drip. When I was playing Little League baseball, I was okay but was unnerved by the pitchers in the league that could really throw that fastball. All I could see was getting nailed by a pitch.

One day before our game started, one of the older kids on the team decided he would give us all a pep talk. His name was Kevin. His dad had been my coach on the minor league team, the Giants. This was now the majors with bigger, faster, and stronger kids. His dad had been my favorite because he was so nice to me. If I struck out, he would encourage me. I needed that.

Mr. Wood had passed from cancer a year or so prior while he was coaching our team. I can remember going to his wake as a seven-year-old. It was my first wake. I got through it with the rest of my team. I was so sad to see him like that. The next game we had just a few days later, a dark cloud hung over the field. I was playing center field. All of a sudden, the clouds parted, and an amazing bright tunnel appeared in the sky that looked like a beautiful walkway cutting through the heavy cloud layer and rose up into the beautiful bright heavens. There were bright sunrays shining down directly onto the field we were playing on.

I was completely stunned! I was absolutely sure that this was Mr. Wood's view of his team playing the baseball game! I'm sure he was looking down on us and watching lovingly! There was no doubt in my mind at all. When the inning was over and we all ran to the bench, I asked the rest of the players what they thought about that amazing cloud tunnel coming down from heaven.

I asked them if they understood that Mr. Wood was watching us from above. Some looked at me like I were completely crazy. Some said, "What tunnel?" Others just looked at me and said nothing. Was I the only one who had experienced that supernatural tunnel with the rays of light beaming down onto the field? Ugh, how could they not have seen it?

Well, back to the majors now. Kevin Wood was pacing back and forth, ranting and raving. Although our coach was there, Kevin assumed the role of the coach for that moment. We were about to face the big, bad Braves. Their pitcher was named Brian, and we all feared his fastball. He was built like a mature man compared to the rest of us and could throw a fastball like a pro! Kevin was trying to rally the troops! The Braves were a better team than us and had only one loss thus far. We were less than five hundred at best. Kevin Wood spoke of *potential*! He told us that all we had to do was really try our best and that we should not hand the Braves the win. We needed to take this game because *we* were going to give it are all!

As he walked along the bench that had been arranged in the batting lineup, he stopped and pointed right at me! I was one of the younger players on the team. He shouted, "Gallucci, you will hit a home run today! Just get up there and keep your eye on the ball and swing for the fences! I have faith in you! You have all the potential, so have faith in yourself! You will do this!" He took my breath away. I looked down at the ground as if to say, "Yes, I will!"

The game started, and we were in for the fight of our lives. In the third inning, the score was 3–2, Braves ahead. I was on deck. Brian threw a wild pitch and nailed our batter in the shoulder. He shook it off and went to first. Now my fear of getting nailed with a fastball was almost out of control. Kevin looked at me and yelled, "Just do it!" I took to the plate and thought of Kevin's dad. "Mr. Wood, I need your help! Kevin says I can do it! I know you think I can! Jesus, help me! I'm scared! God, help me!" Brain wound up and threw a rocket right over the plate! As it came in, I swung as level and as hard as I could. *Crack!* I never saw it. I never felt it! It sailed into the stratosphere over the center field fence and into the sticker bushes! It was an impressive two-run homer! We were ahead 4–3!

Kevin Wood was going wild, jumping up and down. "I told you. I told you!" As I ran the bases, I got emotional and almost started to cry. I thanked Mr. Wood for his help. Then I thanked Jesus for His help. I couldn't believe what had just happened! An inning later I was at bat again. I figured lightning wouldn't strike twice, but I was going to try. I had no fear. I now had the confidence I had never had in my entire life. Kevin looked at me expectantly and said, "Well?"

The pitcher threw a fastball with a vengeance straight over the plate! *Crack!* There went another homer straight and far over the center field fence again! Woodsie was screaming like crazy just as the rest of the kids on my team were. It was now 5–3. Now it was the bottom of the ninth inning, and the score was 7–5. The Braves were winning. It was our last chance. There were three men on base. I was at bat, and the bases were loaded! Brian threw a fastball, and I swung and missed! He threw two balls next, and the count became two and one. I foul-tipped one into the street, and then it was two and two. Oh, and there were two outs. Brian then pitched a third ball, so the count was full now. The tension was as thick as it could be. The pitcher finally threw another rocket right over the plate, and I followed it in and swung like I was going to kill it dead! *Crack!* It was a grand slam homer! Everyone went wild! Brian put his glove up on his head as I ran the bases, bringing in all the runs! What had just occurred went against all the odds!

I thought I was in a dream. It was one of the most amazing events of my life. That unforgettable game took place at Blasi field at the corner of Bradford Avenue and Grove Avenue in Cedar Grove, New Jersey. Years later when I would drive past that field with my small children in the car, I would tell them that this was where I had hit three homers in one game and that the last one had been a game-winning grand slam against the Braves and their feared fastball pitcher.

I'd tell them this several times over the years. Whenever we were about to drive by the field, they would say, "Yeah, we know. Three homers in one game against the Braves." I can't blame them for getting sick of that story. Every time I passed that field, the energy would come back to me, and I'd relive the event.

Well, I know that everything happens for a reason, and by the end-of-the-year all-star game, I was picked to play along with others for our division. Going into the game, I was the leading home-run hitter in the league with seven homers. Not only were my dad and mom there, but so were my grandparents, friends, and siblings. I had a crowd!

The game started with me on the bench. I didn't mind. The game was nine innings long. They'd put me in at some time. By the fifth inning, I was still on the bench. I was a little concerned, but it was no sweat. They had to put the league's home-run leader in the game at some point. They would for sure.

During the seventh inning, I noticed that all the kids who were playing without interruption had fathers who were on our coaching staff. I stood up and grabbed a hold of the chain-link fence so the coaches could see me. They saw me for sure. I felt like a caged animal. I felt anger like never before. One of them looked my way and said, "Yeah, yeah, Gallucci. You're going in next inning." Well, the eighth inning came and went. Now it was the ninth inning, and we're winning by four runs. I was put in the outfield, though I typically played third base. We got three quick outs, and the game was over.

I never got a chance to get up to bat. The coaches' sons all played the whole game. I was beyond mortified. I was so embarrassed. My parents, grandparents, friends, brother, and sister all came to watch me sit the bench. The home run leader sat the bench and never got up to bat. I didn't say a word. On the way home in the car, you could hear a pin drop. Halfway home I said, "Dad, I will never ever play baseball again."

He looked at me, and all he said was, "Yep." Well, things happened for a reason, but I didn't understand that in 1968.

Baseball season was the same time of year as track and field in high school. My dad was a great track and field coach. He had coached a few teams that went to the state championships. I would go whenever I could with him and his Nutley High School team to all their meets. My favorites by far were the weight events. I had a deep inner love for the javelin, hammer, shot put, and the discus. The hammer throw was illegal in New Jersey, so I didn't experience that until college. My favorite event was the discus throw. I would have dreams of throwing in the Olympics. I made a discus at home out of an old sports measuring tape and threw it as often as I could in my backyard. I took books out of the library on the Olympics in both ancient and modern times.

By the time I got to high school, I was a better discus thrower than most upperclassmen but not very big. I would win most dual meets as a freshman. The biggest event of the year for me was the Essex County championships held every year at Montclair High School. Through the years I watched athletes there astound the crowds, and some of those amazing athletes then went on to play high-level division-one collegiate sports and then on to the professional ranks. New Jersey is a very densely populated state, so when you had a championship *anything* going on, it was a high-caliber event. I had the opportunity to compete against several guys who played in the NFL and the NBA.

All year round I would engage in weight lifting with my dear friends Phil DeAngelo and John Sessa. We were more or less the discus relay team for Memorial High in Cedar Grove, New Jersey. I would study the weight events. I would get my hands on loop films of world-class throwers. I would watch the loop films over and over and over until I couldn't see straight. I would visualize my form. I would see myself performing flawlessly in a meet! This is a combination of prayer, the law of attraction, and a technique called psycho-cybernetics. It worked for me. I was investing my heart, mind, body, and soul into this sport. If you love something, how can you not be all in?

Tony Naclerio was a *brother* and coach at Essex Catholic. I asked him for some spiritual advice along with his award-winning coaching techniques. Tony was one of the Olympic developmental coaches. I literally did everything I could to be the very best I could possibly be given the body God had given me. Lots of people thought I was barking up the wrong tree. During my junior year, I surprised many by taking the gold medal! I beat guys who were twice my size and usually threw farther than me.

In my senior year, I was determined to repeat my victory. It meant everything to me! The shot put went off prior to the discus. I threw fifty-one feet! That was my high school best, but because it failed to make the top six for the finals, they didn't record the measurement in the book. I was livid! Who made these rules anyway?

One of my archrivals was a very large guy from Maplewood High named Phil Hartung. He was about six foot six and weighed in at about 240 pounds. I knew we really liked and respected each other deep down. But hey, competition was competition, and this was the Essex County Championships! Phil's dad had been a weight thrower, and so had mine. This was a serious showdown!

After he medaled in the shot put and I didn't, he figured he would try to psych me out for the discus throw coming up. He came up to me and said, "Hey, Gallucci, you're just too damn small and just not good enough to beat me." He laughed in my face. I don't think he had any idea what sore spot he hit with the old "you're too small" comment. It was being the little guy in a large family all over again! Well, that was his miscalculation. It was like Rocky getting his nose broken. Rocky was hit so hard that he would either stay down or … well, you know the rest.

I told my coach George Jenkins what Phil Hartung said to me. Mr. Jenkins looked at me and said, "For the love of God, John, make that guy eat his words!" The field of throwers looked good. There were guys from Livingston, Nutley, Belleville, Essex Catholic, East Orange, Barringer, Bloomfield, Central High in Newark, Westfield, Maplewood, and of course, Cedar Grove. On my first throw, I just needed to put one relaxed good throw out there to assure I was in the finals, usually the top six guys. I did just that. Phil Hartung let loose with a throw you may expect from a guy his size and with his love and dedication to this noble and ancient event. He went into the finals well in first place with a throw of about 171 feet. He continued his psych-out attempts on me.

By the grace of God, I turned his energy into mine. I was stoking a blast furnace deep in my heart. It was my last throw, and I wasn't going to lose to this big guy from Maplewood! *No way.* Besides, all my life I was the runt of my family. I was the small one. I was always in the shadow of very large people. I couldn't let this day end like so many other days routinely did in my life. I wasn't going to take second place to yet another physically large person!

Here's what performing in the Spirit means. I spoke to Jesus and said, "Jesus, my brother! Jesus, my master. Let all that I have put into this event for many years show itself now!" All the heart and effort, the off-season weight lifting, the practices, the loop films, the prayers all had to come together right now in one super Herculean effort! I stared out at the discus sector and its end fence. The fence stood out at about 180 feet along the high school property's border. There had never been anything I wanted more in my entire life than to hit that fence on a fly. The field planners never imagined anyone would ever throw that far. Some had in the past but usually in the warm-ups. Come time for the official throws, most had either thrown themselves out in warm-ups or choked and performed poorly under the pressure.

This moment was all about looking deep within myself. There were no bias Little League coaches to keep me down or on the bench. I had to allow myself to totally let go, trust my inner spirit, and perform maximally and perfectly. An Olympian really competes with him or herself and not the opponent, especially not in this sport. Some performances are flawless while others are not. I calmly stepped into the circle and took my starting position. I went into my relaxed single back windup, and I remember absolutely nothing after that at all. I was being controlled by the Spirit totally and completely. You can call it muscle memory, but it was much more than that. To perform in the spirit, you give your *higher self* the control. You must get out of the way of your God center and let it fly.

The next bit of consciousness I experienced was a loud scream. That's the explosion of physical and psychic energy most weight throwers let loose with just at that ballistic moment of release. Then I pirouetted down to a relaxed and smooth standstill. I looked out into the sky and saw my disc sailing in slow motion. It was so high, maybe too high. If you don't have enough kinetic energy behind a high trajectory, the disc will eventually fall back and not continue to fly and finish its arc of flight.

I was still in a dream world. I could hear nothing and saw only my disc flying. It made the summit of its flight and continued on its flight arc. In the last twenty feet or so of its flight, the scene went into real time, and my disc crashed into the fence on a fly. *Clang!* The metal rim on metal fence snapped me out of my dream. I stood there silent. My whole world stood still. I looked at the official, and he nodded to say, "Good throw. No foul." All I needed to do to make it official was step out the back of the circle the way I came in. Walking out the front is a foul and renders even a world record null and void.

I stood there for a moment, not really comprehending what had just happened. For a second I knew this was a sacred moment in time for me. It dawned on me that the second I left that concrete circle, the moment of a lifetime for me was history! It would be one for the record books.

The rest of my life would come and go—college, career, marriage, children, the passing of loved ones—and this moment would be forever etched in who John Gerard Gallucci was for all eternity. That's how much it meant to me to hit that fence on a fly and win the gold medal again as a senior in high school. It represented my love for my father (my chief mentor), my mother, my brother (a former thrower), my sister who was suffering from brain cancer, my friends, my coaches, my team, my connection to ancient Greece, and God the Father Almighty, who had instilled in me a drive and a spirit that would ultimately prove unbeatable against all odds.

I calmly stepped out from the back of the circle, and every emotion in my body and soul came rushing out of me. I stood there as the officials grabbed the end of the measuring tape and ran it out to the fence. For a thrower there is nothing like the sound of that measuring tape whining and whining as it was run out to where your disc had landed. You want it to never end. You want the tape in the spool to end before they even reach your mark. I watched as numbers flew by my eyes—140, 150, 160, 170, 172, 175, 177. Then the official at the circle called off the number 177 feet and four inches. Extremely close to crying, I ran through the crowd.

I saw my coach Mr. Jenkins. He stood there stunned with a huge smile from ear to ear as I jumped through the air into his arms. I screamed loudly, "I did it! I did it! I hit the fence!"

He screamed, "Way to go, Galluch! Way to go! You showed him! You did it!"

Then we turned toward the circle, and our jubilation was cut short. Phil Hartung had one more throw. Mr. Jenkins and I looked at each other. He raised an eyebrow silently as if to say, "Here we go." The crowd went silent. Phil stepped into the circle and went into deep concentration. I could see the pressure all over him. He went into his spin, and he let loose with an immense throw. Up, up, up it went—up to the summit. Then it came down the other side to continue its full arc. *Clang!* Phil

Hartung had hit the fence. The crowd went wild! The back-and-forth competition between us was remarkable, and the crowd knew it! I was staring at the fence. I started to see that the fence came across the outfield obliquely. In a split second, I knew that where I had hit the fence was farther out than where Phil's disc had hit! They measured Phil's throw. I had won the gold. I was the discus champion of all Essex County for the second year in a row.

I ran through the crowd, hugging and high-fiving my buddies from Cedar Grove and Nutley, where my dad was the athletic director. The statisticians informed me that not only had I won the gold medal but that I had indeed broken the record for the county meet. For all those great throwers who threw off that circle, NFL and NBA athletes, Tony Naclerio's unbeatable Essex Catholic boys, and many others who were New Jersey track-and-field icons who had all inspired me to be like them, I was the best on record! I broke that county record at five foot ten inches tall and 165 pounds. Those guys were all at the top of the hill, the very best of the best, and certainly larger than life for me.

On that spring day in 1978, I had to be perfect and give everything my heart, mind, body, and soul could give. Just like everything else in my life, I lived that entire day and all that was unfolding around me with a spiritual heart and eyes. On that day heaven granted me the grace of God and allowed the Holy Spirit to move in me and control me. Without the Holy Spirit and the grace of God, there was simply no other way an event like that with such an outcome could have ever happened, but it did … against all odds.

"And you shall know the truth, and the truth shall set you free" (John 8:32 NIV).

And we impart this in words not taught by human wisdom but taught by the Spirit, interpreting spiritual truths to those who are spiritual (1 Corinthians 2:13 ESV).

I appeal to you therefore, brothers, by the mercies of God, to present your bodies as a living sacrifice, Holy and acceptable to God, which is your spiritual worship (Romans 12:1 ESV).

"Blessed be the God and Father of our Lord Jesus Christ, who hath blessed us with all spiritual blessings in Heavenly places in Christ" (Ephesians 1:3 KJV).

John Gerard Gallucci and Phil Hartung

Phil Hartung went on to a glorious division-one collegiate career as a discus thrower and weight man. I threw in college as well, but at the division-three level. The collegiate discus gains in diameter and a full pound in weight. That made it essentially impossible for me to keep up with those throwers who were built to be weight men. Phil and I became friends, and we still are. He and I share a great love and respect for the ancient sport of track and field, especially the discus throw. We stay in touch by social media as he lives very far away. I lamented for quite some time that I couldn't keep up with the bigger guys. You see, God gave me that incredible moment for my effort, devotion, and pure love of the sport. God also had other plans for me, and I knew it. I took God with me in every aspect of my life from that moment on. You see, with God, my future would eventually take me places I could never have dreamed.

The Spirit that moves and works in us all also moves and works in our brothers and sisters of the animal kingdom as you will see in the next chapter. Since the beginning of man's existence on earth, animals have shared our lives and have acted as intermediaries between humanity and the Creator. Animals are certainly as capable spiritually as most people. Understand that, and respect it. Regard them as the brothers and sisters they truly are.

Chapter 2

Our Animal Spirit Guides

I have always loved animals. As far back as I can remember, I've always shared my life with animals of every sort. I always knew that animals have souls. They have feelings and emotions and are certainly connected to us in spiritual, emotional, and physical ways. I knew this as a toddler. Nobody needed to tell me about it. Admittedly, some forms of life certainly react more to stimuli by their natures; however, if you just take a good look at the people around you, you will see that many humans act more like reptiles than the creatures in a terrarium.

Tippy and me

Through the years our family had all sorts of pets. Anyone who has loved a pet knows that the relationship is a two-way street of love, energy, and emotions. Most will tell of the love they share with dogs, cats, horses, goats, birds, or any animals that are typically considered human companions. As a child, I even had gratifying relationships with tropical fish that responded to me in ways I couldn't have anticipated. I had a freshwater puffer fish that would signal me to turn on a bubble maker so he could ride in the bubble stream over and over.

As the years passed, I had the benefit of loving many animals ranging from my own pets to many wild beach dogs in the Caribbean. The animals that know you will anticipate your every move and respond accordingly. Some animals can surely premeditate evoking a desired response in you. Your pets will absolutely intentionally manipulate you for their gain. I don't need scientific commentary or affirmation on this.

What I didn't anticipate in my early life was that animals would serve as messengers from God to me. I've seen this written, and I've surely been aware as a child of indigenous people's folklore on totems and spirit animals. Early on, I didn't give this the proper attention and respect.

The classic example for me growing up as a child was Noah on the ark. To me, the ark was all about saving God's innocence in the form of animals. After the rain stopped, they floated around for quite some time without any sign of dry land. Noah prayed and prayed. What message did God send Noah? Noah sent out a raven. The raven flew back and forth until the waters nearly dried up. He then sent out a dove to see if the waters had dried from the surface of the ground. The dove could not find dry land, so it came back into the ark. Noah waited seven more days and once again sent out his dove. This time the dove returned with a freshly plucked olive leaf. Noah waited seven more days and sent the dove out again. This time it did not return. He knew then that there was dry land.

There was a period for me as an adult that could be termed "the dark night of the soul" for several years. There have been several periods of undue stress and angst for me over my lifetime that could have been labeled this way. My marriage had become almost entirely problematic, and along with the stress of work, life was unbearable. At night I would be filled with the stress and frustration of the day, put all three kids to bed, and then go to bed myself. Many times I would either read or play my guitar softly until I was so exhausted I was finally ready for sleep.

When it was time for me to actually turn the lights out and lie down, the following would happen: I would lie down and close my eyes, and as soon as I did, I would see the vision of the inside of a barn. I would always be standing in this large barn on a dirt floor with hay piled up on the right of me. I would look up, and I would see a hay loft across the back of the barn. At the center of the wall up on that loft, there was a large barn door on sliders. The door was a typical barn door with wooden support members that crisscrossed.

I would open my eyes, and I would see that I was in my bedroom. I would close my eyes, and there was the barn and the barn door up above the hay loft. Open my eyes, bedroom. Close my eyes, barn door. This went on for nearly a year. I didn't know what to make of it. I guess I just thought it was my imagination during a very stressful, unhappy time. I really didn't know what to think. It was just always there. I had to figure this out. So I thought, *What's in that barn hay loft?* I hadn't actually thought about making the climb and going in. I was determined to find out.

That night I went to bed, closed my eyes, and bingo! There was the barn door. A ladder appeared leaning against the edge of the hay loft. I climbed the ladder and stood in front of the door. I slid the door open from right to left, and all I could see was pitch black. I needed to step down about two feet onto the floor of the inside of the hay loft. When I did step in, I realized the floor was made of dirt just like the barn floor on the ground. I thought this was interesting considering the loft was about twelve feet off the barn floor.

Well, there I was inside the loft behind the barn door I had seen hundreds of times. I closed the door behind me. It was pitch black. There was nothing. I had no fear. I was just in a pitch-black room with no sight, sound, or smell. Then out of nowhere to my left, I saw a piercing bright light. It was a spotlight like one that shined on an actor doing a monologue on a stage. In that light was a large bald eagle sitting on a perch. I froze, not out of fear but out of complete amazement. I turned to face it square on. It was sitting there in high definition. I looked at it and saw that it was alive and not a facsimile of a bald eagle. It turned its head to look at me better.

I said, "Who are you?"

He looked at me and telepathically said, "Preston."

I know I must have given away my thoughts on hearing that, so I just looked at him and said in a puzzled tone, "Preston?"

He looked at me and repeated to me, "Preston." Then he told me that he was my guide and that I should call upon him whenever I needed him.

All I said was, "Okay." With that, Preston vanished, and I climbed out of the loft. Then I was back in my bedroom.

The next day I went to the bookstore and picked up books on animal totems and guides. I learned that the bald eagle was the chief avian archetype (fundamental pattern of behavior, characteristic, or energy). Preston represented the whole of the energy that was on the wing. The eagle represents many things, but one significant attribute is that they fly very high and can see much more than other avian archetypes and other animals. So the eagle carries with it the attribute of the seer. He is one of my animal spirit guides.

I also have other animal spirit guides that aren't birds; however, the eagle plays a central role in a number of teaching traditions, mainly as a messenger of the Creator. Although a number of birds can fulfill that role from time to time, no other bird can replace the eagle because of its purity of spirit.[1] You can interact fully with your power animal in the spirit world. Each person has a unique power animal, and it will stay with the person throughout his or her entire life, whether the individual knows it or not. You have a power animal.[2]

The very first time to my understanding that I had a learning encounter with a bird was when I was about twenty years of age. My dear friend Tom Mantone and I went up to northwest New Jersey to spend the day in the woods with our shotguns. The main agenda was for us to have fun and shoot at inanimate objects for target practice. Tom was an expert with a shotgun. I saw him shoot a hundred out of a hundred clay pigeons with doubles thrown into the mix. He did that with no difficulty at all. He made it look so easy.

As for me, it looked easy, but somehow I couldn't hit the broadside of a barn. I was remedial. At the end of the day with some adequate sunlight still left, we started walking the half mile or so out of the woods across a large field. It was late autumn, and so the trees were bare.

I looked up and saw a bird fly across the sky and perch itself at the very top of a tree about a hundred yards away. I said to Tom, "Hey, do you think I can hit that bird at the top of that tree?" It was far enough away that I had to show him where it was. He said, "No way. It's too far for a shotgun with bird shot in it." I agreed, but I thought I'd give it a go. I shouldered my Ithaca twelve-gauge and took a look down the barrel, and with no thought of hitting the bird whatsoever, I figured I'd shoot my last round of the day.

Bam! I watched for several seconds as the bird never flinched from its perch. As I knew all along, I was just shooting the last round with no intention of hitting that bird. As I ejected the empty and made sure my gun was now completely unloaded, the bird dropped from the tree. Tom and I looked at each other in amazement. My mind was now racing. *What in God's name have I done?* I hadn't really hit any of the intended inanimate targets all day.

Against all odds I shot at a bird clearly too far away without any intention of hitting, and lo and behold, it was down! As we ran to the tree, I could hear the bird somewhere in the tall grass screaming a distress call. I finally located it and saw what I did not want to see—a small bird with a single small hole in its chest and bleeding. It was clearly mortally wounded and at my hand! My cavalier actions had ended this bird's life!

I had spent many days hunting in those woods with a bow and arrow or a shotgun. I couldn't figure out why I never successfully made a kill. I tried so hard to be a successful hunter. Unlike with a shotgun, I was very good with a bow, so my inability to hit a target with a gun wasn't a problem during deer season. Why could I never make a kill?

This small creature gave me the answer as it lie there protesting its violent, senseless, pending death. A wave of utter remorse filled my heart, mind, body, and soul. I couldn't speak a single word. In my heart I profusely apologized to the bird for causing its suffering and pointless death. That bird was merely doing what all God's creatures did. It was flying around in its environment and had taken a rest at the top of a tree on a clear Saturday afternoon in autumn.

Every action in this world is taken for a reason. Every event that occurs does so to hopefully evoke thought and a subsequent reflection upon the event. Never believe that this isn't so. What could this have been all about?

After thinking and reflecting and praying on this for years, the answer now is clear to me. This small creature was part of a greater scheme, and it taught me a very important lesson. My life would not be about hurting or killing anything. The life that awaited me was one of nurturing and healing for *all* God's creation. That included people and animals alike. It also made me reflect upon free will. Our free will is actually a weapon just as lethal as the twelve-gauge shotgun in my hands. Free will comes with consequences.

Animals and people will both play roles in the evolution of others and teach them the lessons of life. This is at the very heart of the matter in regards to events that befall us and why things really happen. Our interactions with others and animals may leave us with the emotions and experience that often appear hurtful and pointless. I can assure you that there is no exchange that is pointless in your life.

I never hunted again after that event. I'm not suggesting that hunting is wrong or an unworthy endeavor. In no way am I demeaning those who hunt. What I am saying is that hunting or killing animals is not to be a part of my life. This small bird gave its life to teach me a serious life lesson. To miss the significance of what happened is to deny the profoundly spiritual truth behind our interactions with animals. Since ancient times people have known that our relationships with animals is often of a profound spiritual significance.

As for the eating of animals, there is arguably a reasonable and an unreasonable way of going about it. I contend that the modern practices of animal agriculture and the way people have lost touch with the spiritual nature of our relationships with animals is a profoundly unreasonable endeavor. When we disrespect the heart, mind, body, and soul of an animal, we disrespect its spirit. When we do so, we in fact disrespect our own spirit. Thus, we disrespect God.

The next encounter I had with the avian archetype playing the role of messenger happened in 1991. I was driving to work as a general surgery intern in Camden, New Jersey, at about four forty-five in the morning. We routinely put in 120 hours per week. I had fallen asleep at the wheel. While driving under an overpass on Route 38, a pigeon fell from its perch under the bridge and smashed into my windshield. The impact woke me up in time to see the pigeon smash and rebound off my windshield, but I also saw I was heading for the concrete divider. I regained control of my car and proceeded to work safely. That pigeon saved my life.

My next encounter with a bird (namely a dove) happened around the time of my sister's passing, and this experience is covered in the chapter titled Franny.

Nearly nineteen years had passed since my sister Fran's departing of this world. I was divorced from my wife, whom I had been with for more than twenty years. I was keeping company with someone I hoped was sincere in their feelings toward me. Truth be told, I was in a situation that seemed to be causing me far more emotional trauma than good.

The spirit world went into action on behalf of both my friend and me, but it took me a while to catch on. Strange things involving birds began happening. I would be driving along in my car and a bird would fly directly into my driver's side window! When does that ever happen? Many times as I was driving, a bird would fly in front of my windshield and fly with me at about three feet in front of the glass. The bird would fly like that for about ten seconds or so. This unusual event happens often to me even to the present day.

I often told my kids about this strange phenomenon, but I wasn't really sure if they believed me or not. One day while driving with my daughters Arielle and Gemma, a hawk flew directly in front of my window as we drove. I was driving about thirty-five miles per hour, and apparently, so was the hawk. The hawk flew with us for about five seconds as we stared at its beating wings and its tail feathers only four or five feet from our faces. Then the hawk peeled off and disappeared.

Another time on Route 22, I was going about sixty miles per hour, and a hawk flew straight at my windshield and diverted off to my right with what seemed like no room to avoid getting smashed. It scared the daylights out of my daughter Gemma and me. Now my kids believed me.

One day as I walked in a nature preserve in the woods of the town I live in, I looked up out of nowhere, and in the distance I saw a small bird flying through the sky. Time seemed to stand still for me at that moment. I stopped and followed the bird's flight. Why that particular bird? There were several here and there. It seemed like a scene from an Alfred Hitchcock movie. Everything about it was surreal.

Why would I focus on a single bird hundreds of feet away? As I visually tracked this bird, I said the words out loud, "I see you, and I see how beautiful you are. I can see you landed on a branch high in that scrub pine. Through hundreds of branches, I still had a completely clear view of this light green bird and the branch it sat on. I could see it was approaching a nest. I was excited that I had followed the flight of this random bird all the way to its nest.

I said again, "I see you, and you are so beautiful." Then I could see the bird become frantic with fear. It was hopping in and out of its nest, screaming bloody murder. I looked to the right of the nest and could clearly see that its partner was entangled in a spider web. It was fighting for its life. I could see the spider clearly from a good thirty feet down, spinning its web and biting the bird over and over again. I stood there horrified as I watched the methodical murder of the bird's mate by this sinister spider.

Why would I have paid any attention to this specific bird from hundreds of feet away and followed its flight path into the top of that scrub pine. How in God's name would it be that no branch obscured my view of what turned out to be a struggle of life and death, light and dark, good and evil? Both birds were clearly helpless here. I was completely stunned by what I had witnessed. Needless to say the scene disturbed me deeply.

These avian powers are clearly part of my spiritual guidance system. We all have them. You can't see them or benefit from them if you don't believe they exist. I'm not saying that they don't exist if you don't believe. What I mean is that you won't benefit from them if you fail to regard them. Those who deny would simply dismiss this as pure coincidence. Given the turmoil I felt, I understood the message. I knew what I had to do. I decided the time was right to end my relationship. I knew deep down that the relationship was not in the best interests of either of us in the long term. This was not an easy task by any means.

I agreed to meet my friend at a local restaurant not far from our respective homes. I really wanted to avoid having an emotional discussion in public. As I pulled into the parking lot, I saw she was there in her car waiting for me. I pulled up in the next space. She waved me over to her car as if to say, "Let's chat out here." I got out of my car and hopped into her passenger seat. As we spoke, things were tight and emotional as expected during a breakup. Most of us have been through this at least several times.

As the moment heated up, I found myself not completely sure about what I was doing. I had second thoughts. Was I being too hard on her? Was I missing something? I was suddenly full of doubt that I hadn't had the day prior. I needed help and clarity, and I needed it fast! I asked Jesus for wisdom and for the strength to do what I knew I must do. I made my sincere distress call to God silently but also energetically!

All of a sudden, a flock of sparrows came flying over the ridge that separated the parking lot from the street. They made a spectacular circle around our cars and landed on my car just next to us. There had to be easily several hundred birds hopping all over my car. My roof and hood were standing room only. I had never ever seen anything like this before in my entire life.

The birds seemed confused. All at once the entire flock stopped and literally turned toward me and realized I was in fact in the car next to them. They all jumped simultaneously into the air and came down on the car I was actually in. They were all over it, chirping and hopping on their little talons! They looked through the windshield at me as if to say, "We're here! We got this!"

I was completely stunned at what was going on outside the car. My friend just shook her head at me and dismissed the drama going on outside the windshield. As quickly as they all assembled, they jumped up and flew off in a flash. I looked upward through the windshield to follow them. Then I saw six large blackbirds fly over us and land on the electrical wires just above the car. These blackbirds looked down at us just as the sparrows flew off. This was totally amazing. I read the situation as follows:

1) I was in a relationship and suffering badly for it. I was actually sacrificing myself to teach my friend a life lesson. The span of the relationship would bring about a huge positive change for both parties. I was momentarily in need of spiritual help and support, and I asked Jesus for help.
2) Then the spiritual cavalry arrived to do just that.
3) They landed on my car, but I was not in my car. Then they saw me and hopped over to where I was.
4) They were summarily dismissed by my friend.
5) Six large blackbirds appeared on the wires above us. They chased off the army of smaller birds.
6) These blackbirds clearly did not support me.

This was another spectacular play between the light and the dark by my avian guides.

What ultimately came out of this relationship was very positive for me and my friend. My animal spirit guides helped me carry out the plan that best benefitted both of us in the long run. We will always be very dear friends but not a couple. Both of our spiritual gains from this relationship and its closure turned out to be life-changing.

Birds are for sure spiritual messengers and have been recognized as such for thousands of years. Look closely at the encounters you may have with birds and/or other animals, and consider that these were not mistakes and that there was something you needed to learn. God has used all creatures large and small to help humanity along its path.

The late Russell Means, a Native American rights activist and actor, once said that nothing happens by accident. This even extends to the passing of a bird or its shadow across your path. These are considered signs in Native American culture, especially if they are unusual. He tells the following story:

> I lived in a house for eight months that was next to a forest where a very loud hawk lived. Just before I moved out, I explored the forest and visited the hawk's abode, and he made his usual racket. A few days later was my official moving day. As I was standing out in the driveway, he came out over my head and did figure eights over me for a while, singing his farewell song. For the first time he wasn't hundreds of feet in the sky, but was low above my head. It was my last day living there. The next day I had to come back for a few more items. He brought two friends with him—hawks I'd never seen before—and they flew high overhead making noises. It was a memorable bon voyage![3]

Look up Russell Means on YouTube, and assimilate his messages. It will bring insight and blessings to you. In real life, birds seldom speak in audible sentences. But according to the traditional lore of bird medicine, they speak volumes through their songs and motions. These messages are mainly meaningful in relation to the environment and the observer's situation at that time. It could be said that no two bird signs will ever be exactly the same. The variations seem infinite and ingenious.[4]

My other animal spirit guide is certainly the wolf. I have had a fascination with wolves and dogs all my life. I believe my three kids feel the same way. My daughter Arielle recognized our relationship with wolves very early on. As soon as she was old enough to speak in sentences, she began to tell me that she wanted a wolf. I would tell her, "No, sweetheart, we can't have a wolf. We live in New Jersey, and it's not allowed to own a wolf."

After my divorce my kids started in on me about a dog. They all had ideas of their own regarding what kind of dog and what its name should be. I realized it was time. This is right around the same time I got to know my patient Jorge Garrido and his family. (Jorge's story will be covered in another chapter.) When we were so graciously offered one of the husky pups Jorge had bred, I said yes. How could I know that Lucky was a wolf-dog hybrid? He quickly became the love of our lives. I knew that being given a puppy from my dear friends the Garrido family was a big deal. Jorge had bred Lucky and named him just before his passing, and I knew that was an even bigger clue that Lucky was certainly part of a much bigger spirit play. I am not suggesting that you seek a wolf-dog hybrid. They can be unmanageable at best. This is just something that I had no control over.

I didn't understand just how important Lucky was to us all until I realized that he would follow me into the spirit world when I did my meditation healings at night. One night I went into meditation with the agenda of healing several children from work. As I walked up a grassy hill toward a rendezvous site, Lucky came trotting up from my right side and passed me. I was caught off guard by this, but it was no surprise to me at all. I was in my healing dimension, and Lucky was just showing up to be with me. He was not invited by me, and he knew it.

He schooled me right then and there about who had access to the spirit world. He had access. He had always had access. Truly, everyone has access to the spirit world, but you must be in resonance with it. The natural world does resonate with the spirit world, but humans so frequently do not. Being out of resonance with the spirit world is very much a consequence of how we are mentally controlled by the prevailing powers and principalities that surround us.

Access to the spirit world is granted by the power of our Father God, who created both the spirit world and this physical world. Indigenous populations have known this fact and used it through their shamans and medicine men or women for many thousands of years. Lucky is a power animal for me just as Preston is, but Lucky shares my physical life with me too.

There was a time when Lucky was nearly a year old and he took a very negative hit from a dark energy source that was meant for me and my children. As a prayer warrior and healer, it isn't a surprise to be spiritually attacked. Saint Padre Pio was often attacked by dark forces. I was under spiritual attack from a dark force attempting to stop me from healing others.

As this dark force asserted its disruptive energy, Lucky became sicker and sicker. This went on for a week or so. I took me a while to figure out that the spiritual attack and Lucky's sickness were related.

When Lucky's vomiting turned to hematemesis (bloody vomiting), a friend of mine and I rushed him to the local animal hospital. Lucky required an emergency laparotomy (abdominal exploratory surgery) that night. The veterinarian found nothing inside Lucky's abdomen that could explain the vomiting or bleeding. It was a negative laparotomy.

Although I had been praying for Lucky to be well again, this very disturbing happenstance prompted me to pray and meditate on what had happened. I found my answer in the spirit world through prayer and meditation. Needless to say that I removed the source of the negativity and Lucky never threw up again.

If this sounds a bit like shamanism, then so be it. It's my life, and these are the things that occur in it, although I don't consider myself a shaman. Shamans connect with the *source,* and they often do so via animals and the earth itself. This is in no way a contradiction to us connecting to our Creator. In fact, shamanism is all about being connected to our creative force or God.

About two months later, Lucky and I hunkered down with each other during Hurricane Sandy. We were there for each other with no electricity and no heat for three weeks. He grounded me and showed me that this hurricane, which resulted in no power or heat, meant nothing to him. I slept under a buffalo pelt, and he was right next to me the whole time. Lucky didn't need a buffalo pelt, but I did. He acted as though it was all just quality time with Dad.

On one Saturday afternoon about six months after Hurricane Sandy, I had Lucky running around my yard. I was tossing a bone around, and Lucky was chasing it all over. Then he would play keep away from me. As I tossed the bone across the yard, he ran for it and then stopped dead in his tracks. He looked straight up into a completely clear sky and then stood on his hind legs. He began jumping straight up in the air and whining as if he were so desperately trying to touch something or someone who was teasing him playfully and just out of his reach.

He was so entranced by what he saw that he hopped across the yard totally on his hind legs, standing up like a human. He never lost sight of whatever he was seeing. I couldn't see anything at all. *What in the world is going on here?* I thought. Then he hopped all the way to my shed. He stood against it and tried his best to jump up on top of the shed, but that was clearly way out of his reach.

Lucky was staring at something that had clearly engaged him and had slowly moved to the top of the shed. He was obviously happy about what he was seeing. There was not a shred of aggression or hostility in Lucky at all. He stayed focused on the top of my shed for about three minutes or so. Then whatever was there departed. He ran all around the yard, barking at me and trying to tell me what he had witnessed. Dogs can hear sounds at frequencies that are inaudible to humans. Dogs can also see energies that are beyond our range of vision. To this day, I don't know if it was Jorge coming to see him or some other benevolent spirit watching over us both.

Several days later I got a visit from a beautiful spirit as I slept in my room one night. I had finished my prayer and meditation for that night, and it was time to close my eyes. I had a big day at work tomorrow. I went to sleep, but I was awoken by a blinding white light shining in my face. It shone right through closed eyelids and woke me up. Imagine an old World War II searchlight about ten feet in front of you and in your face.

I sat up and opened my eyes only to find my room was as dark as it had been when I fell asleep. I hit my pillow and closed my eyes, and there in my face again was this blinding white light. I rolled to my right side, and it followed me. I rolled onto my left, and it followed me again. Now I'm getting angry because I wanted to be left alone so that I could go back to sleep. I turned over, and then I lay on my stomach. Now the light was behind me, and it was so bright that I couldn't sleep anymore. I jumped up on all fours. I was on my hands and my knees. I opened my eyes, and I could see the area around me illuminated so brightly that I almost couldn't keep my eyes open.

What I did see was the shadow of my head and shoulders on my pillow as this light source shone behind me. I sat up and resigned myself to the fact that I wasn't going to sleep and that this source obviously wanted to get my attention.

Now I was up, and I was not amused at all by what was going on. I spun around on my bed and faced this amazing white light. As I did, it vanished out my bedroom window. I sat there in silence. I was beyond stunned. I knew that some great power much bigger than me had just paid me a visit. I immediately made a connection in my heart and mind that this was the same energy that had been playing with Lucky in the yard.

We decided to get Lucky a friend when he was about one and a half years old. Then Rina, a pure bred husky, came into our lives. She challenged us in every way you could imagine. With the grace and the love of God, it all worked out very well. We couldn't love Rina more, and she certainly loved us. Both dogs clearly had my back here in this physical realm. Lucky, however, had my back in both the physical and spirit realms. He was my guide and my protector from spiritual attack as I did God's work in this world.

To some, the concept of animal spirit guides may seem fanciful or absurd. In fact, the concept and truth behind it is as ancient, as real, and as spiritual as the pyramids of Giza are. The animals guide us and are intentional cast members in God's greater plan.

God created the creatures of the sea, air, and land on the fourth and fifth days of creation, and He created man on the sixth day. God made every kind of wild animal, every kind of tame animal, and every kind of thing that crawls on the ground (Genesis 1:25 NAB).

Then God said, "Let us make man in our image and our likeness" (Genesis 1:26 NAB).

"And Jesus said to the demons, 'Go.' So when they had come out, they went into the herd of swine. And suddenly the whole herd of swine ran violently down the steep place into the sea, and perished in the waters" (Matthew 8:32 NIV).

Animals have sacrificed themselves for us and have been sacrificed by us in many ways from the beginning of man's reign on earth. We must honor them in body and soul and treat them far better than we do, for they are also God's beloved creation.

"And he was in the wilderness forty days, being tempted by Satan, and he was with the wild animals, and the angels were ministering to Him" (Mark 1:13 ESV).

Some Thoughts on Our Friends of the Animal Kingdom

If you talk to the animals, they will talk with you, and you will know one another. If you do not talk to them, you will not know them. And you will fear what you do not know. What one fears, one destroys.[5]

Haven't we already ravaged the earth enough? Think about modern animal agriculture for a few moments. Watch a few YouTube videos on how our brothers and sisters of the animal kingdom are terrorized, abused, unceremoniously killed, parceled, packaged, and shipped off to the market. As consumers, we are completely disconnected from the process in making fish, beef, chicken, pork, turkey, or veal available to us.

In total and stark contrast, indigenous peoples honor the animals and thank them for their sacrifices. They do this as individuals but also through their shamans and medicine women or men. This has been true for thousands of years and is also true today.

How many other people actually pray over their food before they eat it? Far too many don't give it a thought. This is so sad. Consider that the energy of your prayers actually changes the object of your prayers. Look up the rice experiment on YouTube. It turns out if you seal freshly cooked rice in two different jars and pray for one but scream, holler, and curse the other, fungus grows in the ravaged rice, and the rice you honor and pray for remains pure! The *energy of intent* is a very real thing.

I believe much of the sicknesses and diseases in our society come by way of the ravages of modern animal farming. You reap what you sow, and what you give comes back to you tenfold! This does not consider the different drugs we pump into the animals that we consume. Steroids are used to grow the animals so they're ready for market faster and grow to bigger sizes. The antibiotics are needed because of the deplorable conditions the animals are grown in. Farmed fish are often fed chicken feces. It's all about money and the bottom line like the rest of our societies.

In turn, we consume animals that are very poorly treated and completely disregarded spiritually. Our willingness to turn a blind eye to the horrors of how we treat what we eat certainly comes back at us. This speaks volumes about what we have become as people and as a society. We must rethink this whole issue of how we treat what we eat and the lack of gratitude and thanks we give to the animals and to God.

My very favorite YouTube video is titled "AMAZING Adorable girl refuses to eat meat because she likes animals." I recommend you watch this video over and over. Out of the mouth of babes comes a profound truth.

Realizing that visible bodies are only symbols of invisible forces, the ancients worshipped the divine power through the lower kingdoms of nature. The sages of old studied living things to a point of realization that God was most perfectly understood through knowledge of His supreme handiwork as well as animate and inanimate nature. Every existing creature manifests some aspect of the intelligence or power of the eternal one.[6]

Terrestrial animals have always had a strong symbology associated with them. They have represented the emotional side of life, often reflecting qualities that must be overcome, controlled, and/or expressed again. They are also symbols of power that's often associated with the invisible realm that we can learn to manifest within the visible.[7]

To discover your spirit animal and/or totems, meditate on them, and practice the following steps:

1) Relax.
2) Enter a cave or tree in a meditative state.
3) Leave the cave or tree to enter a meadow or natural area.
4) Experience the peacefulness of nature.
5) Allow the totem or animal to enter the scene.
6) Allow the animal to speak to you. Its movement, sound, form, color, and other attributes will give you a message about its power. You may even hear its thoughts in your own. Allow it to tell you or show you how it has helped you in the past and how it will do so in the future.[8]

And God blessed them. And God said to them, "Be fruitful and multiply and fill the earth and subdue it, and have dominion over the fish of the sea and over the birds of the heavens and over every living thing that moves on the earth" (Genesis 1:28 ESV).

Having *dominion* over the animals doesn't mean we should terrorize and mistreat them. We must see and treat them as God's creation. I believe our dominion over the animals is one of humanity's many tests. Every healthy tree bears good fruit, but the diseased tree bears bad fruit (Matthew 7:17). This Bible verse isn't talking about trees. It's a metaphor. What goes around comes around. How we treat our brothers and sisters in the animal kingdom matters a great deal. It shapes the world we live in.

On the third anniversary of my dad's passing, July 11, 2017, I was besieged by birds (spirit messengers) from every direction. Starlings and sparrows flew with me as I drove to work while other birds were dive-bombing my car as I drove. I knew immediately these were messengers telling me that my dad was visiting me for his anniversary. It was breathtaking to witness God's messengers in action. It was such an emotional moment that I had to pull my car over to collect myself.

When I got to the parking garage, I was met by a large crow sitting on the concrete ledge and waiting for me. As I got out of my car, he began pumping up and down while sounding off a greeting. I thanked him for his message and thanked my dad for sending him.

As if this weren't enough, I got a call from my daughter Arielle. She said that Lucky had been barking that morning to call her out of her bedroom. As she and Gemma looked into the second-floor hallway from their rooms, Lucky looked at them and then looked straight up at the skylight in the ceiling as if to say, "Look! Look and see who's here!" To both my daughter's astonishment, there was a beautiful hawk sitting on the edge of the glass ceiling panel and looking down at them. The hawk then walked across the glass panel and stopped at the center of the window to spread its plumage and pose for them. It stayed there long enough for them to take videos and still shots of the glorious event.

Earlier that morning as I walked through the yard to my garden, I heard this beautiful creature up in the tall oaks. I couldn't see him, but he was certainly screeching a greeting to me. Although this was no surprise to me, we were all stunned to know his message was important enough that he subsequently found my skylight and got Lucky's attention, who in turn alerted my girls so that they would bear witness to his spirit message of glory and splendor! Clacking across the skylight and looking down upon them was one thing, but posing with full plumage so that my daughters could take pictures was an unbelievable gift!

Getting in touch with your true spirit allows you to see your animal brothers and sisters as they were meant to be seen. As you regard them spiritually, you must pay close attention and listen to them. They have stories to tell you.

Lucky   Lucky and Rina

Gemma and spirit drums   Dad's messenger

My cardinal messenger

Although our bodies of flesh appear to be all there is while we are in them, they are perishable and are only meant to last for just so long. Our permanent state is that of the spirit. Thus, when the body has served its purpose and falls away, we merely transition back to where we came from, namely a higher existence. Yes, we can still communicate with those still in the flesh if we so choose. The next chapter is all about communication from the other side.

Chapter 3

Walter

Out of undergraduate school, I attended dental school at a major University College of Dentistry in Manhattan. This was my first time living away from home. New York City wasn't far, but it sure felt that way. I had great expectations for this entire endeavor, but I especially couldn't wait for the first day of gross anatomy. There were 146 freshman students, and the gross anatomy lab had about thirty-five cadavers.

A cadaver is a human body that has been procured for teaching and research. It was explained to us that each cadaver had been donated to science. Each one was to have been preserved in formalin for two full years prior to reaching a laboratory. By the time students experience them, they are rubberlike to the touch, and they display a tan-blanched color and have a very heavy formaldehyde stench that certainly lingers in your clothing, skin, and nose. It's always advisable to wear a good pair of exam gloves.

The cadavers shouldn't come with any identification regarding their lives. It's generally all very impersonal—that is, unless you're me. The goal of the class was to teach human gross anatomy (i.e., the visible and ostensible construct of how we are made). We would study one body system after another.

Like any major dental or medical school basic science class, there was the textbook side of the class and the laboratory end of it. The lab is the hands-on part of the teaching experience. By the end of the semester, we should have covered the entire body from head to toe, inside and out, emphasizing great detail in the head and neck. After all, this was dental school. There isn't a great need for a dentist to know the intricacies of the lower extremities.

Day one in that anatomy lab would be indelibly etched in the hearts and minds of all 146 of us. We were given strict rules of engagement regarding the cadavers and how they should and should not be treated. Numbers were assigned to each of us, and those numbers correlated to cadaver tables. This way, we would have the benefit of step-by-step continuous dissection with our own specimens.

We were free to walk around and look at other cadavers and help as we were invited. On test day each cadaver would have several labeled body parts that we would have to identify on a timed basis. The test could have up to two hundred questions. As students, we quickly realized that each body was actually different in its own way. It would certainly behoove all of us to experience and quiz one another on all of them and not just our own. Certain parts dissected on one cadaver could look very different from those in another.

As I got familiar with the look and feel of all thirty-five cadavers, I began to wonder about who they were in life. There were several middle-aged males and some females, some morbidly obese men and women, and also several very aged men and women. There were certainly Caucasians and people of color. There were no children or teens though. We all wondered and discussed what we thought each cadaver's cause of death may have been. I believe that curiosity was just human nature.

The curiosities mentioned were generally irrelevant for the purposes of the class, but we still all wondered about it. With time invested at each table, I couldn't help but feel sad, reflective, and grateful for each and every brother and sister of mine that had been born, lived, reared a family, made friends, and then eventually met with their fate and died, ultimately ending up on these cold, stainless steel tables.

Not a single cadaver came with any life story or markings that could identify who they were—except mine, of course. My cadaver came with a hospital wrist band that had been turned inside out. None of us saw for quite a while that it was, in fact, an ID band with his full name and the hospital he had passed in. My cadaver was an elderly white male, and he looked like he had lived well into his late eighties or nineties when he passed. He was cachectic and basically skin and bones.

Our instructors assured us that none of the cadavers regardless of the cause of death were contagious in any way. As time went on, I found myself doing what came naturally to me. I would have a conversation with my cadaver—silently, of course. How could I not do this? I knew there was life after this world. It never occurred to me that there wasn't. That meant that this man who had donated his body to science was surely aware of me (from afar) and the other students.

I'm sure I would have been laughed out of the lab had I addressed him out loud. I pictured *my guy* Walter as a child up in the Massachusetts rural countryside, probably growing up on a farm. I could see him with his grandparents, siblings, mom, and dad. I could see him playing with the family cats and dogs. I would then see him as a young man with friends. He probably played baseball and maybe football. He had big, strong, calloused hands. I bet he was in the military at one point in his life. Then I imagined him as a married man, a husband and father. As I saw him growing old, I could see how he loved his family and his grandchildren.

Walter was now my friend. The only thing that separated me from him was the veil that separated this life from the next. I prayed for my friend every night. I prayed that he was in God's hands, and I told him that I hoped that he liked what I was doing with his dissection. I promised him that I would take all that I learned from him and put it to good use helping people for the rest of my life.

As the class was coming to an end, months after our first encounter, I was growing sad because Walter would no longer be useful as a teaching specimen. This body that he had so lovingly donated to science had now fulfilled its objective. From the time he was conceived in his mother's womb to the present as a teaching specimen, nearly a century would have passed. Soon there would be no trace of Walter left in this world other than his next of kin. Where was that person? Did his family miss him?

With just several days of class left in that semester and several final exams bearing down on us, the stress levels were high to say the least. Many of us would study all night and skip some classroom time to cram all we could into our brains prior to our exams. All of us were completely exhausted from the rigors of eleven classes going at the same time—physiology, biochemistry, dental materials, and dental anatomy just to name a few.

One late night after walking home from a dental materials lab, I made it back to my building and took the elevator up to my dorm room on the twenty-second floor. I staggered over to my room, set my alarm, and flopped onto my bed. My last thoughts were of being consumed by too many classes and not enough time or energy to assimilate all that was being shoved down our throats. Like many of us, I thought that I didn't know anything and that I was going to get killed on these exams!

I quickly entered that sweet, peaceful, silent, black realm of sleep. At some point thereafter, my consciousness awoke, and I found myself stepping into a scene! I was transported to a beautiful, brightly lit ballroom with a black-tie gala in full swing! It looked like a scene from the very late 1800s or very early 1900s. I took notice of what the guests were wearing. This wasn't a contemporary affair at all. I was there, but nobody there could see me. I couldn't see myself. I could see, hear, and smell the event though. I marveled at the high ceilings with exquisite crystal chandeliers. The entire scene was spectacular! The music was classical, and musicians were performing live!

Everyone was either dancing a waltz in three-quarter time or standing around the perimeter and chatting with champagne glasses in their hands. As I marveled at this scene and moved slowly around the room, I briefly asked myself why I had been transported to such a place and to this particular affair. I was calm and peaceful, but I felt a certain underlying anticipation that something would be revealed to me.

I eventually found myself at a vantage point where I had an unobstructed view of the beautiful dancing at the center of the room and was quite mesmerized by it. I slowly turned my head to the right as if something was willing me to do so. The room was crowded. I saw several men in tuxedos with tails and old-fashioned cummerbunds drinking champagne. There were young and middle-aged men, and they appeared to be in the best shape of their lives and very well groomed.

As two guests parted a bit, there came into very clear view … my cadaver in a tuxedo! He stood there among the other very alive and well-groomed men as if it were business as usual. He stood there as if someone had stuffed his very old, rubbery, cold cadaver into a pressed tuxedo, bow tie and all. I froze for a moment wondering if he would know that I was there. I was staring at his left side, and he looked straight ahead.

As I gazed at him, his cold rubberlike gray body slowly began to reanimate. As he did so, he regained his original height and color. There were scattered silver and gold sparkles emanating from him that were shining so brightly that I had to squint my eyes. The scintillating sparkles multiplied until they completely filled his image.

With the completion of this unbelievable reanimation, Walter stood there, no longer a cadaver. Now he was alive! He was well-groomed and in the best shape of his life. He was clearly among some of his best friends. He looked to be about twenty-two years of age and very happy and healthy.

As I stood there watching this unbelievable transfiguration come to completion, Walter turned to me, looked straight at me, and gave me a big healthy smile as if he had known me for a thousand years. He could see me, but nobody else could. Walter had a full head of flowing blond hair that was slicked back, and he also had smooth perfect skin and a radiance not seen in this realm. He raised his glass of champagne to me and toasted our relationship. He nodded his head and telepathically said the following four words with a beautiful smile from ear to ear: "Thank you. Good job." With that, I was immediately transported back to my dorm room on east Twenty-Third Street in New York City. I sat up on my bed with an energy running through me that I had never experienced before.

I went over and over what I had just experienced. I was stunned yet so full of gratitude that God had granted me a brief moment with my friend Walter. I was transported to the other side. This was no dream. It was a *visitation*. I was given the gift of experiencing Walter in the spirit, the Walter whom God had created to last for all eternity. God bless you, Walter! I will carry the gift of you in my heart forever!

"Truly, truly, I say to you, whoever hears my word and believes him who sent me has *eternal life*. He does not come into judgement, but has passed from death to life" (John 5:24 NIV).

"Who will not receive many times more in this time, and in the age to come eternal life: (Luke 18:30 ESV).

"Keep yourselves in the love of God, waiting for the mercy of our Lord Jesus Christ that leads to eternal life: (Jude 1:21 ESV).

The next chapter shows us that we truly are eternal and that we truly can communicate from either side of life when the love is there to facilitate it. See our existence as eternal. That's exactly what it is!

Chapter 4

Franny

There were three kids in our family—me; my brother Tommy, who was four years older than me; and my sister Franny, who was about two years younger than me. I was the middle child. Although my mom loved us all, my sister was the apple of her eye. Mom had two boys with a dad who was a sports and football coach. And then there was Franny. What's not to love about the only little girl in the house?

There were times when I was very young when I'd have dreams of looking at Franny's photograph in a frame. In the dream I was so sad that she had passed. That's something I never shared with anyone. I didn't know why I had those dreams, but I remember them clearly. They always disturbed me deeply. I didn't want her to die. I used to talk to God and say, "I see that my sister is dead. She left us. I don't like it. I want her back. You can send her back to us now. My mom and dad are sad enough." I was about four or five years old when I had most of these dreams about her.

Franny grew into a physically strong girl. She frequently wrestled with us and our neighborhood friends. She wasn't afraid of any of us, and she was glad to let us know it. Grammar school came and went, and things seemed to be going fairly well for her in high school. She was a twirler, and she had lots of friends. She loved to go skating with us at the South Mountain Arena in West Orange, New Jersey. Franny loved her speed skates. She also went on the winter CYO ski trips to Great Gorge-Vernon Valley Ski Resorts on Wednesday evenings.

Life was going fairly well for my sister until she became a sophomore. Her behavior started to change, and she then suffered her first seizure. Doctors performed tests and diagnosed her with a brain tumor in her right temporal lobe. We were all stunned. The entire extended family and many friends began going to prayer meetings and attending novenas for her. My mom went into permanent prayer mode.

Franny had her surgery to remove the right temporal lobe and its tumor in the summer of 1978. She was sixteen years old. We didn't know what the outcome would be. The night of her surgery, she woke up and spoke to us all. Franny asked us about a party that was set to take place at the town pool. We were all so relieved to see that her recall was good and that she was able to speak.

My father was told several days later that her tumor was cancerous. They called it a high-grade astrocytoma and gave her six months to live. They recommended chemo therapy and radiation treatments. They said it could possibly increase her life expectancy. They also said that if she lived for ten years, they would consider that a cure, but that was very rare.

My dad knew how vulnerable my mom would be to such news. Out of concern for my mom, he never told any of us this information. Right or wrong, he made a decision and went with it. He told us that everything would be okay but that Franny would need treatment and also anti-seizure medication for postoperative seizures. None of us were in the medical field at that time. We were all just so thankful she made it through the operation.

If you were in her presence, you would never know she had been given a diagnosis of brain cancer. She was funny and so very sweet, but she also became very sensitive to physical and emotional stimuli that wouldn't have bothered her prior to her surgery.

As the years went by, it seemed like there was no script left for her life. Everything she tried ended in unfruitful ways. She lost her job at the mall. She rebounded and became a beautician, and she was very good at it. She had that down just great but the chemicals that she came in contact with gave her hands a terrible case of eczema. It was so bad that she often bled from the cracks in her skin. She tried everything, including seeing several dermatologists, but to no avail. Franny had to stop cutting hair. One relationship after the next seemed to let her down and evaporate.

My sister was a gentle soul who eventually became bewildered and at times despondent over how there seemed to be nothing left in life for her. I knew this was going on, and I became very upset for her. I wondered why she apparently needed to suffer as she did for so many years of her young life. I wondered why there was so much suffering and sadness in the world in general.

As a surgeon in training, the trauma center in Camden, New Jersey, had given me a hands-on, up close, in-your-face view of unmatched sorrow, horror, and destruction. There was just too much murder and mayhem to go around. After several years of scooping up brains and blood off the floor of a trauma center, I was becoming more and more certain that nobody was looking after humanity.

The old familiar question would come up over and over in my mind: "If God really did exist, why would He allow such horrible things happen to people?" This was true for the sister I loved dearly and for all the other unfortunates I came across as a surgical resident. I was just about ready to proclaim myself an agnostic (one who doesn't know if God exists).

I traveled to Seattle to present a research paper at a major national surgical conference. A day or so after I flew in from Seattle, my sister was rushed to the hospital. The workup revealed a tumor in her brain stem. How could anything be worse? I guess the statistics were wrong.

Tumor-free for fifteen years apparently meant nothing. Some wanted to biopsy her brain stem while others said not to. This tumor was probably from her prior radiation treatments. Back in 1978, the radiation beam used wasn't as well focused or sophisticated as it is today.

My baby sister had suffered for fifteen years, and now she was going to die a slow, debilitating death. What was fair about this? Anger set in. We did all we could. We took Franny on several trips so that she could enjoy life while we were feverishly researching potential treatments that could possibly change her prognosis. Our cousin Angela took her to California, and we also went with her to Mystic Seaport in Connecticut for a weekend. While we were there, Franny, who had her great sense of humor, bought me and my dad a toilet paper roll insert that would play the tune "Anchors Aweigh" when you dispensed the paper. (Dad had been in the navy.)

By now, my proclamation of agnosticism had completely vanished. I threw myself in front of the Lord! "God, I'll do anything for my sister's life! Take my life, but let her live!" I began what I recognize now as my vision quest or spirit quest. I read every book I could on God, life after death, reincarnation, Buddhism, Jesus Christ, and other similar topics. I was slowly starting to catch on to how God worked and how He interacted with His people through trial and tribulation. This spirit quest was absolutely started because of my sister's illness. The very beginning of my quest spanned form 1978 to 1993. I'm still on that spirit quest today and will be as long as I'm alive.

We were so desperate that we even took her to see a doctor that was in the newspaper for treating brain tumors with shark cartilage enemas. I knew the theory behind anti-angiogenesis, and I read the book *Sharks Don't Get Cancer*.[9] There was nothing else left to try.

I would travel from Camden to Cedar Grove, New Jersey, which was about eighty-five miles, several times each week to reinsert her feeding tube as she could no longer swallow. We couldn't let her starve to death. As a result of all the traveling, Franny and I spent many nights watching reruns of M*A*S*H together on TV to take away our pain and fear of what was to come. We would laugh and laugh for an hour before heading off to bed. These were very sweet and poignant times for us. I would need to get up at three thirty a.m. to get to work by five o'clock at the Hospital in Camden.

Franny was on one of her hospital admissions when a big snowstorm hit the area. I'm not sure how none of us stayed over with her. I think we just didn't buy the forecast. The storm came in hard, and we got nailed with three feet of snow and snowdrifts more than six feet high. People called it the "1993 Storm of the Century" and the "'93 Super Storm."

I felt sick to my stomach that she was in the hospital alone. I prayed to God with everything I had well into the night, hoping that Franny would be okay while alone in the hospital. I literally asked Jesus for a sign that would tell me everything would be okay for the time being. My entire family was praying that Franny would be all right. She was sick enough, and her condition was terminal, so we really didn't know when she might pass.

It was the morning after, but the storm still raged on. I was filled with despair for my sister as I gazed into the storm through the window of my dad's front door. I was lost in the thought of her suffering. Then I saw something out of the corner of my eye. There on my dad's railing leading up to his front door sat a beautiful dove. It was brown with speckles. There was no refuge on that rail for this creature. There was no roof or shelter for it at all. I stood there in total awe of what I was seeing.

In this terrible storm, what on earth would cause this dove to sit on my dad's rail exposed to the high winds, cold, and driving snow? The answer was obvious to me. This dove was God's messenger. I asked God fervently for a sign that Franny would be okay through this storm. God sent us his Holy Spirit in the form of a dove. I burst into tears. I called everyone who may have been awake to come see the dove. My mom saw it for a brief moment, and then it disappeared into the storm.

Traditional Native Americans have considered birds their allies for at least ten thousand years. Birds bring many blessings and play many roles in the life of indigenous peoples and people all over the world. Birds are messengers, healers, communicators, guardians, life-changers, teachers, meteorologists, musicians, storytellers, role models, and so much more.[10]

During one of Franny's last times as a patient at the hospital, I was sure to stay over with her. She was in the ICU. I sat at the foot of her bed, talking to her and giving her a gentle foot message. We talked about lots of things. She was only able to speak a little as a result of high dose steroids she was on to reduce the swelling adjacent to her tumor. I told her how much I loved her. She thought about what I had said and began to cry. She said, "You do?"

I said, "Franny, why would you ask me if I love you? You're my sister. You know I love you."

She looked at me and said, "Well, I guess I know it. But it's so beautiful to hear you say it, and you never say it."

So many things raced through my mind. That very moment of her testimony was stunning and life-changing. I thought of all the times I could have said, "I love you," to my sister but just didn't. I had no real reason. I just didn't. Maybe it was from when we were kids. We just wouldn't say that as kids, and maybe we just carried that bad habit through the years. "What a person desires is unfailing love" (Proverbs 19:22 NIV).

A few days later, we had a hospital room full of friends and relatives. Franny wasn't going to last much longer. That night my cousin Angela and I sat on chairs on either side of her hospital bed. We wouldn't leave her. We were completely spent, but where would we go? As family filed back into her room that morning, my brother Tommy, Angela, and I figured we would go to the coffee shop for a sandwich.

Franny was unresponsive most of the night, but she was still breathing. As we took the elevator down to the coffee shop, the elevator stopped, and the doors opened just two floors below. I looked at Angela and said, "Get off, and go back to her! We'll bring you something to eat." She did so, and we proceeded to the coffee shop. We sat down and had just ordered when the cashier's phone rang. We both knew it was for us. We raced up to the room.

As I entered the room, everyone was just standing there, waiting for someone to help, for someone to just say it. I went to the far side of the bed and approached her from her left. I looked deeply into her eyes as I lifted her lids. Her pupils were fixed and dilated. My sister was gone after all those years! All the fear and the worry, all the nights of suffering for her had just come to an abrupt end.

We always knew this moment would inevitably come. The concept of Franny's eventual passing took on a surreal feeling as though it was just the way it was and that the end would never come. The threat of her passing was like looking at the moon in the night sky for fifteen years and waiting for it to fall. It was always there. It became perpetual for us all.

When Franny passed, it hit like a freight train slamming into a semi. It was done. Franny was actually dead. The moon had finally fallen from the sky. She wasn't coming back ever again. I leaned into her and put my forehead on hers, and all that came out of my mouth was, "Oh, Franny." Then I heard the strangest sound I'd ever heard in my life—the sound of my father sobbing like a baby. That was like nothing I had ever heard before. I didn't know it was possible.

My mom, on the other hand, just stood there on Franny's right side with one hand in the other. She never said a word. She was the woman with a heart of gold that was as big as the sky. My mom, an tremendous empath, never cried a single tear. My mom went into a relative silent, blunted mode that took her years to get through. Twenty-one years would pass before my father would die from leukemia. My dad and sister were my mom's world. To this very day, I have never seen my mother cry a single tear ever.

In spite of my spiritual beginnings as a small child, my sister's passing vaulted me into a spiritual world that I couldn't imagine. When we parked the limousine for her burial at the cemetery, I watched the pallbearers from a distance carry the casket to the grave site. As I watched, the song "From a Distance" by Bette Middler came into my head. I was singing that song in my head as I thought of those appropriate words, "God is watching us. God is watching us … from a distance." As I cleared my head of the tune, the driver started the engine to pull up closer to the grave. When he did so, somebody from the family turned on the radio of the limo. Bette Middler's "From a Distance" started playing on the radio. Was it a coincidence? I don't believe coincidences exist.

One day while at home in Cherry Hill, I found the gag gift Franny had given to me while on a trip to Mystic, Connecticut. The item was designed to play "Anchors Aweigh" when it dispensed toilet paper. I knew well that it hadn't worked in more than a year. Franny had been gone for more than a year and a half by then. As I stood there, all the emotions came crashing back in on me. I started to sob over the loss of my sister. In that moment I relived her life with us through all her joys, sorrows, disappointments, and suffering.

As I stood there sobbing, that musical insert began to play "Anchors Aweigh." It hadn't worked in a long time, and I hadn't even touched it. I stopped sobbing immediately. Franny loved me, and she was telling me she was there. She wasn't gone for good. She was just gone from my physical world. She persisted, and she was making sure I knew it. That gift never made another sound after that moment.

Several months after that incident, I had a stunning and amazing visitation with my sister. I awoke from my sleep to a scene where I was walking on a beach. I came upon a very large and most beautiful sand dune. I climbed up the dune to a wood and wire snow fence at the crest of the dune. The plants on the dune were spectacular. I saw dune grass and beautiful dune flowers of every variety and color. I could smell the ocean and feel the sun on my skin. This was no dream. I was in an alternate dimension for sure. The breeze and the sounds of the ocean were all perfect.

As I gazed over the dune to the ocean, there to my right I saw the most beautiful beach house made of redwood. It had steep vaulted ceilings and high peaks with glass that went all the way to the crests. There was also a large beautiful redwood deck surrounding the house.

What was most interesting was that this gorgeous beach house was on the ocean side of the dunes. In our world, that would not happen at all. The anger of the ocean would destroy the house. The dunes here in our world protect the beach and homes from the rage of the ocean.

I began to float up over the snow fence, and soon I made a gentle landing on the deck of this home. As I gently made my landing, I saw my sister Franny about fifteen feet away and to my right. She walked up to me and gave me a big smile. I said loudly with surprise in my voice, "Franny, what are you doing here?"

She looked at me, wagged her finger, smiled, and said, "Oh, no, no, no. What are *you* doing *here?*" I was on her turf.

She looked absolutely fabulous. She had a new short haircut, and her skin was healthy and a bit sunburned but with a beautiful glow. She had on navy blue gym shorts with a pure white short-sleeved blouse made for a sunny beach day. I also loved her new white sneakers with no socks.

I went on a visitation to my sister in her realm. To make matters more interesting, my dear friend Teddy was there with her on her deck. Teddy and I had been very dear friends back in grammar school, and we had also been lifeguards together at the Cedar Grove Pool in the town we grew up in. Teddy had passed several months prior to Franny.

This visit was such a happy moment for us all, but I couldn't resist asking her how it was dying like she did. She looked down at the deck as she moved her foot back and forth, thinking of how to answer me. Franny looked up at me and said, "It was horrible." Then she smiled a big happy smile and shrugged her shoulders as if to say, "Hey, here I am, and I'm so good!" She then waved to me with her left arm and said jubilantly, "Come see my house!"

The inside of her home was more beautiful than the outside. There were family members and friends inside. Some had passed, and some had not. My dad was there setting the table for a feast. The table was long and made of beautiful heavy timber. It could easily fit thirty people, and it was set along the main front windows overlooking the ocean. The ceiling was steeply vaulted with huge open beams made of redwood. There was a gorgeous forest green tablecloth, and my dad was setting the table with thick bone-colored dishes and silverware. The chairs were high-backed and hand-carved from a dark wood that looked like teak.

I was so very happy and grateful or this visit. I was so thankful to God in heaven that He had granted me the privilege to see that my dear sister and dear friend Teddy were better than just okay. As a matter of fact, they were fantastic! They were in a beautiful realm where there was no pain and no sickness and where the ocean would never rise to destroy my sister's beautiful home.

We were just about to sit down, and I said to her, "Franny, I have so many questions for you."

My dad looked at me and said, "Not now. There will be another time for all that. Leave her alone for now." With my dad's proclamation, I found myself sitting up in my bed in Cherry Hill, New Jersey.

Every so often Franny and I see each other. Sometimes she's the ghost visiting me, and sometimes it's me visiting her realm. Yes, we do traverse the veil that separates us from the other side, where our passed loved ones are. Not long ago while I was asleep, my consciousness brought me to the cocktail hour of a wedding. I was present at the side of the room much like in my visitation with Walter in the previous chapter. I just stood there wondering where the heck I was. I knew this was no ordinary dream. It was a visitation for sure.

As I stood there, I saw my dad, who had passed on about two years ago. His passing hadn't been pretty. He had fought hard for his life against kidney cancer, a lengthy cardiac operation, and then leukemia. When he passed, he weighed less than one hundred pounds. As a younger healthy man, he stood six foot three and weighed 245 pounds. Dad was wearing a beautiful blue blazer with a red patterned tie, white shirt, and tan pants. He looked terrific. He was tan and very healthy. He also had a full head of thick black hair as he did most of his life. He was holding a dish with hors d'oeuvres under his chin with his left hand and stuffing his face with the right hand. That was exactly what he would be doing at a cocktail hour. As he walked past me, he saw me and subtly raised his eyebrow as if to say, "Yup, I see you!" He knew I was totally capable of the visit. Quite frankly, he expected it.

Then I saw an extraordinarily beautiful buffet table adorned with crystal carvings and full of gourmet food items beautifully displayed. There at the end of the table in a gorgeous flowing mauve gown was my sister Franny. She was picking food items with buffet tongs in her right hand and holding a dish in her left. She felt my presence and turned to look over her left shoulder. Franny looked straight at me with her mouth agape as if she were seeing a ghost. I smiled at her from ear to ear as if teasing her as brothers and sisters do.

I miss my sister and my dad fiercely. However, I see them rather frequently. My dad has been showing up in all sorts of dreams and visions quite a bit lately. I'd say I see him at least once a month. Franny and I see each other once every six months or so. We all absolutely know we are part of one another's eternity, and that's a very good feeling. I know for sure where I'm going when I pass.

Recently, I was with my dad. I went to him. He knew I had been lonely and overworked, so he stepped up to give me some encouragement. I found myself in a car with my dad as the driver and me as the passenger. He was taking me to a job site not far from where he lived. My dad always loved woodworking.

When I was about ten years old, my dad remodeled our house in Cedar Grove, New Jersey. He loved the American West and things like cabins and the Ponderosa from Bonanza. My dad transformed our home into a western lodge with hand-carved open beams and a full-length carved mantelpiece over our stone fireplace. I was his faithful helper, but dad was so very creative, artistic, and talented in so many ways.

This job site was in a neighborhood with very large homes. They were arranged around a cul-de-sac with very narrow alleys between the houses. All the garages faced the cul-de-sac, but the front of the homes all faced the water of a beautiful lake or ocean.

As we pulled up to the house, the garage door opened. It was a single-door, four-car garage. The owner came out and greeted us. He wanted to show me what my dad had done on his first floor, which was one floor above the garage. When we ascended to the first floor, I was awestruck! Never have I seen such beautiful woodwork. The entire first floor was one single room with vaulted ceilings and large windows. The whole thing had been clad in my dad's handiwork. I had never seen wood like this before. It had grain and color reminiscent of cedar but even more beautiful. I knew that this wood was not of our world.

My dad was so happy to show me the work he loved so dearly. He also knew clearly that I would revel in his work just as he did. My dad was right where he wanted to be and doing just what he loved to do. He was free to express himself as he saw fit. He was there to manifest his God-given talents and passions all for the benefit of others. That's what my dad was all about.

My sister and dad are happy and in a far better place. I have no fear of death. There is no power or force in this dark world that can alter or detract from God's divine plan. God, our Father, has shown me His salvation and His grace one time after another. My dad and sister certainly led the way for our family. One day I'll be with my dad and sister as often as we please. Expressing your God-given talents and passions is in itself one way of praising the Lord. Glory to God in the highest.

"I consider that our present sufferings are not worth comparing with the glory that will be revealed to us. For the creation waits in eager expectation for the children of God to be revealed. For the creation was subject to frustration, not by its own choice, but by the will of the one who subjected it, in hope that the creation itself will be liberated from its bondage to decay and brought into the freedom and glory of the children of God" (Romans 8:18–21 NIV).

"For God so loved the world, that he gave his only Son, that whoever believes in him should not perish but have eternal life" (John 3:16 ESV).

Who shall separate us from the love of Christ? Shall tribulation, or distress, or persecution, or famine, or nakedness, or danger, or sword? (Romans 8:35 ESV).

But, as it is written, "What no eye has seen, nor ear heard, nor the heart of man imagined, what God has prepared for those who love him" (1 Corinthians 2:9 ESV).

Love never ends. As for prophecies, they will pass away; as for tongues, they will cease; as for knowledge, it will pass away (1 Corinthians 13:8 ESV).

"Do not work for the food that perishes, but for the food that endures to eternal life, which the Son of Man will give to you. For on him God the Father has set his seal" (John 6:27 ESV).

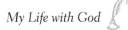

Franny   Franny and Me

Cousin Angela, Franny, me and Tommy

People are connected through love. That love never dies. Thus, relationships and friendships endure forever! As you will see in the next chapter, we do not forget those left behind. Love is a never-ending cycle of giving and taking, receiving and returning. Love never dies!

Chapter 5

Nathan and Grace

My surgical residency was certainly an amazing time in my life. My general surgical residency was six full years of utter inhumane torture and cruelty that nobody should ever be subject to! That being said, I actually miss those crazy days. The Medical Center I trained in was one of several level-one trauma centers in the state of New Jersey at that time. To say the least, we were a very busy place, and that's exactly where you would want to train in general surgery. I truly only have fond memories of my time in training. I guess that's all that really matters. They were very tough years but such a huge positive impression had been left upon me. The cruel punishing times just served to make the good times that much better.

The Medical Center was also a designated regional cardiac surgery center that did about four pump cases each day. There was a fairly busy pediatrics ward, pediatric intensive care unit, and neonatal intensive care unit. We were also a state-designated pediatric trauma center. I can honestly say that I miss the patients, the staff, the nurses, my residency mates, and *almost* all the surgical teaching staff members who trained us.

Our lords and masters (surgical teaching staff) were an interesting bunch of surgeons we either loved or hated with a passion. Some were caring, gentle human beings who wouldn't hurt a fly, were very good at their trades, and really cared about our growth as surgeons and physicians. Others were indifferent to us. Some were scary, powerful, and revered figures of the surgical world, and then there were a few who were clearly psychopaths that apparently got some perverse thrill out of making our lives as miserable as they possibly could in any way they could. They were the minority but indelible all the same.

The residents I trained with had personalities that paralleled those of the attendings in uncanny ways. My residency mates were either my contemporaries, juniors, or seniors and also had the same mental and emotional stratification the attendings did. Some were truly good people, some were indifferent, and some were very nasty, arrogant characters. Some had great surgical ability, and others had very little surgical acumen. All these years later, having trained many surgical residents in many hospitals, I can say this stratification holds true no matter what hospital you may be in. People are people.

I started my internship in general surgery on July 1, 1990. As a medical student at the very same institution, I thought I really knew what would unfold in the event I matched at our hospital for my residency as opposed to somewhere else. In reality, I had no clue. I can remember asking one of the chief surgical residents on day one of internship if I were expected to be in the hospital at work on a Saturday if I wasn't on call that Friday or that Saturday. He looked at me with a look I had gotten only once prior in my life. That other look came from a realtor when I asked her about the steady flow of water that was coursing through the basement of a house she was showing my wife and me at the time. I asked the realtor whether the water was a steady issue or one that came from the recent torrent that the area had experienced over the last three days. She looked at me and said, "Oh, well, think of how great this is! You can grow plants down here all year round, and all you need to do is put the pots right were the water is. Then you never need to water them!" Well, if you ask a really stupid question, you'll get a really stupid answer right back at you. The chief resident said, "Well, I think it's a good idea that you show up and jump in with some of the work just to show that you're a team player. You'll probably leave really early." I thought I saw him roll his eyes as he turned away. The reality was that I was in that hospital every day all day and all night for nearly five months straight. My first day off was sometime in late November.

One of the pediatric surgical attendings whom I grew to love and respect very much saw us so exhausted one day that he gathered us around and asked us if we knew how many hours there were in a week. We all looked at one another like idiots. None of us knew. He dismissed us with a flip of his hand and a chuckle and said, "Well, if you don't know that answer, then you're just not working hard enough. The answer is 168." We all knew it from that point on. It was common place for any of us to work a hundred to 120 hours per week. The good old days.

Some of us fell asleep at the wheel driving to or from work. Once while I was driving home after work, I pulled up to a line of cars at a red light in a snowstorm. I jammed my leg and foot onto the brake pedal, and the next thing I knew a hospital administrator was banging on my driver side window with a look of horror on her face. When the sound of the pounding pierced my deep sleep, I turned my head and looked at her as if to say, "What in God's name are you doing here standing in the snow outside my car?" I rolled the window down. She screamed at me, "Are you okay?"

"Yes. Why?" I asked.

"You slept through two light changes!"

"Oh, my God!" I looked around and then thanked her and drove off. That's just the tip of the iceberg for sure, but somehow I think most surgery residents across America have similar stories. We didn't invent surgical residency cruelty.

When you are on call on any given night, you are responsible for every single surgery and trauma patient in house and on any floor except orthopedics—that is, unless you are on that rotation by day. If you are, then all the patients are your responsibility through the night. During one crazy busy night, I counted nearly two hundred patients that I was covering as I went through my list. All you needed was for one patient to have an issue, and you were dead meat. You were consumed all night with that one patient.

What about the other 199 patients? Oh, let's not forget the consults in the adult emergency room or the pediatric emergency room. They were yours too. New trauma admissions? Yep, yours as well. There were nights we would admit sixteen new trauma patients from the trauma admitting area. Guess where they would go? The worst of them usually went to the ten-bed trauma intensive care unit (TICU). Guess where the TICU patients who were fresh admits the day before would go with each new night? You got it. To the floors of the hospital in general. So trauma patients would end up all over the hospital even on the OB-GYN floor. Thank God things have changed regarding work hours and conditions since I did my training, but I do believe it's a bigger story and a double-edged sword that's beyond the scope of this book.

General surgery residents got really good really fast at responding to issues that adults had. Admittedly, some of us were better, quicker, and more aggressive than others. This is why a surgical residency was anywhere from five to seven years long. Oh, remember, you're supposed to study while all this is going on for the yearly in-service exam. Now that you have all that in hand (or so you think), the beeper goes off, and it's a call from either the pediatrics floor or worse yet, the NICU. The last place most surgical resident want to get beeped to is the pediatric floor or the neonatal intensive care unit (NICU). I think that's because as a surgeon in training, you are so overloaded with all kinds of adult surgical issues that most residents don't really have a clue what to do when faced with a child or a neonate.

One of the most dreaded calls we could ever get as surgical residents was a call from pediatrics regarding certain patients who were chronic repeat admissions. Nathan Fleet was one of those children who would be admitted every so often to our pediatric unit. He was an unfortunate five-year-old who had severe mental retardation, cerebral palsy (MRCP), and cystic fibrosis. Yes, this is a real medical term, and no, I'm not being politically incorrect. He didn't speak as far as we were ever aware. Nathan would get admitted with pulmonary issues that usually required a pulmonary tune-up. This requires that he have a good working IV.

The call usually came because the pediatric residents either couldn't get an IV on Nathan, or more commonly, he would rip his IV out in protest. Then what? Sometimes we would need to disimpact feces he couldn't pass on his own. We all knew him well. That poor child usually felt pretty tortured by the time we got to him. As a consequence, when we did approach him, it was like approaching a panicked wild animal. Poor Nathan would fend us off any way he could. He would bite, kick, scratch, grab, pull hair, and throw feces at us. He did all he knew to keep us away.

For some reason, the pediatrics residents figured we were better at pediatric IVs than they were. I also think no medical or pediatric resident ever disimpacted anyone. They just conveniently figured our fingers were somehow better at it than theirs. They were better than us at pediatric IVs for sure. They did it every damn day.

Several of us had been inducted into that elite group of fearless soldiers who were duly bitten by Nathan or smeared with his feces as they skillfully achieved a good working IV while others held him down. He would come in for his tune-up, get better, and finally be discharged. This cycle was never-ending. I knew him like this for the first several years of my residency. Several months had passed, and I hadn't been made aware that Nathan was in house. It was a conspicuous absence. A month or more passed, and no Nate.

While on the pediatric floor one day, I asked about him, "Hey, where's Nathan Fleet? I haven't seen him in months."

"Oh, didn't you hear? Nathan won't be coming in anymore for his pulmonary tune-up." It turned out that he had somehow slipped past his family, out of the house, and into the street. He was hit by a car and was pronounced dead at the scene.

Nathan, our nemesis, our challenge, the kid we loved to tell stories of heroism about and measure our worth against, was gone. Poor Nathan. God rest his beautiful soul! Some laughed, some cried. I felt great remorse for such a warrior as my little brother Nathan Fleet. The hell he endured on this earth in just five or so years was unparalleled. What that poor soul went through and what we were put through was unspeakable. God had taken him home. I saw it as sorrowful yet merciful all at the same time. I prayed for Nathan for weeks on end after learning of his passing. I wondered where he was and if he ever came back spiritually to the Hospital to visit those who cared for him or some of the other chronic patients who knew him.

The next day I would begin a new rotation. It was back to trauma for me. Somehow I was always put on trauma for June, July, and August. Hey, these were the ungodly crazy summer trauma months in "inner city" New Jersey. If you were going to be on the trauma rotation, you may as well be there when the "you-know-what" hits the fan.

On a rare night off when I was not there and not on call, a woman named Grace came in. She was a middle-aged victim of a severe car crash and rollover. She was in bed one of our trauma ICU. Her internal organs had been so badly injured that after her trauma laparotomy, the team couldn't safely get her abdomen closed because of massive swelling. When this happens, we can employ several techniques to save our patient's life. In one of these techniques, we get a sterile IV bag, cut it open, and use it as an impermeable but temporary patch to close the open abdomen. The bag is transparent, so we can see through it as well. This way we can see the color of the bowel. The bag holds the moisture and liquid in too. As an added benefit, nothing in the patient's abdomen sticks to the plastic. So when we go back to the OR to remove the plastic patch and properly close the abdomen after swelling has lessened, we can easily remove the person's sutures and just slip the bag off. This was how this woman's abdomen was temporarily closed.

She was on the edge of passing every day for weeks. She remained intubated for that time as well. She was as sick as any trauma patient could be. She eventually received a tracheostomy to facilitate her chronic ventilator status. Every day for two months, Grace was my responsibility. I changed her IVs. I changed her central lines on schedule to minimize line sepsis. I would change her abdominal packing, inspect her bowel, irrigate her open abdomen, and place new sterile packing gently on her bowel and other solid organs after her IV bag closure had been removed.

The IV bag used to close her abdomen worked initially, and her abdomen was officially closed. However, she needed to be reopened, and now we were dealing with a long-term chronic open belly. Typically in this situation, the bare bowel and solid organs will eventually granulate and fuse to one another. This is in part how an open abdomen can eventually close, but if you need to get to other deeper areas of the abdomen, you're in big trouble because everything is literally fused together and very bloody. It's nearly impossible to safely operate again on a chronically open, granulating abdomen.

Nearing the end of my three-month trauma rotation, Grace developed a severe upper GI hemorrhage. This complication could be the result of a peptic ulcer or the more dreaded hemorrhagic gastritis that severely physiologically stressed patients could develop. This can occur in spite of state-of-the-art medical prophylaxis that guards against gastritis and ulceration. You can scope a patient with a bleeding ulcer and potentially cauterize the bleeding or use several techniques to stop the bleeding. In hemorrhagic gastritis, the situation is much more difficult. Generally, the entire inside of the stomach becomes one inflamed mess that's granulating and bleeding. You can't cauterize the entire gastric mucosa and hope to stop it from bleeding. The stomach has a very rich blood supply. Many arteries provide overlapping blood flow to the stomach. When hemorrhagic gastritis is severe, one way of stopping the exsanguination is to remove some of or all the stomach. In Grace's case, nobody could get to her stomach because her entire open abdomen had fused solid.

There's an old surgical saying, "All bleeding eventually stops." If *you* can't stop the bleeding, it will eventually stop on its own. That means you've lost the patient! It was going to be one or the other for this patient. The trauma team was well aware of the predicament they were in. I can remember squeezing bags of platelets into Grace with my left hand and a bag of fresh frozen plasma (FFP) with my right. Then I'd give her a bag of packed red blood cells (PRBCs) with the left hand, and this process would be repeated over and over and over.

As my trauma rotation came to an end, I said a very sincere prayer for Grace. I wished her well and hoped that she would survive somehow. When I left, she still had an open abdomen and still required aggressive transfusions and the maximal medical management of her bleeding diathesis. The odds of her surviving were not great.

About three months had passed since I had left the trauma unit. I was on call one night, and the surgical trauma floor called me for a routine Tylenol order at nearly midnight. I called the nurse and gave her a hard time for calling me at that time for that type of order. We all knew one another well, so it was all in good fun. I was busy, so I said I'd be up in about thirty minutes. When I arrived, I asked sarcastically why they hadn't seen that this patient didn't have a Tylenol order hours ago. The nurse jokingly shoved the chart into my stomach and said, "Here. Just do your damn job please, and leave me to reading the *Enquirer*!"

"Ha! Okay, but who's this patient? Tell me something about them please."

This woman was in an MVA (motor vehicle accident), and she'd had a laparotomy, an open abdomen, and a tracheostomy. She'd come out here about a week or so ago from TICU. Well, it was almost one in the morning, and months had passed since I left the trauma service. Many things had filled my life since then. I wasn't thinking about Grace Carry, but could it be? I thought she was surely dead. I opened the chart and saw her name. It was her. I threw the chart on the counter and did a

71

quick step for the room. I entered, and I saw her in the glow of the TV screen—Grace Carry!

I wanted to genuflect! I wanted to burst into tears. I felt as though I was entering a sacred space. I knocked gently on the door. "Hello," I said. "Mrs. Carry?"

She turned her head and said, "Yes? Come in." I approached her and couldn't believe my eyes. There she was, alive, watching late-night TV. She didn't have a tracheostomy either. I asked her if I could turn the light on. She said, "Yes, of course you can." I was looking into the face of an angel. I couldn't believe what or who I was seeing.

"Mrs. Carry, I'm Dr. Gallucci from the trauma team. Do you remember me?"

She looked at me and smiled and said, "No, sweetheart, I don't remember you."

"That's okay, Mrs. Carry, I remember you so very well. Frankly, the last time I saw you, you were so sick I didn't know—"

She interrupted, "Yes, so they tell me. I was in a terrible accident. I remember nothing of it at all."

I asked her if I could pull up a chair so that we could chat for a bit. She said that would be fine. So I slid a chair over and sat next to her. I swear I felt like I was sitting with a relative. I felt at home with her. I told her how we took care of her for months in the TICU and some of the things that had happened. Just as we were getting to some interesting things, my beeper went off, and I was called away with an emergency. I asked her if I could come back the next day to chat some more. She said she would like that very much.

Two days later I found some downtime, so I went back to see her. She smiled and said she didn't think I was coming back. I apologized, and she said she wanted to finish the conversation we started the other night.

I asked her what she remembered of the whole incident, particularly her time in the TICU when she was so deathly ill. She told me that she remembered that every time she looked to the wall on her right (and there was one), she could see her beautiful meadow and the garden she cared for at home. She said, "I was actually there, but I couldn't walk to it." She could see it, smell the soil and the flowers, and even feel the breeze on her face.

She then told me that she found herself several times walking through the halls of a school. She told me that she was a teacher but that this wasn't her school. She would walk to a classroom, and she would see another teacher she knew. To see him, she would have to look through a glass and wire window on a wooden classroom door like so many older schools have. She would try to open the door to go to him, but the door would not open for her. He saw that she wanted to join him in his teaching, but he would hold up a Bible and gesture to her that she couldn't come in right now. He was saying, "Grace, go back. It's not your time to come here and teach with me yet. It's not your time." He would smile and then turn away. The vision would then end.

She didn't know what to make of this vision. She said that it all seemed so real as if she were really there. She got very sad as she related this story to me. I asked her why she was so sad, and she said that the man in the classroom was in fact a beloved coworker of hers. As she got better and was nearly ready to be discharged, her family told her that her friend and coworker had passed away unexpectedly while Grace was so deathly ill for months on end. I just looked at her. I didn't know what to say. It was obvious to me that she had routinely crossed over to the next dimension and indeed had visited her friend. She naturally was drawn to join him, but he knew better. It wasn't her time. She still had work to do here on earth.

As if that weren't amazing enough, the next thing she told me floored me. She said that every day a child would come to visit her and that he would be walking a black-and-white cow on a rope with a cowbell. They would come right through the door adjacent to the foot of her bed (and there was one). The cow would graze, and the child would play around her bedside for hours. Then after they were done, they would say goodbye and walk out the door that they had come through. I said, "Gee, that's a little strange that a child would come to you with a cow." I laughed about it but not to convey that I didn't believe her.

Had Grace had some type of narcotic-induced hallucination? A child is one thing, but walking a cow around sounded like hallucination time to me. Maybe it was ICU psychosis. I asked her if the same child and cow came to visit her each day. She replied, "Oh, you know I love cows and animals and all. I just don't have the time for them. A garden is enough. But that little Nathan lives near a farm here in South Jersey. He loves farm animals. We would play with toy farm animals all the time. We had a whole set of farm animals. We had the happiest times when we gave the animals names. He loved to take care of them."

I said, "So who are you talking about? Who is Nathan? Is Nathan the child with the cow? Do you know him?"

She said, "Of course I know him. I'm his teacher at school."

"Really? So you are a teacher, aren't you?"

"Yes, dear. I'm a teacher. Oh my, he must miss me. I've been gone so long. I hope he's okay. Well, there are several teachers there, but I seemed to have a special connection with that little Nathan Fleet."

With those words, my brain just exploded! "What? Who did you say that child was? Nathan who? Nathan Fleet? You know Nathan Fleet?"

"Yes, dear. I'm his special education teacher. Little Nate can be a handful, but I had a special relationship with him. We always seemed to know what the other was thinking."

"Mrs. Carry, I know Nathan Fleet too. He comes here to this Hospital for his treatments."

"Yes," she said. "He does indeed. I wonder if he misses me."

I dared not say a thing! My heart was in my throat. What were the odds that this trauma patient who'd had such a slim chance of survival would have seen her coworker and her little friend Nathan and that both had passed just prior to or just after her accident?

Several days later I saw one of Grace's family members. I asked about her friend and coworker who had passed away while Grace was so ill. Yes, they confirmed that he had indeed passed. Then I told them about Grace's visions while she was so ill in the ICU. I told them about her seeing her friend who had told her that it wasn't her time and that she had to go back. Her work wasn't done here yet. Then I told them about Grace's visitations by little Nathan. I also told them that he had passed away right around the same time as Grace's accident. I didn't have the heart to tell her that her little friend had passed. Grace's family member told me that I should tell her. If I didn't, she would. "Okay, let's go, and we'll both tell her that her visitation was the real thing and not a hallucination." So we did. She was certainly well enough to hear the truth as her discharge to rehab was imminent. When she heard what we had to say, she wasn't surprised at all. She said she'd thought that might be the case because he was so sick all the time, but she was saddened and surprised to hear about how he had passed. She emphasized that during the times when he would come to her with his cow, he was happy and normal and well. He didn't have cystic fibrosis, cognitive impairments, or cerebral palsy. Nathan was a happy, healthy child doing exactly what he wanted to do, playing with his beloved farm animals and returning the favor to Grace, the teacher whom he loved, by helping her get better when she was so sick.

Jesus said, "The person old in days won't hesitate to ask a little child seven days old about the place of life, and that person will live" The Gospel of Saint Thomas. The Gnostic Society Library. Robert J. Miller, ed., The Complete Gospels: Annotated Scholars version. (Polebridge Press, 1992, 1994).

"Truly, I say to you, unless you turn and become like children, you will never enter the Kingdom of Heaven" (Matthew 18:3 ESV).

And we know that for those who love God all things work together for good, for those who are called according to his purpose (Romans 8:28 ESV).

Being true to your word transcends the physical-spiritual boundary. The next chapter shows how a dying child's pledge to me was kept. A promise is a promise, even if the means its fruition requires is a convoluted, improbable path.

Chapter 6

Lena

I got a call from the pediatric intensive care unit one afternoon for a surgery consult on a very sweet twelve-year-old girl who was suffering from the ravages of AIDS. Lena was a known AIDS patient for about four years now. She would on occasion be admitted so that we could treat various infections she would develop.

Her story wasn't the usual story of an adult AIDS patient since she was a child. She hadn't spent a lifetime shooting heroin, sharing needles, or living a high-risk lifestyle. It's not that those things matter to a physician. They don't. We still treat all people regardless of their situations or how they got there. Lena had done nothing to contract the HIV virus and was truly an innocent victim.

Lena was born with a congenital anomaly of her gastrointestinal tract that required major surgery. She underwent successful surgery for that issue in the first few weeks of life, and things went well; however, apparently, she was given a transfusion. Baby Lena had received 40 mL of packed red blood cells in the perioperative period. She was transfused to keep her oxygen-carrying capacity maximized during anesthesia and surgery.

Lena grew as a normal child and did all the things any other child would do. She began to get unusual infections, and by the time she was eight years old, she was diagnosed with HIV/AIDS. She stumped her doctors for many months, but then she was finally diagnosed with AIDS when her constellation of infections, including recurrent pneumonia, heightened her doctor's suspicions. She contracted the HIV virus from her transfusion as an infant. The screening of blood and blood products back then wasn't what it is today. The treatment and care of AIDS patients wasn't as good in the 1980s as it is now.

For this particular admission, Lena had developed a large and painful abscess. In fact, when we examined her, it was obvious that she had what is known as a horseshoe abscess. A horseshoe abscess is one that starts near the vaginal labia, works its way back to the anus, encircles the anus, and tracks its way around to the other side of the vagina, forming the shape of a horseshoe. We discussed the case with her parents and the intensivist.

Lena would require an incision and drainage of her abscess and most likely deep wound packing and many trips back to the operating room to wash out her abscess cavity and to change her packing. This is one method we can employ to help a large abscess heal. It can take weeks to heal a large abscess cavity in a healthy patient. In an AIDS patient, we definitely had our hands full.

It didn't matter that we would potentially be exposed to her body fluids quite often. We had a job to do, and we were professionals. Every contemporary gold-standard precaution was taken when we started treating her and patients like her. The area was so painful for her that we would go to the OR and only work on her when she was under sedation.

As several weeks passed into her ongoing treatment, I noticed that Lena would look forward to seeing us on our rounds. She didn't undergo any painful procedures at this time. She would engage us in small talk. Most of the residents and students just wanted to finish the list of patients to see so that we could get ready for attending rounds or the operating room. They had no interest in chatting with her or any other patient. Chatting is something that might seem impossible to surgical residents because they aren't afforded the time to do so.

It was obvious to me that Lena desperately needed that human touch. She longed for some personal interaction and hated being seen as the kid with AIDS who had an infection. I would go to see her in the PICU when my work was done. If she wasn't sleeping, I would pull up a chair and have long talks with her, time permitting. All she wanted was to tell her story to someone with an ear and a heart that cared. Well, that was me for sure.

How could I not want to hear about her life? She told me about her grandparents and how they lived on a farm in southern New Jersey. She loved to go to her grandpa and grandma's farm. She used to play with the goats and chickens. Her favorite was to feed the horses and cows. Since she had been diagnosed with AIDS, she had very limited interaction with her animal friends. She still went when she could, but she wasn't allowed to touch the animals. She was very upset over this.

Lena also told me about her dog. The family had a golden retriever. She loved that dog and spent as much time with him as possible. Apparently, the dog was the exception to the "no animal" rule. Lena explained to me that when she was diagnosed with AIDS, she was pulled out of school. She missed her classmates and friends very much. Her neighborhood friends require parent-supervised visits that were timed and limited in their content and contact.

I sat with Lena and talked about life for many weeks. I had a new friend, and it was amazing. My day wasn't complete unless I sat with her and chatted. There were times when I would go late at night to see her because my work consumed the entire day. If she were already sleeping, I would sometimes feel badly since she may have thought I had skipped out on her. I never did.

When Lena was finally discharged, I made her promise that if she needed to come back to the hospital, she should tell the nurses to let me know so that I could come and see her. She lit up and said she didn't want to come back but that if she had to, she wanted me to take care of her. I told her I certainly would even if I were on another rotation. She smiled and said, "It's a deal!"

Months went by, and I often thought about my little friend Lena and how life might be going for her. I was so happy for her that she was home with her family and her dog and not in the hospital. I wondered if she were getting to see her friends. Had she been to her grandparents' farm? Did she have a reasonable quality of life? I prayed for her all the time. If I thought of her, I prayed for her. That's something that comes natural to me. My mom instilled in me a tremendous capacity for empathy. I think she passed that trait to me in both a genetic and emotional sense.

One evening as I was seeing a child in the PICU for a consult, I noticed that Lena had been admitted that morning with another case of pneumonia. She was fairly sick and sleeping, so I let her be. She apparently had developed pneumocystis pneumonia, and it was bilateral (i.e., in both lungs). She was on an oxygen mask; however, she looked comfortable, and she appeared to be breathing easily. I didn't think too much of it as she had been in for that same thing several times prior. The next day I stopped by, and she was awake and eating something for lunch. She was very happy to see me but very tired and upset that she was back in the PICU. She was on several different antibiotics and an antifungal medication too. She didn't have much energy to speak for long, but we caught up on life as she was able.

Lena made me promise that I would come back to chat with her each day she was there. Days went by, and she was getting better. One day we got good news that she was transferring out of the PICU and into an isolation room on the pediatrics floor. Well, at least she would get a change of scenery, and going to the pediatrics floor was a clear sign she was getting better.

Life got extremely busy for me during the next week or so. I was on the trauma service, and it was one trauma after another with sleepless nights between backbreaking days in the trauma intensive care unit. I would stop in to see her as often as I could. The doctors finally told her parents that Lena could go home soon as her blood counts looked better. She was very close to meeting her doctors' discharge criteria. Lena had a framed picture of her dog with her too. She would talk to him and let him know that she would be home soon.

I felt good about what I was seeing, and apparently, so did her doctors. The last time we saw each other, we agreed that no matter what, we would always look for each other whenever Lena was in the hospital. She told me, "Whenever I'm going home, I promise I'll let you know." She emphasized and promised me she would be sure to say, "So long." After all, we were friends! Two days later Lena was discharged. We didn't get to say goodbye this time as I was very consumed by my responsibilities on the trauma service.

Several months passed, and I was unaware of any subsequent admissions for Lena. I was relieved for her and her family. I would run into her doctors every so often, and they would tell me she was doing well at home. Almost four months had passed, and I would think of her often and pray for her. This cycle never ended for me. I figured if I prayed for her, she would stay home and be well. She wasn't the only patient I did this for. Admittedly, that kind of spiritual involvement can be daunting. There were days when I would pray for a dozen people, adults and children alike.

I always thought that the monastics (monks in a monastery) had it easy as they would pray all day and didn't need to worry about going to the operating room or the trauma admitting area or to take severely traumatized patients from a helicopter that was doing a hot drop-off. I mixed my days and nights with hospital work and prayer for my sick brothers and sisters every day and every night. One could say I was in a state of constant prayer. As for the Monastics, God bless them. They keep the holy flame burning as the rest of us live our lives completely unaware of their penance.

There was one thing I did notice about children with chronic illnesses, terminal cancers, or AIDS. They had a sophistication and an emotional maturity about them that most adults didn't have. I really believe they have an emotional awareness that's advanced beyond most people in general. Maybe it was the difficulty and stress of the illness that matured them early. It was as if time was compressed for them. They seemed to live full lives or even several lifetimes all densely packed into their short lives. I believe they are old souls here on missions to evoke spiritual change in those who surround them. Some regard it as compressed karma. Lena certainly had that very same maturity and emotional perspective about her.

To further the illustration, I can remember one five-year-old who was in our PACU (the post anesthesia care unit or recovery room). He had undergone a lengthy surgery for a tumor debulking by the pediatric surgery team. I was on call, so the team had signed him out to me. Apparently, his tumor recurrence had been quite extensive and unresectable (not removable). Thus, he was placed under hospice care. The only thing to do for him was to keep him comfortable. There would be no chemo or radiation for him. He was terminal. He had been through so much in his short five years, including multiple procedures and painful surgeries.

I was in the PACU tending to another patient when I witnessed this poor unfortunate child's mother and aunt being brought in to see him for the first time after his surgery. He was in obvious pain because he was moaning terribly. This could have been his reaction to coming out from under anesthesia, but our job was to keep him comfortable. I asked the nurse to give him some morphine, and that seemed to help him. His mom and aunt were emotional basket cases as anyone would expect. How do you act when you have been told your five-year-old has no future? Nothing could help him. Everything to be done had been done. The tumor was everywhere and rapidly advancing.

They were all over him. They were shouting as if they desperately needed him to hear what they had to say. I thought the shouting was also an emotional attempt at shouting away the horror of the situation, drowning out the pain they had in their hearts. His mom started talking to him about his birthday that was coming up a month or so away and how they would have a big party. All the relatives and friends would be there. He would receive so many nice gifts. Then Christmas was only a month after that. They went on and on.

This child's mom and aunt were out of their minds with grief. I could only think, *God, please help them! This torture is so very intense and inescapable.* It was nearly unbearable for me just watching this all play itself out. I was tending to another patient, so I had to quietly stay put and bear witness to their horror.

Just as I thought I couldn't hear any more talk, her five-year-old son sat upright in his bed with a fresh incision on his abdomen. He screamed at them to be quiet. They stood stunned and in perfect silence. He then shouted, "Don't you get it? Don't you understand? What is it that you can't understand?" There was a deafening and uneasy silence for a moment. He then shouted out, "I won't be here on my birthday! Don't you see? Can't you understand? I won't be here on Christmas either! I don't have a choice in the matter, and you don't either!"

With that, the mother, the aunt, the nurse, and I all stood straight up and froze like statues. Time stood still. The earth stood still. All the air in the room was now gone. The nurse slid a chair under the mom. The child lay back down and put his hands over his face. The aunt turned to me and began to sob. I got the aunt a chair and told them to just have the nurses call me if they needed anything as I went in search of pastoral care.

That child's time was compressed as was many of the other terminal children I had worked with. He had a full understanding of his situation and spoke about it more clearly than an adult would. He made it crystal clear to his mom, who wasn't able to deal with what she was faced with at that time. There but for the grace of God go all of us.

The next day was a very busy trauma day for us. It seemed like one trauma after another came in. There were also several emergency room surgical admissions. As the evening grinded on, I thought I heard a code called in the PICU. (A code takes place when a patient is dying and doctors are trying to resuscitate him or her.) We're using paddles, jump-starting the heart, and intubating, all that stuff that the public sees on TV shows. I wasn't on that service, and I had to juggle one trauma after the next in addition to one inpatient surgical consult after another. There was no way I was going to the PICU for a code. The PICU had a full team complete with an attending intensivist, a fellow in training, residents from pediatrics, and a surgery resident. I really didn't give it a second thought.

In the next two hours or so, I found myself running from one emergency to another like a madman—trauma ICU (TICU), the emergency room, trauma admitting. The hospital operators would make a well-known trauma protocol announcement that carried throughout the entire hospital, "Trauma alert! Shock trauma STAT!" over and over again. At the same time, all the trauma beepers would begin screaming about a trauma alert. That meant anyone on the trauma team had to get to the trauma admitting area STAT! You never knew whether multiple choppers were bearing down on you all at once with multiple wounded or a ground transport was arriving because of a shooting or stabbing right outside the hospital.

Things finally calmed down for a few minutes. I had time to run to the cafeteria before it closed to grab a bite to eat, but then I got a phone call that they needed me STAT in the TICU. It was getting late in the evening, so running down the hall was more acceptable than doing so at one in the afternoon. A repair crew was working on the usual elevators to the TICU. I had to run down another hall to a different wing and then go up the stairs to another set of elevators. As I turned the corner to approach the double doors of the TICU, I saw that the floor was being waxed. It was a little unusual to shut down this busy area this time of the evening. The floors were typically done around two in the morning or so when traffic was low. The crew doing the floor just glared at me as if to say, "No, you don't!"

I stopped and thought, *Okay, I'll go around the back hallway.*

There was a back hall that wasn't meant for traffic. It ran behind the PICU but also continued behind the TICU though. This back hallway was frequently jammed with gurneys, beds, IV poles, and wheelchairs. To get through from one end to the other could be a real chore. As I threw the doors open to the back hall, I started to fight my way through the unorganized cluster of items with wheels. I wasn't looking down the hall. I was looking at each item in front of me that I needed to negotiate. As I was almost to the other end, I was just about to really shove the next gurney in my way, and I stopped just in time to see a black body bag on it.

For a second I was startled as if I were a layperson who had never been near a dead body. I felt some momentary fright come and go in about two seconds. I was caught off guard. I looked it over and thought, *why in God's name is this body sitting back here in this hallway? Who would do this?* This was not the usual way the deceased made their way to the morgue. I did notice that the body was apparently that of a child or a very small adult. I did what came naturally for me. I said a quick prayer for whoever was in that bag. Hmm, there was that code in PICU earlier.

Off I ran to the TICU. When I got there, I was out of breath, and I asked what the STAT call was all about. They were all sitting around, grazing like buffalo, jaws grinding and faces stuffed with submarine sandwiches and pizza. One nurse chuckled at me and said, "Surprise!" The attending knew we were pressed all day, so he had treated everyone to the eats. That wasn't uncommon. This was a typical scene in that TICU. You really never knew what you were up against. Usually, it was injury, death, and/or destruction, but occasionally, it was pizza and subs and even sometimes sushi!

After I stuffed my face, I went over to the PICU. I was curious. Did they know they had a body in the back hallway, or did they somehow forget?

I asked the desk clerk about the code I had heard earlier and if that person had lived or died. Was that who was in the bag in the back hall, and why was anyone in the back hall at all? Without emotion, she said, "Oh that was a girl who was here all the time. She came in very ill, and she coded not long after she arrived. It was a quick code."

"What was her name?" I asked.

She looked it up. "The funeral home just picked up Lena Harlan thirty minutes ago. She's gone, not back there anymore." I just looked at her. I thanked her and slowly walked back to my call room.

I wasn't upset at first. I just pondered the whole thing. I thought back to when I first met Lena. I remembered how I had felt so bad for her. I thought about her diagnosis and how it all came down. She was a real victim in every sense of the word. Oh, how she loved her family and her friends and her dog. All the conversations her grandfather had with me regarding his "little lamb" were etched in my heart and mind. That was how he referred to her. He was a devastated grandfather to the core. I remembered how she suffered so terribly in her short life. I remembered how we got to know each other and how we promised that I would take care of her if she ever needed surgery again.

As I sat there on the bed in my call room, I kicked off my sneakers and began to rub my aching feet. All I could see was her smiling face. I pictured her playing with her dog. She always had a framed picture of him at her bedside. She always had a smiling face for me. No matter how terrible the pain or how grim the report, she wasn't going to burden anyone with outward sadness or emotion. Then I remembered her words to me the last time I saw her. "Promise me you will always look for me." Yes was my reply, and I told her to always look for me too. She said, "If I'm going home, I promise I will look for you to say, 'So long.' I promise." With this, I burst into tears. I was so grief-stricken for her and for her family … and for me!

I was so relieved that nobody else was in the call room at that time. It gave me my time to grieve, and I certainly did. To this day, it was obvious to me that somehow, my dear little friend arranged for me to run around an elevator being serviced and a floor being waxed so that I had to take that completely unorthodox path to the TICU and run right into her body on that gurney *against all odds*. I know she was there, waiting for me just like she promised she would. She fulfilled her promise to look for me to say goodbye if she were going home. Then she was taken away.

I'm so thankful for my time with Lena. She taught me so much about life in her very brief time here with us. Her life had been filled with so much sorrow and suffering but also lots of love and joy from her friends, family, nurses and physicians. She held her faith and uplifted all who knew her. Lena held God's love and light for herself and others through unspeakable heartache and suffering. I will never forget my dear friend. I know that she is part of my forever and that I am part of hers. May God bless you, Lena Harlan. May God, the Father of the universe, raise you to the highest Heaven. Yes, Lena, we are brother and sister in God's kingdom forever!

"But Jesus said, Let the little children come to me, and do not forbid them; for of such is the Kingdom of Heaven" (Matthew 19:29 NIV).

"Whoever receives one of these little children in my name receives me; and whoever receives me, receives not me but Him who sent me" (Mark 9:37 NIV).

"Then the woman said to Elijah, 'Now I know you are a man of God and the Lord's word from your mouth is true'" (1 Kings 17:24 CSB).

People can and do have spiritual connections to one another. This includes beloved pets as well as places and cities all over this earth. Often dreams can be of a prophetic nature. The next chapter shows us how Montreal is the city of my heart and how the relationship goes way beyond what meets the eye.

Chapter 7

Montreal, City of My Heart

What did it mean for me to be named after my mom's uncle John? My dad was my hero and mentor, but let's take a look at John Marchese. He was the first one on either side of the family at that point in time to go on to professional school and become a pharmacist. Although I never met him as my older brother Tom had, I was named after him. There were six Tom Galluccis, but I was the very first and only John Gallucci. John Marchese was married to my aunt Theresa, "Aunt T," on my mom's side of the family.

John Marchese was an avid ice hockey fan and became friends with several of the New York Rangers way back in the 1940s and '50s. This would have been somewhat uncommon in those days as other sports were much more readily accepted by the contemporary American society. Apparently, he attended lots of their games at the original Madison Square Garden in New York City and was also a poker buddy of the same crew.

I was the second son of a man who was a football hero. My dad was given a full football scholarship by Georgia University. So I grew up loving football in a very big way. How I became such a fan of ice hockey is a bit of a mystery to all of us. I feel like it's in my blood. Against all odds, I became a big ice hockey fan. I also went through college and on to professional school (health care) just like John Marchese did. I don't think that's just coincidence. Yes, everything really does happen for a reason and naming me after Our Uncle John Marchese had to be inspired by Heaven.

As a young child, I became fascinated with the city of Montreal. Of all the cities that were famous for or synonymous with ice hockey, Montreal was the pinnacle. Even the Russians considered the Montreal Forum to be the shrine of ice hockey. I took out every book I could from our township library on ice hockey and Montreal. I literally dreamed of going to Montreal one day. I didn't know how or why I would go, but the attraction was beyond words for me.

When I was in my teens, I would have this recurring dream that I was walking down a street at night in a strange city that was ice cold. The snow was falling, and I really didn't know where I was or why I was there. As I walked this city sidewalk, I would take note of the gray stone steps that led up to brownstones and other apartments made of stone and brick. I stopped to see the snow sticking to and building up on the stone steps. The wrought-iron railings going up the steps were old, thick, and black. As I made my way along this cold city street, I would come upon a cross street. Kids were walking in the street with hockey sticks, batting an ice chunk back and forth to one another just like I would have done if my friends were with me. There was a park with a statue and benches to the right with brightly lit buildings behind it. There was also a very large old brick building across a parking lot to my left. The dream would end with me walking across the street and up to that old brick building.

I never went in the building. Nor did I know what or where it was. I had the feeling I was in another world, another time and place. I would get as far as the front doors made of glass but never farther. Why did I have this recurring dream of walking in a strange cold city at night that felt so real yet so very far away as the snow fell? I didn't know this place. I used to imagine that this was Canada. Maybe it was Montreal. Why else would it be snowing and kids passing a chunk of ice back and forth to one another with their hockey sticks?

The only time I ever heard anyone in my family mention Montreal was when my dad would tell me about Dr. Marie Braun from Panzer College. She was one of my dad's college mentors. He described her as a caring and mentoring soul who made it a point to guide my dad while in college. She apparently went to college at McGill University in Montreal and got her PhD there as well. She became a folk hero to me while growing up. After my freshman year in college at Panzer, which was part of Montclair State College, I received an award. Who was there to present this award? It was none other than Marie Braun. She was in her nineties by then. I was humbled and so very privileged to meet her and receive an award from her. After the ceremony I asked Dr. Braun about McGill University and Montreal. How could I not? As she talked about Montreal and McGill, her face lit up, and she took on a youthful glow. I felt as though I were speaking face-to-face with a celebrity and one who had actually *lived* in Montreal.

One day a letter came in the mail from Tony Naclerio. As previously stated, Brother Naclerio was a very well regarded track and field coach. He would be chosen as one of the throwing coaches at the 1996 US Olympics and many other world events. I had known him fairly well as did my father. I attended two of his summer camps for the throwing events. I loved track and field and the throwing events as much as ice hockey, although they were two very different sports.

Brother Naclerio was running a trip to see the 1979 World Cup Track and Field Championships. Wow, I'd love to go! The event was also held in … Montreal! Here was my chance to spend a few days with Tony Naclerio, watch the World Cup of track and field, and see Montreal all at once. I sent in the registration form with a check and waited patiently for that great day. I had a blast. *Montreal, I finally found you! The language! The city! The people! The World Cup!* I got to be an insider chatting with Tony about the athletes and their techniques.

My experience in Montreal was all that I hoped it would be and more. I was in love with the city that I had thought so incessantly about. It didn't let me down. Years would pass, and life would take me away from my childhood passions of football, ice hockey, and track and field; however, I never lost the love for Montreal. I believed deeply that my relationship with that city was in no way over.

On a glorious but fairly serpiginous path, life ultimately found me applying for training spots in pediatric surgery. This was in my fifth year of a six-year general surgery residency. There were approximately twenty-six centers in the United States and Canada where one could match for training in that field. This would mean two years of intense training after my six years of general surgery training. I was advised to apply to all centers so as to maximize my chances of matching, and so I did.

I can remember my very first interview like it was yesterday. Of all places, my first interview would be in Montreal. I flew into Montreal, the city of my heart, on the evening of November 3, 1994. When I got to my destination and settled into my room, I quickly dressed up for the cold and hit the sidewalk with my map in hand, setting out to find my destination for the next morning. I always knew being lost or late was a big no-no on an interview, so I figured that if I walked to my destination the night before and timed it, I'd have no issue when we went live the next day. Off I went into the cold. The snow was lightly falling.

I didn't get far along my path before I realized there was something very familiar about where I was. As I walked down Rue Du Fort, I made a right turn onto Rue Tupper. The snow came down harder and harder as I walked, but I liked the cold and the snow, so it was all good. As I hit the middle of Rue Tupper, I stopped in my tracks. I became overwhelmed by a tremendous wave of déjà vu! I stood in perfect silence and reverence of what lay before me. There I was. This was my recurring dream from my teens. I was there in the exact scene I would see over and over again but had no explanation for at the time.

I walked Rue Tupper on a cold night in a strange city with the snow falling. I looked at the gray stone steps that led up to the brownstone and brick apartment buildings to my right. As the snow fell, it was sticking to and building up on the stone steps. I looked for the wrought-iron railings, and there they were just as I had seen many times before. I had chills and goose bumps all over me, and it wasn't from the cold. As I got to the cross streets, I looked to the right, and I saw the park with its statue and benches. And there was that very large old brick building to my left. There were kids crossing through the park and carrying their hockey sticks. I knew they would be there somewhere!

This whole supernatural seen took on a sacred energy. The emotion I was experiencing was nearly overpowering me. It was abundantly clear to me that I had all those dreams for a reason. I had been led here by a supernatural force, the force of destiny.

Then I saw a marquee up high on a pole in the parking lot of the old brick building that read, "L'Hopital de Montreal pour Enfants" (Montreal Children's Hospital)! Although this was my very first interview out of twenty-six, I had arrived at the destination that I had seen in my dreams over and over again. In fact, I had been seeing the Montreal Children's Hospital in my dreams since the 1970s as a teenager in New Jersey!

As I went to bed that night, my mind was racing with all that had just happened. I couldn't wait for tomorrow to come! The next day I was a nervous wreck. I guess it was first-interview syndrome. I made my way to the program director's office and introduced myself. I was politely asked by the secretary to take a seat on a bench just outside the office.

The program director walked over to me and introduced himself. He must have seen that I was nervous, so he immediately put me at ease by making some small talk and asking me about my flight and hotel. Then he said something that took me by total surprise. He said, "Let's go, Johnny Boy. We have a busy day planned out, and you're going to be here all day." The use of the familiar term "Johnny Boy" may or may not be common here and there, but to my family, I had always been Johnny Boy since I was born.

Things moved along quickly, and the day went by like lightning. I walked into that place the morning of November 4, 1994, a stranger, but as I left, I knew in my heart that this wasn't over. I felt like I was home. I felt like I knew these people from another time and place. I knew beyond any doubt that this was where I belonged, and I knew this was where I would match. I didn't want to be anywhere else.

I prayed to God that this surely had to be in His plans for me. I knew it. I could feel it. I prayed every day and night that this was a done deal. I was sure that God was sure. If not, why all the dreams of the Montreal Children's Hospital from when I was a teen?

As I left the Montreal Children's Hospital after a long day of interviews, I thought I would walk around the greater area for a bit. My flight wasn't until the next morning, so why not? As I walked to Cabot Park right across the street from the hospital, I went up to the monument I'd seen over and over in my dreams. I looked up to see the lights of the building across the street on the other side of the park. As I jumped the curb onto the sidewalk, I could see that this building was in fact the famed Montreal Forum! I was standing in front of the shrine of hockey right across from the park near the hospital!

This may sound juvenile to many, but this whole situation was just knocking me out. My agenda was to train as a pediatric surgeon for sure. It wasn't to be where my childhood sports heroes had played. Nonetheless, if I could have signed a contract for my fellowship at the Montreal Children's Hospital right then and canceled all the other interviews, I would have done it without hesitation. For me it was all about how amazingly comfortable I was with the entire situation. I just had the feeling of being *home*. Now I had to go through twenty-five more interviews in Los Angeles, Boston, Memphis, Toronto, and many other places.

I can vividly remember interviewing all day in Memphis, Tennessee, after a sleepless night in a cheap hotel. Drug deals and violence was happening literally right outside my room door, and it had kept me awake all night. With no sleep from the previous day, I was supposed to fly from Memphis to Buffalo only to then get in a rental car and drive on to Toronto.

Our plane was delayed in Tennessee for hours of deicing. The wings and fuselage of our jet had become encased in ice. I was supposed to have arrived in Buffalo by nine in the evening, but I didn't get in until after midnight. The SUV on reserve for me was no longer available. I climbed into a subcompact car with front-wheel drive, and off I went with a map in my hand.

I was completely exhausted and starved, and I had no idea where I was going. Oh, and it was snowing fiercely and around negative five degrees Fahrenheit. As I set out, I knew I needed to get to some roadway called the Queens Elizabeth Way (QEW). I found that road and thought, *Great! I'm on my way.*

As I drove from Buffalo across the Canadian border, the weather got worse and worse. I looked at my car thermometer, and it read negative twenty. The snow was falling sideways. I saw road signs along the QEW that displayed names like The Chippewa, Lake Ontario, and Lake Erie. Those names conjured up thoughts of Gordon Lightfoot's ominously famous song "The Wreck of the Edmund Fitzgerald," which said, "The legend lived on from the Chippewa on down to the big lake they called Gitche Gumee. Superior they said never gives up her dead when the skies of November turn gloomy!" This wasn't November. It was January.

As I sped along my frozen path, I realized that I wasn't exactly sure where the roadway began and where it ended. Tractor trailers were passing me doing what seemed like a hundred miles per hour. I had reduced my speed to about fifty miles per hour because I was sure I would drive off the side of the highway if I didn't. How could these guys know where the road was? I was now in a dreaded whiteout! The snow was falling so hard and fast that I got the sensation that my car had just lifted off the ground and I was up in the air. It was very dark out, so my headlights shone only on the snow falling, and that was all I could see. I was moving in one direction, and the snow was whipping in another, so I was badly disoriented. I felt as though I had just taken flight. I actually got dizzy, not knowing what was up, down, left, or right. If you have never experienced this, I promise you that you don't want to.

What in God's name was John Gallucci from New Jersey doing in this situation? "The Wreck of the Edmund Fitzgerald" was playing in my head. There was nothing remotely fun about this. I loved adventure, and I'd done many things in my life, including flying through a severe lightning and hailstorm in a helicopter in Florida, living on the island of Grenada on a campus full of bullet holes and grenade blasts, and climbing an active volcano on the island of Saint Vincent and hanging over the lip of the crater. I've been through hurricanes down in the Caribbean where three-hundred-foot steel tankers were tossed five blocks inland. I've taken tankers and freighters to nearby islands just for the fun of it. Part of my life was very much like a Jimmy Buffet song. I did stuff most people don't ever get to do.

My adventures all always turned out just fine, even though they certainly didn't have to. I can remember when we were all held in our cabins at night under martial law for several nights in Grenada because the trial of those allegedly involved in the killing of the former prime minister was going on. Death threats had come our way several times. We were a bit scared.

However, nothing scared me like this night on the QEW from Buffalo to Toronto. I felt as though I had no control over my fate. I began to pray and pray hard! "Jesus, if one of these trucks hits me, please let them find the car and my frozen body. If I drive off the road and into the lake, let the ice not break." I was in a sweat on the QEW at one in the morning in a whiteout, at minus 20 degrees Fahrenheit and the wind was unreal!

I pulled my car over to what I thought was the side of the road to collect my thoughts. The tractor trailers were flying by me and making visibility even worse because the snow would go into a swirl in their wake. I could feel the suction on my car as they whooshed by me. Now my visibility was nil. This was not good at all. Now I felt that I was more likely to get rear-ended by a speeding tractor trailer than driving off the road. I had to make a move and do it fast! It was do or die for me.

I prayed fervently, "Dear Lord, please get me to Toronto alive and in one piece!" I was completely exhausted and nearly in a panic. Then the idea came to me. These trucks were probably going to Toronto. I didn't know for sure, but I couldn't stay where I was either. So I made a plan and a deal with God. I would have faith that these trucks were indeed going from Buffalo to Toronto. The likelihood was great as there wasn't much else in between. Or was there?

I carefully got back onto what I believed was roadway, and off I went. I followed the first truck to fly by me. I had to speed to stay with him. Doing that wasn't easy. I had to floor the tiny car I was in. I was doing eighty-five miles per hour in a very cheap rental in a whiteout, and the wind was pushing me nearly off the road, drafting a tractor trailer on the QEW. I stayed on that truck for about an hour until I saw city lights up ahead.

Even at two in the morning, Toronto was lit up like a Christmas tree. The snow had subsided. All the signage showed that I was right where I wanted to be. Once I got into the city of Toronto proper, I actually found my hotel quickly and pulled into the parking garage underground.

Thank You, God, for those tractor trailers. They didn't kill me. They guided me and paved the path for me right into Toronto. Thank You, Jesus, for Toronto! I made my way to the check-in desk and headed up to my room on the seventeenth floor.

I opened the room door, and it was absolutely freezing inside. I turned up the gas wall heater and waited for something good to happen. The wind was coming right through the single pained windows and curtains like I had never experienced before. I pushed the couch across the room, pulled the curtains and set it in front of the windows to reduce the wind chill on me across the room where the bed was. The next thing I did was turn on all the hot water in the sink and shower. This actually raised the temp of the room so that I could fall asleep. I eventually turned off the water. Off to sleep I went at about three o'clock.

I had to be at the Toronto Sick Children's Hospital for a full day of interviewing by seven thirty. In the morning I grabbed a bagel and asked the concierge how to get to the hospital. I was wearing a black woolen dress overcoat, a suit, and a tie underneath, and I held a briefcase in my hand. I followed the directions to the hospital. Luckily, it was only two blocks away. No matter how cold, I could go two blocks and be okay. I walked up to the doors and made my way to the elevators.

It was a little strange that so few people were around; however, it was early, and I was focused on getting to my destination. I went to the second floor as directed. As I got off the elevator, a full team of people met me. One asked if they could take my coat, and the other asked if I wanted any tea or coffee. A team leader then asked me if anyone else was with me. I looked at him in a puzzled way. Just then a very attractive woman walked over to me and offered her hand in greeting.

I started to feel like something wasn't right. I asked her if she knew where the department of surgery was. She looked at me and chuckled as if I were making a joke. She playfully dismissed this and asked if I had any questions about the scene we would be shooting that morning. I looked up at her and said, "Excuse me. Shooting what scene? Hang on here please. Where am I, and who are you all? Is this not the children's hospital?"

They all looked at me as if I were making a joke. Then another crew member asked me seriously if I weren't there to shoot the scene they were setting up that morning in whatever production they were involved in. Apparently, this truly was a film crew, and they were shooting a scene for a major motion picture.

Just for a very brief moment, I remembered my dream as a teen of being an actor and eventually making it to Broadway and maybe Hollywood. For a second I thought, *Hmm, I can do this and change history right here and now.* I looked at my gorgeous costar. I looked all around me. I thought of the sleepless nights back at the Hospital and the trauma center. That was when I saw the cameras and all the lighting paraphernalia. All I had to do was step into this life, and nobody would know. *John, snap out of it!*

"Oh, my God! You think I'm an actor? This is a film scene location? This is not a hospital? Oh no! I'm gonna be late for my interview! Where am I?" This was a hospital for sure just like the concierge directed me to. They then all realized what was going on. They were all very helpful as they told me that I could go down to the entrance and that the guard would show me how to get to the Toronto Sick Children's Hospital. This place was apparently a hospital that had been closed and was now being used by a film crew. I thought jokingly, *do I still have time to change my mind?* My heart was surely with pediatric surgery. "You will seek me and find me, when you seek me with all your heart" (Jeremiah 29:13 ESV).

Academically, I had my share of outright rejections over and over again. I was rejected by colleges I wanted to attend, dental schools, and medical schools. I never let this dissuade me. I had truly found my calling, and I was resolute that I had no other choice but to succeed.

All these years later when I mentor and teach undergraduate students, medical students, pediatric and/or surgical residents, I usually tell them of going with what their hearts tell them. When you work with your heart and work in the spirit, you increase your chances of overcoming the odds and overcoming rejection. I tell them the greatest story of overcoming rejection I know. Jesus was referred to as "the key-stone rejected by the builders." This Jesus is the stone that was rejected by you, the builders, which has become the cornerstone (Acts 4:11 ESV).

A well-known singer-songwriter was rejected seventeen times in a row for a recording contract at the start of his career. The power brokers of the elite music industry obviously thought too much of themselves and their ability to recognize true talent. Most people would be discouraged and very likely quit trying after a single rejection or two. Something told this talented individual to keep going. After seventeen consecutive rejections, John Denver was finally given a recording contract. Today he and his music are at number four on the all-time leading record sales list, and he passed away in 1997! A few elite people who thought they knew better weren't going to stop John Denver. Destiny is destiny, and nobody was going to stop me either. Like so many other things in my life, I matched in pediatric surgery against all odds.

I can remember *match day* as if it were yesterday. Match day is the day the training programs reveal their choices for training. Match day tells you if in fact you have matched and been given the opportunity to train in your chosen field and where you have matched. Needless to say that it's a very big day for all concerned. Think of it like the NFL or NHL draft.

I was scrubbing for a case with Dr. James Alexander, one of my mentors. Dr. Alexander is an excellent vascular and general surgeon. Early in my residency when I became overwhelmed by everything, he was chosen by the chairman of surgery to keep an eye on me and mentor me. I believe he got me through a very tough time. I was ready to throw in the towel. With his mentorship, I persevered. He and I were about to do an abdominal aortic aneurysm resection. I remembered that he went to McGill University in Montreal for his undergraduate studies. Every once in a while, he would tell me stories of Montreal.

As we scrubbed for the case, he said to me, "Hey, isn't it match day today?"

I said, "Uh-huh, yeah, it is."

He said, "What time do the programs make their phone calls to tell the candidates that they have matched?"

"It's supposed to be noon."

He looked up at the clock on the wall and said, "Hey, it's noon!" We momentarily stared at each other. Just then we both heard an overhead page, "Dr. Gallucci, call the operator." That meant an outside call was coming in. We looked at each other, and he said, "Go! Get your call! We can wait!"

I ran down the hallway and picked up the first phone I saw. I called the operator, and she said, "Oh, great, your wife is on the phone."

I held my breath. "Hello?"

"John, you matched!"

"What? I matched?"

"Yes!" My world turned pure white. My vision left me. I couldn't feel my surroundings anymore. The tears welled up in my eyes. "Oh, my God! Oh, my God! I matched!"

I collected myself for the next bit of news. Where would we be moving to? There were a few places I did not want to go to in a big way, but I would have if need be. It could have been any of twenty-six places I interviewed. It would have been nice to stay within driving distance of our families in New Jersey and New York. However, my secret wish was Montreal. It was my very first interview followed by all the others. I felt at home there and had a love for that city from when I was a kid. I felt like a relative of every person I interviewed with there, and I knew I didn't want to be anywhere else. I had dreams and visions of Montreal. When I said I would have signed a contract to stay and canceled all the other interviews, I wasn't kidding. I would have signed with my blood! "OK, where did I match?" I asked.

These were her exact words to me: "We're going to Montreal!"

I was in momentary shock. The breath was sucked out of me. I had never felt overwhelming happiness and excitation like that ever in my life. Words written here will not convey the thrill and gratitude I felt running through my entire body. It was much more than happiness I was feeling. I was feeling the pure energy of the Holy Spirit running through me because it was an affirmation that God had put this entire process together long ago.

Thank You, God! You allowed me to see it. I knew it. I felt it in my heart, mind, body, and soul! I walked back to the scrub sink where Dr. Alexander was waiting. He must have either already known or read my face, but he was smiling from ear to ear. "Well?" he said.

I looked at him and said, "I going to Montreal! To McGill!"

He burst out with happiness. He shouted, "All right!" He shook my hand with true sincerity and excitement. I was numb. I was in a dream world. We both scrubbed and did the case. He let me do most of it. My confidence level that day took a great jump up. I was floating on cloud nine.

Several years would pass since I finished my training at McGill University in Montreal. I miss the city and the people I came to know so well. I hold so very dear to my heart the countless exhausting days and nights at the Montreal Children's Hospital as well as the children and families I encountered all with their own poignant stories. From the restaurants and patisseries to watching the Montreal Canadians play hockey in the Montreal Forum right across the street from the hospital, I loved every day of my two years there.

We also had amazing landlords, the DeNittis family. I loved them, and I miss them in a very big way. It was Terry, Ellio, and their son Dino. It was as if this family were waiting for me in Montreal. There were many nights when Ellio would call me and invite me for dinner.

My wife was in Vermont several days each week working as an anesthesiologist, so if I had time, I would go over for dinner. Many nights my wife and our kids would go over for dinner as well. Terry made the exact same handmade pasta my grandmother used to make in New Jersey. It was all so amazing. Everything about them felt like family. The

DeNittis family took me and my family in as their own. God bless them. They were and still are the heart of my heart.

My parents would drive up to Montreal every so often for a visit. They would stay in a hotel named Ruby Foo's. It wasn't a new place, but it had lots of history and wasn't very far. There was a restaurant and banquette rooms, and in the lobby of the hotel were several small shops and a haircutter.

One day while waiting in the lobby for my parents, I thought I would pop in to see what the haircutter was all about. I had very little time for haircuts, so maybe this place would work for me. I met Gino, the proprietor. He looked at me as if a stranger had walked in. Well, it was a hotel, and I certainly was a stranger. I made an appointment for the next week. When I showed up, I felt comfortable immediately. The haircut was great, but I had this deep conviction that I was right where I belonged. It wasn't long before I got to know Gino fairly well. I swear I thought I was with family all along.

One day as Gino was cutting my hair, I asked him what his last name was. He said it was Chiarella. He said it with a hard "ch" and a soft D for the R (Ki-adella) in his Italian accent. I asked him the spelling. When I thought about it, it was nearly the same name of my very first best friend back when I lived in Bloomfield, New Jersey, on Belleville Avenue. Ricky Chiarello was my best friend long ago. We moved away to Cedar Grove when I was about four years old. I saw Ricky on a play date once or twice and then never again. I was heartbroken to lose my best friend. I couldn't understand why.

All these years later, I heard that similar last name—one I hadn't heard since those days of Ricky and his family. Now I was more than four hundred miles away and in a different country. Gino Chiarella was my friend and my haircutter. I pronounced Ricky's last name with a soft "ch" like as in "Sharello." That's how I knew him. I told Gino about Ricky. Gino told me that it could be pronounced as I had but that it was pronounced his way in Italian.

Gino asked me where in New Jersey we had lived when I knew the Chiarello family. I said, "Bloomfield." He stood straight up and let his arms fall to his sides. He stood there, just looking at me, not saying a single word. Then he asked me if I remembered what Ricky's dad did for a living. I said sure! At the same exact time, Gino and I both said, "They owned a fish market!"

I couldn't believe what was happening. He was in disbelief! Gino shouted, "They are my cousins!" During the immigration, some of the family went north to New York State. Some went on to Montreal, and others went to New Jersey, ending up in Newark and then Bloomfield. We were both completely amazed that my very first friend was part of his family. If that doesn't go against all the odds, I don't know what does.

I sat there with a lump in my throat. I didn't know what to say. I walked in a stranger in a different country and felt as though I was home with relatives in a place I was meant to be in! In actuality, I was being shown yet another connection that revealed God's work in our lives every single day. God's plan is glorious.

I have been back in New Jersey since 1998, and I have dreamed of Montreal over and over again. In many of the dreams, I am walking through the city at night. I am almost always a physician in the dreams. Sometimes I'm at my home in dreams up in Montreal, and family and visitors will come over for a huge party.

In one dream I was walking up the steps of the Cathedral Notre Dame Basilica in Montreal. I walked in and realized in the dream that I was part of the clergy there and that it was my home. The feeling that dream imparted to me is still with me as all the dreams are, but this one was different. I felt as if I couldn't go any higher in my service to others. It was a blessed and extremely warm feeling that bought me much joy.

I stepped into yet another Montreal dream where I was walking all alone down a city street at about three in the morning. It was early autumn, so there wasn't any snow yet. The night was extraordinarily dark, and I couldn't see any city lights anywhere. As I walked down a hill, I came upon a crowded bar and grill that had glass doors spanning from the ceiling to the ground at the front. The place was packed. In fact, it was standing room only. People were drinking and smoking and chatting and doing all the things people did in a crowded city bar and grill in the evening, but this was a bit eerie as it was more like three o'clock in the morning and it was the only place open. At three in the morning, it should not have been open at all.

I stood there looking at the scene. I was on the outside looking in. That is a very familiar vantage point for me. During my whole life from the early years as a child to the present day, I'm often on the outside looking in. I've always been different. I didn't know why back then, but I understand it now. My life was never really about the things most other people were routinely preoccupied with. I knew from long ago that I was put here to do a job. I just never seemed to revel in the many things that others typically did.

I wasn't then, and I am still not special or better than anyone on this planet. I've just always been different. I saw things that others didn't see, and I've heard and felt things most others don't appreciate. As I saw what I needed to see from the outside looking in to that bar, on my way I went, but I had no destination that I knew of. I was just walking through a very dark Montreal at three in the morning as a solitary observer.

As I reached the bottom of the hill, I was compelled to make a right turn. I did so and walked down this very old, narrow cobblestone street lined with very old stone buildings from the seventeen and eighteen hundreds. It occurred to me that I was now in Old Montreal. I came upon the end of a T intersection. There were shops on both sides of the street that were all closed up, and none had any lights on. The street was very dark and quiet.

However, across the street there was this one shop facing me that was lit up magnificently from the inside. It was the only place that wasn't completely dark. I crossed the street to get a closer look. There I stood directly in front of an extraordinary old shop the likes of which I had never seen before. It was a small shop with large front display windows. The shop had three rows of ancient suits of armor on display. There were amazingly bright, high-intensity lights that made every item on display jump out at you with untold brilliance. The contrast of those blinding bright lights against the surrounding darkness was certainly stunning yet nearly overwhelming.

The lower row of armor on armless sewing mannequins were made of copper and bronze. The ones on the second tier just above the first row were made of pure silver. They were so full of brilliant luster that I had to adjust my eyes to see them. The top row displayed suites of armor made of pure gold. I had never seen anything as spectacular as this. I stood there in total awe of what I was seeing.

The entire city was shut down and as dark as could be, save for the bar and grill. Then there was this incredible place on a dark side street in Old Montreal. It was waiting for me. I was called to it. My destiny was not to go into that crowded, smoke-filled bar. I observed the stark contrast between the only two places I could observe on that dark Montreal night.

As I stood there in silence, I became aware of what this place really was. This was a place of promise for me and others who had the same calling. This shop held in it God's spiritual armor. It was promised to me a very long time ago. The path of my life brings me closer and closer to my truth, my destiny. My time will come. As for others who have the same calling, I know their time will surely come too.

In God's time I will metaphorically and spiritually wear one of those suits of armor, not just any body armor but God's spiritual armor. Why? That's easy. I will do so to fight in spiritual warfare for my Creator! I will be called to fight the fight of my life!

I was created to fight the war between the light and the dark. This is literally a war for the spiritual survival of humanity. The body always goes the way of the spirit. I have always known this deep down in my soul. It's why I have always been on the outside looking in. This had been at the very core of all my dreams and visions from the time I was very young until the present day. I have always known of my destiny from long ago, and I know that it now draws very near.

I dream of Montreal several times each month to this very day. Sometimes I dream about it several times in one week. One way or another, I'm there in a healer's capacity. The spiritual pull is undeniable for me. I have often through the years wondered why all the visions and dreams of this one particular city. Why Montreal?

Each of us in this world has a destiny. You can move in your thoughts and actions near and far, right or left, north or south. But your destiny will appear, and it will catch you. I suppose it's possible to deny your destiny over and over again, but I truly believe that we have a role in choosing our paths prior to incarnating. If you're off your life's path, you will not feel good about what you're doing. You will know that something is wrong, that you must make a big change.

After working in several New Jersey health-care systems for about six years while cutting my teeth as a young pediatric surgeon, I was ultimately recruited by my present health-care system, and I have been there to this very day. I have found my home. I have finally found where it is that I am destined to be in vocation for the Lord on behalf of my brothers and sisters.

About two years ago, I was involved in a fundraising ceremony at the hospital for the construction of a new emergency department. After everything was all said and done, the hospital created a new lobby display that told the story of the hospital and its early beginnings. I must have walked by it hundreds of times before something compelled me to stop and read it all. I did so, and I was very interested to see how the hospital came into being back at the turn of the previous century. As I read further, I learned that the very first people to staff the hospital as nurses and aides were the Grey Nuns. *Okay,* I thought. *No big surprise in that. I work in a Catholic hospital, and I can see nuns being an integral part of the day-to-day function.*

Unlike other hospitals that have no religious affiliation and are run strictly by businesspeople, the archdiocese really did run the hospital. I had been thinking about the place and all it meant to me over the years. I went online at home and read a bit more of the origins of the hospital and how it had evolved through the many years that it had serviced the local population. As I read into the history online, I found the story of the Grey Nuns. I was sincerely interested in learning more about them. After all, I didn't know who they were.

When the Catholic Church sought people to run the place, the search led to this group of dedicated nuns who would indeed be stationed there to run the daily functions, hands on. Who were these nuns who had staffed the hospital and given it life more than one hundred years ago? Their group was founded in 1737, and they came from very far away. In fact, they were founded in another country. Against all odds, they were the Grey Nuns of Montreal.

"And it shall come to pass afterward, that I will pour out my spirit on all flesh; your sons and your daughters shall prophesy, your old men shall dream dreams, and your young men shall see visions" (Joel 2:28 ESV).

"For where your treasure is, there your heart will be also" (Matthew 6:21 KJV).

Put on the whole armor of God that ye may be able to stand against the wiles of the devil. For we wrestle not against flesh and blood, but against principalities, against powers, against the rulers of the darkness of this world, against spiritual wickedness in high places. Wherefore take unto you the whole armor of God that ye may be able to withstand in the evil day, and having done all to stand. (Ephesians 6:11-13 KJV).

At the completion of the writing of this book, I took a chance on a hunch. I reached out to a gentleman I found online. He returned my email the next day. It said, "Yes, Johnny! It's me, Ricky! Call me!" After nearly fifty-six years, we spoke like the best friends we had been when we were four years old. We were best friends then, and apparently, we still are! It was as if no time had passed. God is good!

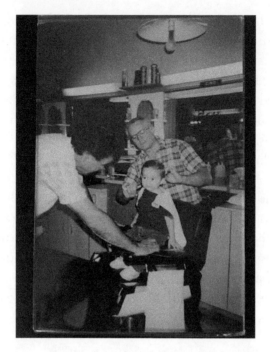

Grandpa, Gino, and Seth at Hotel Ruby Foo's, Montreal, PQ

No encounter is merely by chance. Family, friendships, and relationships are of a spiritual decree. My relationship with Michael Sabella and his family is a classic example. Read on.

Chapter 8

Brother Michael

It was 2002 when I first met Mike and Laurie Sabella. We both had small children signed up to play ice hockey with the Bridgewater Bears hockey organization. My daughter Arielle was born in 1997, and so was their son Michael. The Sabella family eventually grew to four when their daughter Ava was born in 2006.

Mike and I hit it off wonderfully in short order and had lots to talk about. Both our lives were extremely busy. Mike was a contractor, and I was a pediatric surgeon. We always made the time, however, to do some pretty intense workouts together in Mike's basement gym. He had owned a gym in the past and then moved all his equipment into the basement of the home he had built. There was nothing we lacked.

I realized just how spiritually connected Mike and I were when one evening we were doing some super squats. After a proper and formal warm-up period with back squats off a rack and appropriate lead-up sets, you're now ready for the finish. You take whatever amount of weight you can barely get ten full reps with, and you just grind out twenty full back squats. It ends up being a full-body workout that leaves you completely spent. (Do not try this at home, and don't try it if you are not in really great shape and are not experienced at the proper technique or if you don't have a qualified spotter.)

During one of Mike's final sets of super squats, I felt him struggling to get his seventeenth rep. From about fifteen or so feet away, I intentionally but silently sent a well-directed rush of energy to Mike. I then walked over to help him rack the bar as he finished his final set of super squats successfully. As he set the bar down in the rack, caught his breath, and unraveled his knee wraps, he said, "Thank you, my brother, for the energy delivery. The timing was perfect." I was stunned that he knew. I had made no gestures at all.

I eventually came to know that Mike was a very spiritual individual and also very observant of his Catholic upbringing. I found that combination interesting because most Catholics I knew didn't think about things that were truly spiritual and/or metaphysical. Mike was actually both. Mike never missed church on Sundays and also became a Eucharistic minister.

Mike eventually told me about how for many years he would pray for lost souls. He would go to bed at night and would slip into a lucid dream state where he was prone to channeling souls in need. In this in-between state, people would enter his room and attempt to communicate a message through to him. All sorts of people from all walks of life would come to him. One thing is certain. People in this world and those who have passed on come to Mike for help. He is a blessed soul who is holding God's love and light.

Mike and I would often trade metaphysical stories. We were always interested in each other's interpretation of our respective visions, channeling episodes, and the messages that were clearly being sent to us while either meditating or channeling.

We were strangers in 2002, but now we are very dear friends and on the same spiritual path with the same spiritual trajectory. We are part of God's spiritual army. You can consider people like us part of God's sleeper cells (and there are many worldwide). We didn't know for most of our lives what are spiritual paths and functions were all about. I can assure you that we do now. People are bought together seemingly because of day-to-day mundane issues like work, basketball, ice hockey, the theater, among others, but there is absolutely a much bigger story behind it all.

Over the last fifteen years or so, people who were total strangers to me have become now my dear friends. We are all very spiritually based with strong metaphysical capabilities, and I might add that we come from different religious backgrounds. I don't mean just from various Christian backgrounds but from totally different religions like Hinduism, Islam, Judaism, and Buddhism. We all do something completely different for our careers. We have been bought together like thousands and thousands of others all over the world. The end of this age is near. Spiritual warfare is no joke, my friends. God's army is steadily being assembled and positioned with the people who are strong for the Lord and hear His voice.

"So, it will be at the end of the age. The angels will come forth, separating the wicked from among the just" (Matthew 13:49).

In the same manner that more and more people all over the world are becoming aware of the rampant decay of morality in so many ways and the dissolution of civilization, so comes together God's spiritual army. We are being primed to launch the massive spiritual attack of God's love and light upon this very dark and increasingly sinister world.

When enough like-spirited warriors assemble and become activated spiritually, then the light will absolutely overcome the dark, and everything will change on this earth. It will be the dawning of a better world, an ascended humanity. Spiritual warfare will culminate in ushering in the kingdom of God here on earth as it is in heaven. All of this is getting closer and closer, but everything will happen in God's divine time, not ours. Mike Sabella will stand with us as one of God's warriors of light!

"Now we beseech you, brethren, by the coming of our Lord Jesus Christ, and (by) our gathering together unto Him" (2 Thessalonians 2:1 KJV).

Michael and me

Now read about some of Michael's spiritual and metaphysical adventures as told by Michael himself.

Chapter 9

From Brother Michael

Prior to going into my meditative journeys, I would always cleanse myself at a Holy pool that I created spiritually. To achieve complete purity, I would undress first and then enter the pool, say a prayer as in a baptism, step out of the pool, and then put on my traveling robe. My robe is sky blue with white outlines, and on the back is a large cross that can change into a sword.

During my meditations I had several wonderful experiences seeing our Lord, Jesus Christ. One night I found myself walking on the beach near the shoreline. At a far-off distance, I could see a wall made of rock and dirt. The beach ended at this point. As I approached this huge wall, I was able to see narrow steps carved into the side of the wall. I used these steps and went up the wall. There were hundreds of steps before I got to the top. When I reached the top, about three hundred feet in front of me was a structure much like a castle.

No one was around. The structure was tremendous. All I could see to my left and right was this huge structure. I approached the castle to find a very large door that was closed. This door was about twenty feet wide and about sixty feet tall. I stood before the door for a while, wondering if I should try to open it. I tried to open the doors with my hands, but it wouldn't budge. I grabbed my sword and pushed the edge of the sword into the spacing between the frame and the door, and then I tried to pry the door open. After several attempts with all my strength, I got the door to budge a little, and I eventually squeezed through.

I entered and saw a courtyard with many columns. I thought to myself, *Maybe I should leave. Do I belong here?* Again, there was no one around at all. As I stood there looking around, I saw in the far distance a very tiny dot of white light to my left. I decided to follow this light, and it got larger as I went. It bought me to a room that was lit at the rear. I couldn't clearly see what was illuminated. I continued walking toward the light, and as I approached, I could see in front of me Jesus on the cross. It was as if He were still alive and pure. Many thoughts raced through my mind. I got very nervous and thought maybe I shouldn't have come here. With that, I came out of my meditation abruptly. My heart was racing, and my breathing was heavy as if I had physically exerted myself.

Another time while in meditation, I was inside a dark room. I could see many different single streams of colors moving very fast almost like shooting stars. Over time the room I was in became brighter; however, it was nighttime, and no lights were on. I felt cool damp air around me, and when I turned to my right, Jesus Christ was standing next to me. I was startled, and with that, He vanished. He was wearing an off-white robe almost like sackcloth.

Through my life I have had many souls come to me when I am either sleeping or trying to sleep. When this happens, the lighting of my room will begin to change. Often I'll see small white lights in the corner of my room, lights that don't exist physically. My ceiling will begin to reflect light too. Some people will present themselves to me from one side or another while others will hover right over me. Sometimes these souls will speed toward me in light forms but reach me in their human forms. There are times when I feel very threatened before they come as if I can sense there impending arrival, yet other times there is apparently no feeling of threat or uneasiness at all. I can routinely encounter adults or children.

Other times I will see prophetic visions of the near future like a week or so off. When they actually occur, I'm always amazed. For many years I've wondered why this ability was given to me. I now understand what it's all about. My spiritual and metaphysical abilities have been given to me to serve our Lord. The world has fallen into a very dark and scary realm. I am God's light warrior who's here to serve Jesus in the fight against this present and growing darkness. God has bought me together with many people through my life. They are all my brothers and sisters, but not all of them will stand for God in the end. My brother John and I stand shoulder to shoulder for our Lord Jesus. We are ready and at His command always.

God's love to you all,
Michael Sabella

In the last days, God says, I will pour out my Spirit on all people. Your sons and daughters will prophecy, your young men will see visions, and your old men will dream dreams. Even on my servants, both men and woman, I will pour out my Spirit in those days, and they will prophesy. I will show wonders in the Heavens above and signs on the earth below, blood and fire and billows of smoke. The sun will be turned to darkness and the moon to blood before the coming of the great and glorious day of the Lord. And everyone who calls on the name of the Lord will be saved.

—Acts 2:17–21 (NIV)

Every relationship is meaningful. We are all connected by God's river of love and light. The next chapter tells us how even when circumstances may seem hopeless and even fanciful, there is a greater significance to it all. Some relationships would appear to go completely against all the odds and seem frankly impossible. Then Serguie Starikov and his family entered my life, and I entered theirs.

Chapter 10

Serguie

On a peaceful sleepy Sunday in May 1970, my family and I headed out to my aunt Dolly and Uncle Charlie's house for Sunday dinner. They lived in Hackensack, New Jersey, which was about a forty-minute drive for us. Sunday dinner is a big deal for people of Italian heritage. It's a reason to get together with family. You can bet there's always lots of great food and drink and certainly a really good time.

When the kids were good and done, we usually headed off to watch TV. Sunday wasn't typically a good TV day until nighttime. The lineup for Sunday evening was *Wild Kingdom* with Marlin Perkins, *The Wonderful World of Disney*, and then *The Ed Sullivan Show*. We would end the evening by watching Topo Gigio close out *The Ed Sullivan Show*. This was Sunday afternoon in May. That meant no football. I loved football, so I missed it badly. I happened to tune in to a hockey game on TV. I didn't realize it then, but this was a pivotal point in my life. I was mesmerized!

I had no idea that I had stumbled upon the Stanley Cup finals between the Boston Bruins and the St. Louis Blues. Apparently, I stumbled upon game four of the Stanley Cup finals! This was the best thing I had ever seen in my whole life! The Boston Bruins won the cup, and the cup presentation was actually televised. The Bruins had swept the St. Louis Blues in four straight games. I was filled with inspiration, joy, and wonder.

I made up my mind that someday, somehow, John Gallucci was going to play ice hockey. I let a few weeks go by before I told my dad. I will never forget this moment. He was taking his usual nap on his recliner during the time after work but before dinner. I walked up to him and said, "Dad, I want to tell you something. Dad!" I tapped him on his left arm. "I want to tell you something." He opened his eyes and looked at me as if to say, "Really? This better be good. Okay, tell me."

"Dad, I want to play ice hockey." It was nearly summer in New Jersey in 1972.

He looked at me and said, "Okay," and went back to sleep. Hmmm. Did he understand? It didn't matter. I was gonna make sure he got it.

By the fall I had my sights set on skating at the local pond. Bowden's Pond was a shallow pond really perfect for skating in the winter. It always froze when I was a kid. I can remember freezing my tail off as I skated there and then going into the Lion's Den to warm up by the old potbellied stove.

By the spring I had convinced my dad to put me in a hockey initiation camp. I will never forget getting my first hockey uniform, which was purchased at the Verona Sports Shop on Bloomfield Avenue in Verona, New Jersey. The entire uniform cost around $110.00 at the time. That was a lot of money back in 1972. I was so in love with the stuff that I wore it all in the house. I would put it on after school, and I even wore the gloves and my Boston Bruins jersey to bed!

It was the Sunday of my very first hockey initiation at the rink in Branch Brook Park in Newark, New Jersey. I ran across the parking lot with my green duffle bag slung over my shoulder. I was going to look the part of a hockey player as fast as I could!

Dad called me over and introduced me to Mr. Adam Louis. He was very pleasant, and he told me he couldn't wait for me to take the ice for the first time. The Zamboni departed the ice, and the driver shoveled some snow by the doorway and then closed the doors to the rink. Sam gestured for us to step on to the ice. There were about eight of us. He read us the polite riot act about following commands and instructions. It was the thrill of my life!

Mr. Louis had a three-year-old son named Michel who would skate all by himself on the other end of the rink in a full Detroit Red Wings jersey. All the mothers would fawn over little Michel as he methodically skated in circles around and around, to the left, to the right, with the puck and without. Then he would skate while pushing a puck in and out of orange cones set up for him by his dad. Each week little Michel was there skating the full session all by himself in his Detroit Red Wings uniform. He certainly seemed self-motivated.

The hockey initiation class came and went, and I was starved for more. Mr. Louis told us that I needed lots of ice work but that my ambition and heart were great. He said anything was possible for me. My love for ice hockey came from my soul. I understood I was a neophyte, but Sam was right. I had the heart. Mr. Louis and his three-year-old son Michel left a huge impression on me. It wouldn't be for another twenty-five years that I would hear the name Michel Louis again.

I played locally, building my skills as I went. Four years later I made the roster for the New Jersey Golden Blades travel team. I didn't realize my dad didn't have the money to cover the cost, including trips to Canada. I knew what I had to do. I held on to the hope that he knew how much I loved ice hockey and that I had certainly come very far with my skills and abilities on the ice. I would tell him that I didn't think I wanted to play this season but that maybe next year I would. I hoped that he would say, "It's okay, Johnny. You'll play. I know how much you love it."

He was taking a nap on his recliner like he always did after work and before dinner. "Dad, I want to tell you something. Here's the registration form for the Golden Blades for this season. Dad, I think maybe I'm not going to play hockey this year. Maybe next year?"

All he said was, "Okay," and then he went back to sleep.

I stood there in silence. My worst fear had come true. I turned and walked away. I went straight to my room, shut my door, and cried for hours. I still believe I did the right thing, but it sure hurt deeply. My dad was a very understanding and gentle man who loved us all very much. I knew travel hockey was placing an undue burden on him and our family. I stopped hockey because I couldn't bear to put him through the expense and the time that I knew he didn't have, but it left a deep emotional scar in me. Never underestimate seemingly unimportant events and turning points for your children. They can be much bigger in their hearts and minds than you can imagine. That being said, all things happen for a reason.

As an undergraduate student, I got a job as a bartender at a popular national hotel chain. I would tend bar in the lounge here and there, but most of my gigs were for weddings and banquets. The job was fun depending on the gig, and it put a few bucks in my pocket each week. I was now a sophomore in college in 1980. The Winter Olympics were underway in Lake Placid, New York. Although I had experienced my rude awakening with ice hockey long ago, I still wasn't over the game. I still loved it more than anything.

Through the years I would follow the NHL, international hockey like the Canada Cup series, and the Olympics. Either way, if it was ice hockey beyond the NHL, there wasn't anyone who could stand up to the great Soviet National team. Every four years they would kick everyone's butt and win the gold medal in the Olympics or get into a great series with the NHL All-Stars or the Canada Cup. The win-loss record is public knowledge, and they often won against all my childhood hockey heroes.

As for the ice hockey competition at the 1980 Winter Olympics, nobody anticipated anything other than business as usual. Nobody was going to beat the Soviets. The whole world knew it. I hoped to watch a game or so, but why would I bother thinking that anyone would even get close to beating the Soviets? So whatever game was going to be televised, I'd be watching.

It just so happened that the day the US team played the Soviet Union in the game that would eventually be known as the great "miracle on ice," I was scheduled to bartend in a private conference room for a quiet, stuffy, corporate meeting with no TV. The greatest sporting event in modern history took place, and it was on TV a few paces away. I didn't get to see one single second of that game. There were no words for the emotions welling up in me.

Why would God let such an amazing moment in time that meant so much to me personally come and go and shut me out completely? The event was so big that it literally caused reverberations geopolitically all over the world. It also gave birth to US hockey in a real way.

To make matters worse, US hockey decided to lock all memorabilia of the event away legally for twenty-five years. So there were no game tapes or photos. It wouldn't be released until the twenty-five anniversary of the 1980 Winter Olympics. For twenty-five years, I had never seen a single second of that game other than the famous countdown announced by Al Michaels, which had been used in television here and there.

I read of a Christian who said, "I used to have many disappointments, until I changed one letter of the word and chopped it in two, so that instead of 'disappointment,' I read it, 'His appointments.'" That was a wonderful change for "disappointments break your heart," but "His appointments" you accept cheerfully.[11]

Years had come and gone since 1980. I was now working as a busy pediatric surgeon. My wife and I had three kids. The first two were hockey players. I taught them both to skate prior to their second birthdays. I was going to give them the advantages that I certainly never had. Gemma, my youngest child, didn't want a life of ice hockey. She enjoyed the weekend tournaments and hung out with the hockey siblings, but that was it for her. Gemma was headed for a life of acting, singing, playing guitar, and making films.

Somebody had mentioned that the New Jersey Penguins played out of a local rink not far away and that we should try out. I had heard that there was a Russian guy who used to play hockey for the New Jersey Devils involved with that organization. *Okay*, I thought. *Why not?*

No matter how long you may be involved with a sport or any other endeavor, if you have never seen a real professional athlete, singer, or musician up close and personal, you just don't know what you're missing. You can watch basketball on TV for years and even have played the game through high school and local college, but if you haven't been on the court with a Michael Jordan or a Larry Bird, you just don't get it. A friend of mine once said that true professional athletes are freaks of nature. He was spot on. They just aren't normal. If they were, they wouldn't have made it to the pinnacle of their profession.

The kids took to the ice for tryouts. The coaches were generally hockey dads. Then I saw this fellow built like an oak tree step onto the ice. As he did, everyone else seemed to become invisible around him. His strides were smooth and easy, yet they propelled him like a race horse. His edges flawlessly cut the ice like a precision machine. His biomechanics were beyond anything I had ever seen in person. His ability to move his body and propel it one way yet move the puck in an altogether different motion was unreal. All he needed to do was flick his body and the puck would take off like he had shot it out of a cannon.

I asked one of the other dads standing with me and watching the tryouts, "Who is that guy who moves like that?"

He said, "Oh, that's Serguie Starikov. He played for the Soviet National Team, CSKA Moskva, and played in the miracle on ice too. He was also one of the two first Russians to ever play in the NHL, and he played for the New Jersey Devils." I was hypnotized by this man's ability on the ice. At the end of the tryouts, we had our new team. I went home, thinking about what I had just seen.

As the summer came upon us, I realized I should get my two hockey players some private lessons. Parents who were serious about their kids' abilities did the same. I made some calls through our coaching staff and ended up arranging lessons for my son and daughter with Serguie.

I stood in total awe of the picture I had on the ice. Understand that this was something to behold! There they were, my two small children skating and having fun with Serguie Starikov. This man went to battle on the ice with the likes of many of my hockey heroes in the NHL. He was defense for Vladislav Tretiak. He fed passes to Valerie Kharlamov. He was a part of that unbeatable Russian juggernaut, a part of that great Soviet team that nobody could beat. My kids had no idea who they were playing with. They were having fun, but at the same time, they were being challenged with skill development. I had succeeded in giving my kids the advantage that I never had as a kid. It meant everything to me. Wow. God is good!

As the fall-winter hockey season was upon us, we became friends with the Starikov family. We quickly got to know and love Serguie's wife Irina and their two kids Ilya and Ksenia. Irina said she felt *connected* to us, and I totally believe her. Some people are brought together by God's will and wisdom.

Through the years we had lots fun together. Serguie became Seth's coach for several years. Seth took one-on-one private lessons with Serguie every Friday morning at six o'clock for an hour before school at the local Ice Pavillion, which wasn't far from home. He did this for two years. Kudos to my son. He never complained about it and was always up and ready to go.

We would all go to the Starikov family's house for birthday parties, and it was always a great time. The away tournaments were always a blast for us all. It seemed like every year we would end up in Lake Placid, New York, for the annual CAN/AM Hockey tournament with Serguie and Irina.

I can remember seeing Serguie sitting there in the stands of the 1980 rink well before our game and just looking out onto the ice. I knew enough to not say a thing. He looked at me and said in his heavy Russian accent, "It still smells the same in this place." It was twenty-five years after that fateful day, February 22, 1980, when the miracle on ice took place. Serguie and his teammates were in no way over that loss to the US team. What happened that day in Lake Placid, New York, was completely against all odds. It was well, a "miracle".

We both shared a lament over that game, though his was certainly much more serious. He lamented from his heart over the outcome, and I lamented from my heart that I never saw a single second of the game. I had been denied any and all access to the great miracle on ice for more than twenty-five years. Now here I was all these years later with one of my best friends who had played in that game, and we were reliving it.

I can remember taking the team to see the movie *Miracle* while Serguie was our coach. Watching those young kids go from hearing about this big event and its significance to seeing it on screen and then taking to the ice with Serguie was priceless. The kids never looked at Serguie in the same way again.

One day Serguie called me up and said he had tickets to the Devils game at the Meadowlands Arena. It was the twenty-fifth anniversary of the New Jersey Devils. Serguie and another Devils defenseman were going to drop the puck on TV for the start of the game. My very dear friend Mike Sabella and I drove Serguie and played his chauffeurs. We were three friends having a great time. As we pulled up to the parking venue, the guards stopped us and looked into the car. "Can we help you guys? Oh, Serguie! Right this way! Pull right up to the curb and leave the car right here please!" We were given the red carpet treatment in my old 4Runner!

As we walked into the arena, dozens of people, mostly Russians and Eastern Europeans, swarmed Serguie for his autograph. Mike and I stood back and just watched. We were with a living hockey legend, but the average American didn't know him. We were thrilled to see Serguie get the recognition he so deserved.

Not long after this event, Serguie was recruited to be a coach in the prestigious Kontinental Hockey League (KHL). This is the Eastern European NHL. Many NHL players will cross over and play in the KHL. Serguie had to leave home in New Jersey and live where the job was for more than six months each year. We were all very happy for him but also very sad for all of us. It was just one of those things. Serguie told me, "Hockey is my life," and it surely is.

Serguie gave his heart and soul to everyone he ever played for or coached. We were all so very proud of Serguie when he got the call from the Russian Hockey Federation during the Sochi Olympics. They flew him out to the Olympics as a surprise and inducted him into the Russian Hockey Hall of Fame. What an honor! God bless you, my friend. You deserve it!

My son Seth left hockey after the season of his senior year in high school. He had put so much time and effort into it, and he was now finished. Letting ice hockey go was my son's decision, and I have always been good with it. Seth has other fish to fry. I was always in awe of my son and what he achieved in hockey. He played all over the eastern United States. Seth gave it his all, and I'm left awestruck by his tenacity and fortitude. My hockey wish for him had been fulfilled. I'm so very proud of him.

Arielle now plays varsity college hockey in Boston. They just finished their first championship season in school history, and as a freshman, Arielle made the all-tournament team. She even assisted on the winning goal in the championship game. Arielle was then named rookie of the year. I was very proud of her as her pursuit was all her decision.

Serguie, Irina, and their kids are our dear friends, and they always will be. The Starikovs are part of my soul family, and we are part of theirs.

As things come full circle in life, I can see firsthand that God has a plan for each and every one of us. We may not fully understand why things happen at the time. I can assure you that God's plan for you is *always* to your benefit. This is true even in times of great tragedy and strife, and it goes far beyond missing a sporting event. God is focused on eternity, not necessarily the here and now.

If I look back at how this story unfolded, I see two paths that were possible. On path one, John doesn't have to work on February 22, 1980. He watches the miracle on ice like a billion others did, and he remembers watching history in the making. On path two, things happen as they really did in my life. I missed that game and saw none of the footage for twenty-five years.

God heard my prayers and saw my lament. His gift to me was so much more than I could ever have dreamed. Serguie, who played in that very game, became my dear friend and my kids' coach. His family and ours have a blessed destiny together.

Would I go back and choose path one like I thought I wanted in 1980? Not in a million years. The whole thing happened just as it was meant to be, and I thank God for that.

What of little Michel Louis, Adam's three-year-old son who skated all by himself at the other end of the Branch Brook Arena in Newark, New Jersey, back in 1972? Well, he followed the path that God planned for him. What appeared to be a path against all odds was surely God's path of destiny. Michel went on to become an NHL all-star, and his name was etched on Lord Stanley's Cup along with those from the 1993 Montreal Canadians after they defeated Wayne Gretsky and the Los Angeles Kings. He played for many teams in the NHL, including the Detroit Red Wings.

Waiting

"There is no place for faith if we expect God to fulfill immediately what He promises."[12]

"Wait for the Lord; be strong, and let your heart take courage; wait for the Lord!" (Psalm 27:14 ESV).

"But, if we hope for what we do not see, we wait for it with patience" (Romans 8:25 ESV).

"But the fruit of the Spirit is love, joy, peace, patience, kindness, goodness, faithfulness, gentleness, self-control; against such things there is no law" (Galatians 5:22–23 ESV).

Useful

"O Lord, let me not live to be useless."[13]

Relationships

"Life is not a solo but a chorus. We live in relationships from cradle to grave."[14]

"We live in relationships with family members" (Matthew 15:4 ESV).

For this reason I bow my knees before the Father, from whom every family in Heaven and on earth is named, that according to the riches of His glory He may grant you to be strengthened with power through His Spirit in your inner being, so that Christ may dwell in your hearts through faith--that you, being rooted and grounded in love, may have strength to comprehend with all the saints what is the breadth and length and height and depth, and to know the love of Christ that surpasses knowledge, that you may be filled with all the fullness of God. (Ephesians 3:14-19 ESV).

Me, Ilya, and Serguie   Me, Irina, and Serguie

Mike, Arielle and Seth with Coach Sergei

Michael Sabella Jr., Serguie, Arielle and Seth

God's spiritual people find one another. Sometimes it takes calamity and heartache to do so. The next chapter shows us how sickness and sorrow can be overcome by God's love and a strong faith in our own God-given intuition. Deanna Coppola-Rossetter is a fabulous example of just that and certainly one of the strongest people I've ever met. When her child's life was on the line, she trusted in herself and God.

Chapter 11

From Sister Deanna

I have always been a very private person. When I get to know and trust people, I allow them into my world. Mine is a world that many never could understand. At the young age of five, I knew I was different. I knew that Jesus lived within me. I knew I was put on this earth for something way bigger than just being me and growing up the way I was raised. I questioned everything, and I believed nothing. I was told about life. I knew that those teaching me were only passing along what they had been taught from generation to generation. But who's to say what the truth really was?

I went to my mother for answers all the time, but to no avail. I was told that children should be seen and not heard and to do as I was told and shut my mouth. I was told that I was a problem and that I needed to stop questioning everything, and I was punished for that behavior at times. Well, it just made me think, *Why don't they understand me?*

Well, it got worse when I started seeing passed loved ones. Mom didn't believe me. This was not common in my family, and clearly, they had no clue how to handle it. I was scared and confused and just wanted it to stop.

I didn't want to be the outcast or made to feel like I was crazy, so I suppressed it. What a mistake on my part. I was just a kid, and I wanted to be normal and part of my family.

Well, I learned the hard way that I was on my own in this world. If I wanted answers, I only had myself to depend on, and that was when my journey into the spiritual world began. I have never followed societal rules or guidelines for life because they never made sense to me. I have always walked to the beat of my own drummer.

I knew what powers I had within, and I was learning how to use them (self-taught, of course). My grandmother (father's mom) was the only one who understood me and listened to me. She would read me the Bible daily and discuss it all with me. Our time together was a blessing from God. She was the mother to me that mine couldn't be until God took her home when I was fifteen.

Losing my grandmother completely turned my world upside down. She always told me to follow my spirit in life. "You will find what you need, including the family you are meant to be with." So I took that pain and turned it into good. I learned that I was a "self-healer," as I put it. I was able to go deep within and heal myself with my mind (not knowing at that time I was doing it through meditation and prayer). What a power tool the mind is, and so many don't even realize their capabilities and what they can do with their minds.

I knew that life was about love, and I found that love within my grandma and my dad. (They were two peas in a pod, and I was just like them.) My mother was a very abusive woman, and everything was about her. (Needless to say that we didn't get along at all.) She was never a mother to me, and she made that quite clear. So that made it very challenging for me growing up (not to mention having the spiritual gifts I was given). She basically rejected me.

One thing I knew was that if I were ever blessed with a child, I was going to be nothing like the mother I had been given. Believe it or not, all I ever wanted was to be a mom. I never wanted a career. I just wanted to be the best damn mom I could be. After having Will and Ryan (true miracle babies), I understand it all a lot better now. Jesus had a plan for me too, and I never understood it until I had my boys.

Well, at the age of twenty-six, I was pregnant with William, my first. At twenty-six weeks, my water broke, and I was admitted into the hospital. I began getting shots of steroids to try to boost his lung development in the fear that I had gone into labor too soon. Well, at twenty-seven weeks, he was born by emergency C-section because every time I had a contraction, his blood pressure dropped to a very dangerous level. If that wasn't scary enough, he was only two and a half pounds at birth. I was told, "You have a son," and they briefly held him up for me to see. Then they whisked him away to the NICU.

So I got a visit from the doctors once I got back to my room and was told to prepare myself. "Your son has a 50 percent chance of living, and by the chance that he does survive, he will be petite. He will have developmental delay, possible brain damage, breathing disabilities. He may never function and live as a normal child does."

I just couldn't believe what I was being told, and I wasn't going to accept it. After all we just went through, hearing that was my worst nightmare. In my mind, these were just the statistics that they had been taught in medical school or residency. How could they really know what the future held for my son? They only knew what they had been taught.

I did some serious soul searching that night while I lay confined to the hospital bed after my surgery. I prayed and asked Jesus to guide me and show me what I needed to do to gain the strength I would need to heal and to nurture and care for my son.

The next day my husband brought me down to the NICU. What an overwhelming experience it was, especially for a first-time parent. All those tiny little souls fighting for their lives made for a daunting sight. The noises the machines made, the monitors, wires, and tubes that branched out everywhere were overwhelming.

They brought me to my son, and all I could do was cry. It killed me inside to see him like that. I was not allowed to hold him in fear that it would stress his little body out. I knew what I had to do for my son. I knew I had to give him back to Jesus for healing.

I asked to be alone with him and opened the door on his Isolette. I spoke to him, and he heard my voice. I told him how much I loved him and said that I was his mom (the one he had been inside of). I prayed. I put my hands on his little body. I looked up to heaven and said, "He is yours, dear Lord. He is yours for the taking now. If what the doctors said is true and he will not have a normal life and likely not be without machines or continuous medical intervention to live, I am giving him back to you. Please … I don't want him to suffer horribly in life. It would kill me inside to lose him, but I am willing to accept that pain in order for him to not suffer." My heartache was the least of my concerns in that instance.

At that very moment, I felt a warm sensation run through my body and engulf me, and then I felt it transfer from my hands into William's body. His monitors went nuts for a brief moment, and then I felt a sense of peace come over me. I knew at that moment my son was going live and be fine. By the time the nurses came to see if he was okay, his monitors went back to normal.

I looked at my husband and said, "He will be just fine."

He said, "How do you know?"

"I can't explain it. You won't understand. I just know." He still had a long road ahead of him with his health and gaining weight, but I knew that Jesus could heal from within us. He told us so in the Gospels, and Jesus showed me that firsthand.

At sixteen, William is far from petite or tiny. (He's six feet three inches tall.) He's beaten all the odds against him. William has also been given some amazing spiritual gifts. He is a psychic, an empath, a light worker, and a medium. At about six years old, he came to me and told me he often saw a little girl in a yellow dress in the hallway at his school during class but that he was the only one that could see her. I explained to him what he was seeing and how he could help her. When he saw her again, he told her to go toward the white light and that everything would be okay. He never saw her again after that.

That's when his spiritual journey started, but I am so glad that he came to me and didn't suppress it like I did out of fear. He is an amazing young man and super intelligent. William received honors in all his subjects, and he's mostly a straight A student. In his sophomore year, he was already at a 4.0 grade point average. William and I are so spiritually connected that he can read my mind, and he blows me away with some of the stuff he can do and has done. William was sent here to change the world, and I knew that from early on.

Four years later I got pregnant with Ryan, and I was placed under the care of the doctors from a maternal fetal medicine (MFM) group. I went in for my five-month ultrasound to find out the sex of the baby. (My spirit had already told me it was a boy.) However, I knew something was seriously wrong when the doctors came in the room. My husband and I were told there was a problem. William had only a two-vessel umbilical cord. (Three vessels is normal.) I figured they were going to tell us that Ryan had the same issues as William. Well, they said there was an issue with his bowel, and at that point in time, they didn't know what kind of issue it could be. They said it could be one of five things— Down's syndrome, cystic fibrosis, a primary bowel problem, blood he had swallowed, or nothing at all. Wow!

I was trying to process this all, and then they told us to consider termination of the pregnancy!

I was in shock and couldn't believe they just told me what they had, so we left. On the ride home, my husband and I were both upset and confused and couldn't believe what we had heard. He said, "Deanna, do what you do. Go deep within yourself, and find the answers you are seeking. I stand behind you 100 percent with whatever you decide to do."

Well, I did go within, and I thought about everything. I knew it wasn't Down's syndrome because my screening came back normal. I knew it wasn't cystic fibrosis because even though I carried the gene, my husband had undergone the genetic screening, and he didn't carry the gene. A bowel problem could only be diagnosed once he was born. And if there was no issue—well, what can I say about that?

That Monday I had an appointment to see my doctor, and after I told him everything that had happened and how they had told to me to consider terminating the pregnancy, he was just as shocked as we had been. He discussed the odds of what those other doctors had said would happen. I told him that I made my decision. I would not terminate my child. No matter what this brightness in the bowel from the ultrasound turned out to be, I would deal with whatever God saw fit to give me. From that point on, things were pretty stable until I went into labor at thirty-five weeks with Ryan.

I went into labor the weekend my primary ob-gyn was off. Another associate doctor I had never met was going to handle my delivery. I was now in full-blown labor and waiting for my epidural. Then the doctor entered my room and tried to change my birth plan. She tried to convince me to not have the scheduled C-section but to try a VBAC (vaginal birth after C-section). I said no. The doctor was persistent and still trying to push the VBAC. I prayed to God for her to stop. I knew it would not work and a VBAC would put me and my child in serious danger. The issue got ugly, and they finally agreed to go with the repeat C-section as planned. I got my C-section. Ryan was born at seven pounds and eight ounces, and he was taken to the nursery with my husband.

As I was laying there during the C-section, I felt like something was not right because I was on the table a lot longer than the last time, so much longer that I started to feel my feet and legs again, and I told them that. That's when I felt and heard the panic. The anesthesiologist at my head said everything was fine, but I knew better.

I immediately started praying to Jesus. I was not ready to die! I needed to be here for my boys. In my mind, I enveloped my body in the white light of the Holy Spirit, and I knew that if I put it in Jesus's hands, I would be okay. I demanded to know what was going on, and they said, "Sedate her!" However, before I went out, I heard them say, "She is bleeding internally, and it's not stopping."

I woke up in recovery three hours later with my husband holding my hand, crying. I asked him what happened, and he said that there were complications. I got back to my room, and they came to tell me that they had to move Ryan to the NICU because he hadn't been able to hold a feeding down without vomiting it all back up and that he hadn't pooped the meconium plug out yet. Again, I lay there that night, praying to Jesus to guide me and give me His strength to handle whatever I had to deal with in order to get Ryan well.

So Ryan was eventually taken into emergency surgery for a bowel obstruction. After the surgery the doctors had narrowed things down to either cystic fibrosis or a primary intestinal disorder. I allowed them to do a sweat test to rule out CF, which I knew he didn't have, and they got a negative result. I said, "Okay, so now let's figure out what's wrong and fix it please."

They decided to pursue the bowel problem. They did numerous tests and procedures on him and then came back and asked me to allow them to do another sweat test for CF, which was negative again. I now had serious concerns for my son's health. The final straw was when they told me that they were going to start treating him for CF and giving him medicine for it. I refused the medical treatment and told them to find the primary intestinal issue they should be looking for.

I was getting upset over the lack of diagnosis and requested a second opinion. We seemed to be stuck on this diagnosis of cystic fibrosis, which I knew Ryan did not have. The secretary there asked me if I had ever met Dr. Gallucci. I said no, and she explained to me that Dr. Gallucci would come to study the case and then discuss it with me and the NICU team. She asked me to just give Dr. Gallucci a chance. "Trust me. You will not be disappointed in him and his ability." I told her that I was emotionally done, and she said, "Please just trust me." Her name was Joyce Ciancia, and she was an angel in disguise.

Well, our lives changed dramatically when we met Dr. Gallucci. He was the answer to my prayers because he sat with us and listened to every single word I said to him. He took me seriously. I finally had trust in a doctor and felt sure what he was saying was true.

Dr. Gallucci took Ryan to the operating room and found the answers everyone had been looking for. Ryan was diagnosed with Hirschsprung's disease and a micro colon and a case of complicated meconium ileus. That meant his colon was too small because a plug of feces had blocked his bowel at the junction of the small and large intestine. That in turn caused his colon to not expand well enough so feces couldn't pass through. He also had Hirschsprung's disease (a bowel abnormality where the colon can't relax to pass stool) on top of that.

This was a very difficult set of issues to deal with. Fixing this would take multiple operations and many months of urging his colon to expand. Ryan may have complications and abnormal bowel function for his whole life. Apparently, some children could be so dysfunctional that they would have better lives with colostomies. Only time and the grace of God would tell us the answer. My infant son would need a colostomy.

Dr. Gallucci restored my faith in doctors, and that was when our journey began. He always kept me involved with what was happening with Ryan. He made us all understand exactly what we were dealing with, why, and what to do about it. I became my son's nurse overnight. I never imagined all the things that Dr. Gallucci would teach me and have me do. He gave me the strength to keep moving forward to get Ryan's health where it needed to be. I was not a nurse by any means, and I had no clue what I was doing at first. I was a mom, but with his guidance and encouragement, I was able to do everything he asked and expected of me. It wasn't easy, but we did it!

Ryan had been through so many tests and procedures and four major operations before he was even two years old. I clearly remember Dr. Gallucci telling me that he fell in love with Ryan and that no matter what he had to do, Ryan would live a bag-free life. He said, "Positive thoughts and prayers, and it will all work out."

Well, Dr. Gallucci fulfilled his promise to my son the day he decided to do his reversal surgery (his fifth and final major surgery). Sitting across from him at that table and having him tell me, "I don't have any guarantees, Deanna, but I have talked to doctors around the world about Ryan and his case and whether to do the reversal now or wait until his micro colon got even larger, if it would at all. The decision was to go now. We will need to pray for Ryan that this pull-through operation will work for him."

It was possible that he may need his bag as his whole GI tract didn't function well. Well, I looked at him and crossed my fingers, and he said, "Pray for a perfect outcome." I can never thank Dr. Gallucci enough for all he did for my son and my family. He has given my son back his quality of life when no one else could.

Dr. Gallucci was always upfront and honest with me no matter what. I have the utmost respect for him not only as a doctor but as a natural-born healer. His heart and hands are true gifts from Jesus. Dr. Gallucci has been inside my son's body numerous times, and he not only healed his disease but also healed his heart and ours.

Working with both heart and hands at the same time is a rare quality for anyone, let alone a physician. That gift comes from deep within oneself, and he has always shown that to us from the day we met him. I have always looked up to him. When I so often felt I had nowhere to turn to help my son, he was there with his presence and his way with words. The tone in his voice was like no other doctor's I had dealt with.

So many didn't listen to us. So many had gone in the wrong direction but were sure they were right and dismissed what I had to say. Not him. His soul was pure. He never ran off the ego like most doctors did.

He was always smiling and happy, and he would make time to talk to everyone when needed. He never let me down during my worst times. Dr. Gallucci took the time to speak to me to give me strength when I had none left. He guided me to where I needed to be. He allowed me to live outside my comfort zone, and by doing that, he made me realize that I was a lot stronger than I gave myself credit for and that I could do anything I had to.

If Joyce hadn't stepped in and convinced me to give him a chance, things would not have turned out as well as they did. For that, Joyce will always hold a special place in my heart. She brought a true healer into our world.

I knew from early on that Dr. Gallucci was part of our spiritual family, and I have seen that every time he and Ryan were together. There was a glow and special spiritual bond between them. Others told me that when Ryan was about two years old, he had a white glow around him, and they consider him a living angel. (I am still to this day learning and trying to figure out what all this means.) I was also told that Ryan would change the world in ways that I could never imagine and that I was given a divine gift. (I am just repeating what others have told me.)

When Dr. Gallucci met with us the last time we were in New Jersey, I was blown away when he told us how he would astral travel with Ryan's soul and go with him to a healing realm. I wish I could have taken a picture of Dr. Gallucci's face when he realized we all knew what he was talking about. It was priceless.

I know that he was brought into our lives by Jesus through my prayers. We are truly blessed for the gift we have been given. Ryan is doing so very well and functions in a normal fashion. I can't wait to see what the future holds for Ryan and all of us together, and I can only imagine all the good we can do in this world with all these gifts of the Spirit we have been given. I find it amazing and comforting that Ryan also has been given spiritual gifts just as William and I have.

Most doctors do what they do, and then they don't stay in your life. Dr. Gallucci has never intended to leave us. We visit him around the holidays and whenever we visit New Jersey. We stay in touch and interact often. He is certainly a very dear family friend and mentor, and he always will be.

God bless you, Dr. G.

Sending light and love always,
Deanna Rossetter
Ryan's mom

"Or do you not know that your body is a temple of the Holy Spirit within you, whom you have from God? You are not your own, for you were bought with a price. So glorify God in your body" (1 Corinthians 6:19–20 ESV).

"And he said to them, 'Doubtless you will quote to me this proverb, "Physician heal yourself." What we have heard you did at Capernaum, do here in your hometown as well'" (Luke 4:23 ESV).

"Heal the sick, raise the dead, cleanse lepers, cast out demons. You received without paying; give without pay" (Matthew 10:8 ESV).

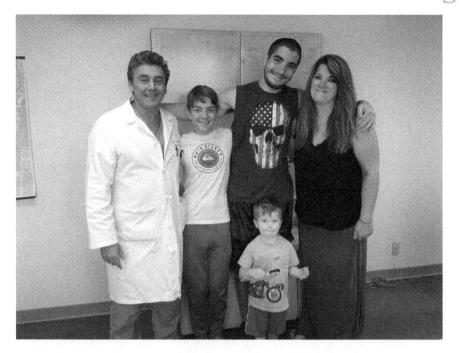

The Family
Me, Ryan, William, Deanna and MJ

The next story is about a family that turned to God for answers when they were told to abort their unborn baby by more than one hospital. Love is the greatest power in the universe and can heal even the worst situations that seem impossible to many. The Mencl family was frightened and badly confused over the plight of their unborn baby. They turned to the Holy Spirit and found their way, their truth, and their life!

Chapter 12

Olivia

I have always known that life is precious. That concept has never been in question for me. There are many who also profess this, but when it comes right down to it, they don't live it. Far too many in this world don't believe it. Life in the flesh is temporary, but it is so dearly precious to every one of us. Why is that so? We know some individuals live to be 108, while others barely make it through the birthing process. I believe (as many do) that life in the flesh holds the key to "maximum spiritual growth."

Our bodies are our earthly temples. You might say we dwell in our flesh, and we use it as a gymnasium for growth and evolution. Every experience is a part of who and what we become. Everything that we experience, say, do, think, and feel are all spiritually stored in what are called the Akashic records. Akasha is a Sanskrit word connoting sky, ether, luminous, or space. So nothing we experience is lost.

The Akashic records are thought of as the Book of Life for many who study the esoteric origins of man. The records are a cosmic eternal library of every single occurrence in our universe. The records are drawn upon by all of us when we are in spirit form and between incarnations.

The life review that we get shortly after passing will become part of the records. Therefore, the records are referenced to guide one's subsequent incarnation and the life experiences that you require and that you must still master. Some believe psychics and seers are able to access these records while here in this physical realm. If this is so, it may explain their metaphysical abilities.

There would be no purpose to living sequential lifetimes (and we do) only to face the same challenges if we have already mastered them. We are here to deal with all the challenges and emotions that life on earth can throw our way while still holding God's love and light. A very large part of our spiritual growth while in the flesh is to deal with and kill off the control our egos have over us and their system of behavior and thinking. An ego-driven life is a life that will only lead to perdition (destruction or damnation), assuring your need for remediation. Could it be that living an ego-driven life only serves to keep you earthbound over and over again? Absolutely!

So if given a chance at life, the opportunity must be taken very seriously. Each spirit-body incarnation is sanctioned by God, the Almighty. Incarnation is a divine occurrence and a chance to advance spiritually and get closer to God through the process of enlightenment (i.e., choosing a God-centered life over an ego-driven one).

It should be clear by now that I don't believe human life is conceived by chance. This then begs the question. What of unplanned pregnancies? What of the unwanted life? What of the child who is conceived but suffers from congenital birth anomalies?

Do we believe we are in a position of judgment? If we have surpassed many developmental milestones, should we have the right to take away another's life because it may not look like our ideal way of coming into this world? The young life you discard may have been exactly what that incarnating spirit required. Subverting that life or discarding it ends up being pointless and troublesome at best and even subversion of God's plan. Many consider abortion or the termination of a viable pregnancy an outright sin (i.e., murder). If you believe that every life is precious, then this issue should weigh heavily on your mind. Judge not, lest you be judged. *That goes both ways in a discussion of the termination of pregnancy.* Live and let live. Let God's divine plan play itself out. The free will they were given by God belongs to them. Regardless of how you feel about the decisions others may make about termination, *don't judge them! You do not have the right to judge others.*

It was a fairly busy day in the office at work. I had already seen nearly a dozen kids thus far. Some were post-ops and pre-ops, some follow-ups, and some new consults not seen before.

My last patient of the day was a new consult. She was an adult in her thirties here with her husband. They were expecting and were about eighteen weeks into the pregnancy. Antenatal consults are done when an expecting mother is carrying a fetus and needs surgical intervention in the postnatal period or when the need for such intervention is suspected.

I picked up the associated paperwork and gave it a quick glance and learned just enough to know why they were here and some basics of the case. I entered the consultation room to find Ron and Aimee Mencl. This was their first pregnancy. After the usual polite greetings and small chat, I then had to establish the fact that Aimee was carrying a female fetus with a giant omphalocele. When Aimee came to me, she was terrified.[15]

Omphalocele is a congenital anomaly (birth defect) where the baby's intestines and usually part of or all of the liver develop outside the baby's abdomen, protruding through a hole at the umbilical ring but usually in a sac. This should not to be confused with gastroschisis, where the large and small bowel and at times stomach (but not typically the liver) are outside the baby's abdomen protruding through a defect to the right of the umbilicus but with no sac at all.

Both conditions can be extremely difficult cases with very poor outcomes and may lead to death. Both can have far-reaching short- and long-term implications. Gastroschisis usually has no associated genetic issues, but omphalocele can often have serious associated issues. Thank God Aimee's child had normal chromosomes in testing.

We discussed exactly what omphalocele was and how it compared to its more serious counterpart, giant omphalocele. Not every case is the same. Babies with giant omphalocele can suffer from a long list of very serious health issues, but nearly all of them suffer from some form of pulmonary compromise early on. In fact, 50 percent of all fetuses with giant omphalocele will ultimately not survive, and very often the morbidity and mortality can be attributed to pulmonary compromise (lung or respiratory failure).

When you surgically attempt to place the organs inside the abdominal cavity, there is no room. The abdominal cavity never expanded to accommodate the growing abdominal organs. Thus, the domain has been lost. It was never created because the organs were never in the fetal abdomen to begin with.

The point of focus of any antenatal consultation is to make the parents as aware as they can be of what's coming for them and their baby, the series of expected events, and the potential outcomes. If the consultation is done early on, it may give the parents perspective on whether they want to go ahead with the pregnancy or not depending on the severity of the birth defect. In any case, it will give them added perspective regarding what life may be like as the pregnancy progresses and certainly after their child is born.

At this point in the consultation, both Ron and Aimee asked me straight away my opinion regarding what they should do. The question was as follows: Should we go ahead with the pregnancy, or should we abort our child? With that, Aimee explained to me that she had already been to two other hospitals in New Jersey for consultation. Both consultations told the Mencls that they should abort their baby. Things would be far too difficult. The baby would most likely not be normal, and the child may not live anyway. As Aimee recounted this to me, she looked lost and devoid of hope and faith. Aimee was staring at me, and Ron gazed down at the floor, awaiting my response.

"Aimee, Ron, do you believe in God?" I asked.

"Yes, we certainly do."

"Okay then. I believe that everything in this life happens for a reason. You have both joined together to conceive this child. You have been presented with a very big challenge. Don't ever believe for a second that God isn't watching us all.

"How badly do you want this child? Are children to be had only if the whole affair is easy and pleasant? If you choose termination, you are saying to your child—and therefore to God—also that the baby's potential life with you is just not important enough to fight for.

"Termination is saying that giving your baby a chance at life would require more effort than what you are willing to give! Choose termination, and it's over and done with regarding your baby. If you do terminate, only each of you as individuals will know deep inside what the implications will be for you spiritually, emotionally, psychologically, and physically.

"However, if you choose life, you are saying to your child—and therefore to God—that you choose this child! 'I will see you through this trial with all my love, heart, and soul. I will fight for you every single day and night as only I can because right now I know you're not able to fight for yourself! I will stand by you and pray for you and love you. Through it all, I choose for you to be my baby, my child! I may fight with all I have and all that I am, and you may still not survive.'

"One thing is for certain. If you choose life, you choose love. When you choose love, you choose to align yourself with the greatest power in the universe. When you choose life for your baby, you choose to become the very embodiment of love! For me, there would never be any choice in the matter. The most precious and helpless thing in the world is an infant. An infant is absolutely a physical manifestation of God's love.

"What to do with God's love? Do you choose God's love only when it suits you? Do you choose God's love only when it's convenient? I say to choose God's love all the time. I say to choose God's love even if it appears to be impossible to grasp and hold. I say to thirst and starve for God's love every day of your life!

"None of us are perfect. In fact, many of us are so far off the mark and so far from God that we don't even think of God in our everyday existence. We challenge God and deny God. Quite frankly, we smite God all too often.

"Are we not God's children? Have we not by our free will and therefore our egos made it difficult for our Lord to choose us? Are we not in a way the same challenge for God as a difficult pregnancy can be for parents? Should we not want to act as if the Holy Spirit lives in us? God will never leave us. God knows we very often are not able to fight for ourselves. Thus, our Creator fights for us! God chooses us. No matter how difficult we may be, God always chooses us.

So I say to choose life and love. Live not as *if* the Holy Spirit were living in you but live *with* the Holy Spirit residing and dwelling in you! Choose your baby! God won't abandon you, so never abandon your child—ever!"

By now, we all had tears in our eyes. I explained to them that it was a good thing that they went for other consultations first and then came to see me. Sometimes contrast is necessary to get a clearer picture of the direction you really must take.

We set a plan in motion. I would send off my consultation to the MFM division and speak to them personally. I also wanted the Mencls to meet with our NICU team and take a tour. If all went as planned, they would be living in that unit for quite a while. They thanked me for the inspiration and encouragement. They knew it was out there somewhere, but it was apparently difficult to find. For the next twenty weeks or so, the Mencls would be engaging in lots of prayer.

Isn't it interesting how we humans so often miss countless opportunities to get close to God? We miss prayer and meditation opportunities every single day. People are way too caught up in the challenges of everyday life.

Today mothers and fathers are separated from each other and their children in their never-ending quest for success in a system of quantitative easing, fiat dollars, and intentionally structured debt. In fact, money is debt itself. (Look it up.). We are fooled into believing that money means happiness and security. It's all too often just a chasing of the wind. As you slave for money to secure your family, you unwittingly deny and forfeit the togetherness, the very core essence of the family unit, which is love in and of itself.

Far too many of us are like the birds that leave the nest in search of food to bring home for the young only to find that a snake has eaten them (the snake being the system). Although we are certainly obligated to meet contemporary survival challenges, if we overplay our parts and buy too much into a fiat system, we lose to the system those we cherish most. *We lose our way.*

So when do we pray? When do we give God our thoughts? When do we share our hearts and minds with God? When do we share quality time with our children? If we don't set loving expectations early (perhaps in the first five years) so that our children spend quality time with us, then when we make a move to do so, it'll be too late! They won't have the love. Don't miss the window of opportunity to instill in your family a true sense of love and togetherness. Their expectations, hearts, and minds will not be with their families, never mind any though of God. A well-known corporatist billionaire whose family controls much of the oil and pharmaceutical industry is quoted as saying, "I can change the hearts and minds of an entire nation in just two generations." Don't lose your children's hearts and minds by chasing the wind.

Suffice it to say that spiritual warfare is at the very heart of the matter we are discussing in this book. This digression into the topic of worldly challenge and spiritual warfare via an intentionally created fiat system of debt may seem puzzling and frankly out of place in a chapter about a very serious congenital anomaly and my interaction with the Mencl family. But I say it has everything to do with the main issue of the chapter. When given a choice, shine God's love and light into this world, and stop chasing the wind!

Many weeks passed, and it came time for Aimee's elective Cesarean section. I was notified days in advance as was the NICU. I communicated with our OR and anesthesia team, and we had all we needed at the ready.

I would never attempt to separate the spiritual side of life from the rest of it. Every night at home, I hold prayer and healing lightings. Each day at work, I stop what I'm doing when I'm able and go to the chapel. I light prayer candles and sit in quiet solitude. I sit and wait on Jesus. I pray, and I meditate on behalf of my patients and their families. I pray for my colleagues at work. I pray for this world. I pray for humanity! I pray for the coming of the Christ consciousness, and I pray for the coming of the kingdom of God here on earth as it is in heaven.

Baby Olivia was taken by Cesarean section and was physically stabilized by myself, my surgery team, and the NICU team. Everyone looked at the defect. It was massive. This particular giant omphalocele had an intact yet extremely thin sac. I wrapped the baby's protruding viscera in warm, moist gauze and put her in a plastic transport bag up to her axillae (underarms), and the NICU nurses placed a nasogastric tube to keep the baby's stomach from expanding because of swallowed air.

Aimee and Ron got a quick look at their daughter, and off to the NICU we went. Everything was done very fast but in a well-orchestrated fashion. Time, temperature, and moisture were crucial. My first order was to surgically remove the natural omphalocele sac because it was so dangerously thin. Olivia's entire liver, most of her large and small bowel, her stomach, and her two spleens were completely outside of her abdomen.

There certainly was a formidable loss of domain too. The differential of the space in Olivia's abdomen available in comparison to what we needed was worrisome to say the least, but that was typical of giant omphalocele. I constructed what is known as a silo to cover and suspend the organs so that they were safe, warm, and moist and also so that they didn't hang dangerously to one side or the other, thereby stretching their blood vessels and potentially putting the organs at risk of ischemia (deficient blood supply).

Olivia was finally stable and well wrapped up and under the radiant heater on her NICU bed. Now the NICU team would monitor her 24-7—intravenous fluid administration, electrolyte evaluation and maintenance, aggressive respiratory care, etc. My plan was to slowly twist down the silo over the course of ten days or so in an attempt to get as much of the organ mass as I could into her abdomen while slowly stretching her abdominal cavity so it would eventually accept the organs. I knew the entire mass would never go in anytime soon.

By the tenth day, I knew I was at an impasse. Any further attempt at reduction would cause Olivia to suffer life-threatening pulmonary compromise. It was time to surgically cover what wasn't going to go in. Skin mobilization all the way around to each flank is routinely done so that we could stretch the skin anteriorly and have it meet in the middle to achieve full skin closure.

I opted to use a biosynthetic material called AlloDerm. This is human dermis that's been treated so that there is no longer any immunogenicity held in its natural micro structure. What you have left is an immunologically nonreactive collagen matrix. The beauty of this product is that you can cover organs directly, and even if you can't completely cover the mesh with your patient's skin, if you keep it moistened with saline-soaked dressing changes, the organs underneath will grow granulation tissue into the collagen matrix. Thus, skin will eventually cover it. Unlike synthetic mesh material, which is historically used in surgery, biosynthetic mesh is nearly impossible to infect, and that has huge implications on morbidity (complications) and thus overall survival.

I constructed an AlloDerm covering for Olivia's organs and stitched it to her musculo-fascial rim that was present laterally around the outside of the giant opening of her abdominal wall. I then mobilized the skin as much as I could and actually got full closure. I waited several minutes and watched as her skin became dark and ischemic. Blood flow was being impeded. I removed about eight of the central skin sutures and watched as her skin once again became pink. This resulted in a circular bare patch with exposed AlloDerm about the size of a silver dollar. That was okay with me.

This was a very big day for Olivia, her family, and the entire team. She was closed, but she still had a very large protruding hernia at the middle of the abdomen. Her natural abdominal wall muscle and fascia were still widely open all around the aperture. So far Olivia had made it past several huge hurdles. She needed lots of time to heal so that she could breathe on her own, digest her food, and expel her waste on her own.

One of the toughest parts of this whole ordeal for Aimee and Ron was not being able to hold Olivia for the first four weeks of her life. Eventually, they were able to hold her and feed her. What a glorious moment for a beautiful family. By the grace of God, the anticipated three- to six-month hospital stay turned into five and a half weeks from delivery to discharge.

Ron, Aimee, and Olivia would be inextricably connected to me for a very long time. They did great at home. They had frequent office visits as well. Now came the next and last phase of the case. We would eventually need to close her abdomen so that her liver was inside and protected and not so vulnerable within a very large hernia that was visible from across the room. This would take lots of time and lots of prayer.

Olivia was growing into quite a special little girl. She spent time at the beach with friends and relatives, went to Manhattan, and had a few birthday parties too. I knew what needed to be done, but that wasn't the issue. I had to wait until I believed her abdominal capacity was large enough to house her amorphous liver and the rest of her viscera.

As she passed her third birthday, I felt things would work safely now. I had her seen by pulmonology before the final reconstruction. This was in anticipation of the eventual closure of her large abdominal wall hernia that contained her entire liver and other organs. Closure now could still cause pulmonary compromise just like so many suffer from during the previous beginning stages of closure. The anticipation of this day was glorious; however, it was also a bit frightening for all of us. Believe me when I say I offered countless heartfelt prayers to our Lord for a straightforward and successful surgery.

The day was finally upon us after more than three years of waiting. The Mencls were ready to conclude the final chapter so that they could devote their time and emotions to raising their little girl and not constantly worry about the next surgery.

I assembled my team. It included my pediatric surgical PA, my colleague, plastic surgeon Matthew Kaufman, and me. The agenda of this phase of Olivia's surgical care was as follows: We would remove the originally placed AlloDerm patch. Then we would perform a component separation so we could move her right and left rectus muscles to the midline and close her original opening. Next we would fortify the areas devoid of fascia with either new AlloDerm or different biosynthetic mesh that was thicker and offered more resilience against stretch and bulge. We planned, hoped, and prayed for the perfect outcome with no pulmonary, vascular, or digestive problems. Off to the OR we went.

I had been quite worried that the original AlloDerm would be incorporated into the liver capsule. After all, the liver granulated through that patch. I thought it may have to be permanently part of her liver. If so, I was prepared to leave the patch and attempt to lift her skin off of it.

As I made her midline incision, I purposely started low, down below her liver. What I found was amazing. Her skin and subcutaneous fat cut like anyone else's. When I opened her AlloDerm patch, what I found was that it had become her fascia. It was tough and resilient but also had a perfect dissection plain above it and below it. When I advanced the incision up toward her liver, I found that her liver had indeed separated from the patch just like the bowel below. I had a clear dissection plain to work with, and her liver was perfect!

I lifted her skin laterally until I reached her rectus muscles, which were splayed far off her midline to either side from her original defect. We dissected farther in a lateral direction until we got to the junction of the oblique musculature and the lateral border of her displaced rectus muscles. This was where we had to perform component separation. If you incise this junction anteriorly, you can then move the rectus muscles medially to hopefully approximate them at center and close the abdomen. It was like stretching out an accordion. I would have to leave the posterior or deeper layers intact. Otherwise, I would have created lateral holes that I didn't want. This technique worked great!

I decided to use a different naturally occurring biosynthetic material to patch the voids of her lateral component separations, and I also did a midline underlay patch to strengthen her abdominal wall under her thin muscles. She ended up with three biosynthetic patches—one on each side laterally and one straight down the center. She now had a newly reconstructed abdominal wall that was shapely, without a hernia, and stronger than most people's natural abdominal wall.

We were all so relieved to finally get this done. Olivia stayed in our PICU for about a week after the operation. After another few days, she was home. The journey took over three years. After the surgery I remember going to the chapel. I sat alone as usual. Nobody but me was there. I looked up and thanked Jesus. I then burst into tears. They were tears of relief and joy all mixed together. I sat in quiet solitude, thinking about Olivia and her life to come. I thought of what could have been had the Mencls chosen termination. Olivia was a beautiful, healthy, vibrant, intelligent, normal child ready to live the life God and her parents had given her!

I prayed that no one else would ever need to operate on Olivia again. After she was eventually discharged from my immediate care, I stayed in touch with Olivia's mom and dad. I watched Olivia grow into a beautiful young lady. She would come in every so often for a checkup. All looked great.

One day nearly five years after her reconstruction, her mom reached out to me. They were terrified. Olivia had developed a swelling over the left side of her abdomen. I was out of state, so my associate Dr. Steven Palder worked up the situation. I went into heavy prayer mode. He told me he thought she had a sterile abscess over the left lateral patch. He took her to the operating room, and that was exactly what he found. Olivia's body had used the secondarily placed reconstruction patches as a template to essentially grow fascia. He removed the patches that were floating in a collection of sterile pus. Her body had rejected the mesh after almost five years.

I wondered how long it would take before the other pieces of mesh did the same thing. One year later the same thing occurred on the opposite side, and I took those pieces out. Olivia healed perfectly well.

Olivia is truly a remarkable child. Her mom sent me a video of her singing. That video was a blessed and joyous gift to me, and she happens to have a great voice too. I have been so very blessed to do my part in the life of such an amazing child with an amazing family. To think that this whole incredible story could have ended before it began more than ten years ago.

Yes, I think about that central patch now and then. I'm giving it to God. God got us all this way from that first antenatal consultation. Olivia's parents had tremendous faith in God and His greater plan. Both Ron and Aimee went with the Holy Spirit and the love of God no matter the outcome.

God bless you, Ron, Aimee, and Olivia, for sharing your incredible life with me. I truly believe something awesome awaits you in this life,

Olivia. I believe I'll be there to see it. Everything happens in God's time, my little sister.

"Then Jesus replied to her, 'Woman, your faith is great. Let it be done for you as you want.' And from that moment her daughter was cured" (Matthew 15:28 NIV).

"Because strait is the gate, and narrow is the way, which leadeth unto life, and few there be that find it" (Matthew 7:14 KJV).

"But Jesus, knowing the reasoning of their hearts, took a child and put him by his side and said to them, 'Whoever receives this child in my name receives me, and whoever receives me receives him who sent me. For he who is least among you all is the one who is great'" (Luke 9:47–48 ESV).

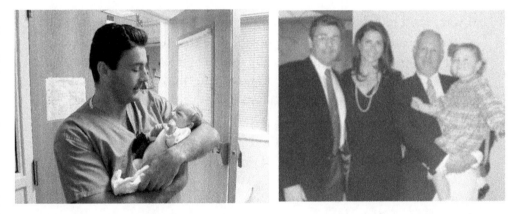

Olivia and Me   March of Dimes Award. Me,
                                 Aimee, Ron and Olivia

In her own words written in the next segment, Amy gave it to God. Her faith and her love for her child overcame what others said was a hopeless case.

Chapter 13

From Aimee

I was raised to believe in God, pray, attend Mass—all the things good Christians are taught. I admit to myself now that my relationship with God was very shallow until the day I found myself expecting a baby with a severe birth defect and doctors suggested we terminate. I have never prayed so diligently in my life. Those weeks were a blur of tests and appointments, of reading horrifying information about the condition our daughter had and praying to God for guidance. Despite the medical advice we had received early on, I continued to seek solutions, and I continued to pray.

It was no accident that we were referred to a place where we would eventually meet God's faithful servant Dr. Gallucci. I can recall our first meeting with him as if it were yesterday because it is something I think about almost daily. I was filled with fear when I entered the room with my husband. We had already been told by several doctors that our baby would likely have insurmountable health problems. Dr. Gallucci's much more conservative assessment of the test results we had gotten were a slight relief. He was the first medical professional we met during the process who was hopeful that he might be able to help our daughter.

He touched on his faith and beliefs, and we were comforted by his willingness to discuss such things. No other medical professional discussed their personal or spiritual beliefs. They merely looked at test results and made determinations.

It has been an emotional journey, but I look at my (now) healthy daughter and know that God guided us to Dr. Gallucci and that his God-given talents were the answer to our prayers. As evidenced by the other amazing stories included with ours, Dr. Gallucci's faith clearly plays an integral role in his ability to bring healing to those who need it. We are immeasurably blessed that he continues to be a part of our lives.

Sincerely,

Aimee McBain

For nothing will be impossible with God. (Luke 1:37 ESV).

The next chapter shows us how complete strangers are meant to interact with us in times of transition and change. They offer support, friendship, and affirmation that our path is worthy and true. They grow with us spiritually and help us through difficult times as we may also help them.

Chapter 14

Sister Renee

In 2010, I rented a house about three blocks away from my wife, from whom I was separated. I was in a rebuilding phase for me and my children. My inclination and nature saw me decorating and outfitting that house so that it took on the look and energy of the loving home it certainly was and not the bare-bones rental it had once been.

There is a local mom-and-pop farmers' market and garden center in the town I live in. It has one of the sweetest old-time feels that I have seen in a long time. This establishment was and still is one of the loveliest places I could every find myself. Some need to fly to far-off places while others need expensive, opulent surroundings to feel good. For me, the farmers' market was a place of peace and grounding.

I would stop in nearly every Friday at the week's end to see what was going on regarding items of décor, good energy, and beauty. Each time I would go, I would find myself in a conversation with a woman who worked there named Renee. We would talk about items such as paintings by local artists, plants, farming, and seasonal decorations.

From the beams on the ceilings and the antique potbellied stove that issued its warmth and enticing scent of a real hardwood fire to the original worn and stressed large-plank flooring came an amazing setting of artistry and country atmosphere.

When I went, I usually did so with the urge and intent to take a piece of that place home with me. I often purchased items for sale, but other times I would fall in love with items that were not for sale, such as the antique barrels and fruit crates that were used for display stands. Renee would talk to the owner and ask him if it was okay to sell me pieces of that nature.

Renee clearly had a connection to the earth and to spirit that I found rare and very comforting. It was no surprise to me at all when she said she was part American Indian by ancestry. Over the next few years, our conversations would shift from the market to family and children and then to spiritual and metaphysical happenstances. It was obvious that both of us loved when the conversation turned spiritual. It's what we are both all about.

I could never separate a place as beautiful and peaceful as that farmers' market from God and the nature of God's creative force. There is a reason why people get warm feelings of heart, hearth, and home in a place like that. Simply stated, it's all about grounding yourself. Grounding is reconnecting with your power source. Your connection to the source or God is almost certainly going to be found in things that connect you to Mother Earth or what shamans call "Pachamama."

When we disconnect from our roots, we become lost in the vortex of the mechanized modern world. Our life force becomes dim, and we long for something we've lost. That something we've lost is our God connection. That's why some recognize that the deep woods, gardens, beaches, or mountaintops are truly earth's cathedrals. If we yield to the forces that lead us astray such as the lust for power, money, and control, we will annihilate the cathedrals of Mother Earth and render ourselves homeless orphans. Renee undoubtedly understood this just as I did.

From the time I first met her, it's become abundantly clear to me that Renee has undergone a transformation. She has always shown me the side of her that reflects her God center, her spark from our divine Creator. Renee's spiritual and metaphysical evolution has taken a quantum leap forward. She has now exhibited her growing abilities.

I may have a difficult day at work regarding a deathly ill child. I may have spent many hours working on that child in and or out of the operating room. I most assuredly would pray for that child in the chapel. Renee would always pick up on it and shoot me a text asking me if I was having difficulties with a small male child and even mention the correct name. I would confirm, and she would send me God's love and light to assist in the healing.

Renee has also been able to discern other sources of angst or challenge in me. We both knew from early on in our friendship that there was something bigger than both of us at hand. God gathers together His elect for His purposes, and it is all done in God's time. There is a storm brewing in heaven and on earth. The spiritual warfare for control of humanity has begun. Renee is clearly my sister in spiritual arms. God bless you, Renee. We will stand together with the coming of the day of our Lord.

"And then He will send out His angels and gather His elect from the four winds, from the ends of the earth, to ends of Heaven" (Mark 13:27 NIV).

In the next segment, Renee describes in her own words how God's Spirit came to her through an elderly gentleman at the end of his time on earth. He knew her spirit and imparted to her affirmation and spiritual wisdom.

Chapter 15

From Sister Renee

When you appeared in my life, it was as if you were on a mission from the lost. It was kind of like a rebirth. You wandered through the farmers' market as though you were on a spiritual retreat. I could see how you were resonating with the place and its energy. When you spoke to me, a stranger, you spoke freely of what was happening in your life as if I were a family member or old friend. By the things you chose to buy for your new place, I could see this was a moment of independence for you. I found myself helping you load old wine barrels into your new car, and you had not a care in the world of what the old dirty barrels may do to the inside of your car.

After that first encounter, you came to the market often. You were always looking, searching, and talking about life. I learned more about you in three visits than anyone else that I had known for years. You were angry and sad, yet you were in a process of liberating yourself. You opened your soul to me, and that amazed me. For all the people who came through that market, you stood out, and I couldn't really say why. My boss Jerry would never sell anything old from the market like antique crates or those barrels used as part of our display to anyone, but when you requested to buy them, he said okay. I thought that was very interesting. I knew this—when you spoke, my job was to listen.

As the months passed, so did your anger. As one season turned to the next and a new year was upon us at the farmers' market, I could see you blooming spiritually. We spoke of many spiritual things, and as we did, I found myself growing spiritually as well. As the years passed, I realized we were truly kindred spirits. Your presence had a calming effect on my restless soul. You were clearly opening a spiritual portal for me to step through, one that I knew had always existed for me. You took me on a journey that I didn't even know I was on. As a result, today I find I have a heightened awareness of everything around me. You are my go-to guru. Over the nearly seven years I've known you, I have seen you become who God intended you to be all along, and you had an inductive effect on me as well. We grew spiritually together.

Fast-forward the story to just the last few months. I met a hugely inspirational person who stopped by the farmers' market. He entered into my existence but for a brief moment and had an indelible and lasting impression on me as you certainly did. This gentleman was an American Indian who was wheelchair-bound. His family kept driving to and from doctors' offices, which led them past the market. He always wanted to stop in, and he finally did. When he rolled up to the entrance of the market, he was placed in his wheelchair, and he greeted me as if he had known me forever. He wanted sweet corn. His granddaughter said she would pick it, but he said, "No, I want her to pick it," meaning me. He said, "I want you to pick my corn. I want you to touch it and choose for me."

We did this for several visits. They would drive. He would chat with me and ask me to pick his corn. He eventually confided in me that what he was doing by going to all these doctors was placating his younger generation, his family. He already knew where he was going and was totally ready for it. He also told me that there was a healer in my life, and he said this healer would guide me too. As always, he held both my hands and touched my cheek. My friend's face was lined with life.

160

He wore his hair in braids, and he wore everything he coveted, all that was spiritually meaningful and dear to him. In a few short visits, I was inextricably drawn to him as I was to you. Several days had passed, and I hadn't seen him. My heart was heavy. This man saw right through me and read my life. We spoke of how he was an American Indian and how I also had American Indian blood in me. There was an incredible bonding of our spirits.

Several days had passed, and my friend's great-grandchild stopped by the market. This person was more traditional in his look and dress. He bought me a feather. He thanked me for my patience and then told me his grandfather had wanted me to have the feather and that he wanted to be sure that I received it. He went on to say that they had passed the market many times but that it was only recently that his grandfather was suddenly adamant that they stop here. I was instructed to place this feather on my windowsill at home. Clearly something larger than life had drawn us together. Losing him was like losing a very close elder from my very own family. His spirit and mine had found each other. The Great Spirit, creator of the universe, saw to it that he and I connected prior to his passing. When we did connect, something magical occurred, and we passed some of our spirits to each other. I know we are connected for all eternity. To this day, his great-grandchild comes in and always holds both my hands.

—Renee DeLong

"And my speech and my message were not in plausible words of wisdom, but in demonstration of the Spirit and of power" (1 Corinthians 2:4 ESV).

"And we impart this in words not taught by human wisdom but taught by the Spirit, interpreting spiritual truths to those who are spiritual: (1 Corinthians 2:13 ESV).

You can create your very own spiritual safe house while embarking on your own meditative and spiritual journeys. The next chapter will tell you how I and many others achieved this.

Chapter 16

Spiritual Safe House and Protection

I was taught a long time ago by friends at the Nutley, New Jersey, Assembly of God (a Pentecostal congregation) that when you side with the Lord and pray earnestly for the light to prevail over darkness, you can expect to be spiritually attacked by dark malevolent forces. Knowing this, you must protect yourself at all times but certainly prior to any spiritual endeavor. I originally imagined this was a fanciful exaggeration; however, over the years I've learned my lesson, and now I know better. Even Padre Pio was routinely attacked spiritually as he engaged in the healing of others. Padre Pio was also a psychic. Many may not know this.

It was suggested to me that before I pray (or go into spiritual battle), I wrap myself in God's protective armor. There are several ways you can do this, but saying lead-up prayers is a good start. I say all the usual prayers my mom taught me like the Lord's Prayer, Hail Mary, and the Jesus prayer. I also love the Prayer of Saint Francis.

You can also imagine yourself standing alone in any setting you wish while envisioning a white beam of light coming from the heavens and engulfing you with the healing protective energy of the Holy Spirit. As the years have passed, I learned how to create a spiritual safe house.

You must create in your heart and mind the perfect place from which you may launch your spiritual endeavor upon the world's darkness (i.e., when you are praying for an individual or humanity in general).

Create in your heart and mind a place that gives you the very deepest feeling of peace and protection. That place can be under a beautiful palm tree on a gorgeous sunny beach in the tropics. For others, it may be sitting in a cathedral in old Europe. For me, it is a small stone cottage with a stone roof and a stone door. The cottage is high on a snow-covered mountain on the edge of a huge canyon. We are so high up that the eagles that soar in the canyon are below us. There is a huge spruce tree with pine cones next to the cottage. There is a treasure chest sitting outside the door and to the left. I can only access my safe house when I am completely devoid of any negative energy.

I'll know when I've reached that state of being by waving my right hand over the treasure chest. If it opens, a skeleton key will be floating there, waiting for me to grab it. When looking down into the chest, I can see a panorama of the heavens and outer space with many stars. I take hold of the key and wave it over the stone door. The door dramatically slides to the left, letting me inside. I drop the key back into the chest, and it closes on its own.

As I enter my safe house, the stone door closes behind me. There is a viewing screen to my right with seven toggle switches. I flip them all up to turn on my screen. This screen is used to contact my spirit guides. There is another screen in front of me on the back wall of this twelve-by-twelve-foot cottage. This screen is where I visualize those who are to be healed. On the left wall is an octagonal window with a thick steel door. This portal window will only open when the heavens know that I am ready to transmit the loving energy of the Holy Spirit to the recipient of my healing. When that happens, there is a crystal white beam of light that comes from the heavens and hits me in my chest. In turn, I focus this energy and direct it to my subject of healing through my outstretched arms and hands.

You don't need to employ the same techniques that anyone else does. What I described here happens to work for me. It's my creation. Find your spiritual fortress of peace and protection. Don't be resistant to using your imagination. I first thought reaching into my imagination was somehow cheating. No, it's not at all. That notion is a fallacy that you must get over. Our imaginations are actually our very own creative forces. The thoughts we think and dwell upon are at their core *creative*. All creation starts with thought. Thoughts precede *words*. The more energy you give to it, the more likely your creation will manifest. You can manifest what you choose spiritually and physically, but the essence of this chapter is the spiritual manifestation of safety and protection from dark forces while you are doing God's work.

"In the beginning was the Word, and the Word was with God, and the Word was God" (John 1:1 KJV).

"Heal the sick, cleanse the lepers, and raise the dead, cast out demons. Freely you have received, freely give" (Matthew 10:8 ESV).

"The Spirit of the LORD is upon me, because He has anointed me to preach the Gospel to the poor; He has sent me to heal the brokenhearted, to proclaim liberty to the captives and recovery of sight to the blind, to set at liberty those who are oppressed" (Luke 4:18 ESV).

The following chapter shows you what moving in the spirit is all about. The story of baby Vanca is an accounting of connecting with our God source through meditation and prayer, and then when it's showtime we must get out of the way of our own higher power, which will guide us to victory. This next chapter shows us that even in deadly circumstances, victory and healing can be achieved by calling upon the Holy Spirit.

Chapter 17

Baby Vanca

A call had come from my office that there was a consult for me in our neonatal intensive care unit. I was told the baby was a female born at just under twenty-five gestational weeks of age and at 512 grams or about 1.1 pounds. The baby had been intubated (a breathing tube inserted into the trachea) immediately at the time of birth (one day ago), and now the baby had mediastinal air on her X-ray. I asked if the baby was stable, and the nurse said yes. I made my way to the NICU ASAP.

An infant born at between twenty-four and twenty-five gestational weeks of age is really like a fetus that is five-eighths or roughly 60 percent done forming, considering thirty-nine weeks is the accepted length of a full gestation by many obstetricians. A pregnancy that has gone on for twenty-four gestational weeks (from fertilization of the ovum) is considered to be at the lower end or junction of second and third trimesters. (Twenty-six weeks is really the exact junction.) This baby was certainly considered to be a micro preemie. That's any baby born at less than twenty-six gestational weeks of age and/or weighing less than eight hundred grams at birth. Many hospitals consider the very end of the second trimester viable.

The mediastinum is that inner central compartment of the chest that houses the heart and its great vessels, the aorta, thymus gland, the thoracic portion of the trachea, the esophagus, lymph nodes, and nerves. I examined the baby, reviewed the X-rays, and then discussed the issue with the director of our NICU. We both agreed that we would monitor the baby closely to see if the air that was visible in the mediastinum on the X-ray would simply go away over a day or so. Gradual resolution of the mediastinal gas is actually the most likely scenario, depending upon the nature or suspected volume of mediastinal gas.

The NICU and I came up with a fairly rigid plan to monitor the baby's physiology and her radiographic course. We would do an X-ray to monitor the mediastinal air seen every six hours for the first twenty-four hours if the baby continued in a stable condition. If things seemed to be getting better, we would then extend the interval and back off with the X-rays to every eight hours for a day, and then we'd check every twelve hours after that.

If the baby's oxygen saturations and ventilatory parameters were also going in the right direction, then this would further our assertion that things were getting better, moving away from a surgical encounter and toward a gradual spontaneous resolution. The baby was placed on what's known as an oscillating ventilator to reduce the airway pressures that may actually worsen the situation.

I also put this baby on my prayer list for all the right reasons. Any baby born at 512 grams and on the cusp of viability (i.e., twenty-four to twenty-five weeks gestational age) needs all the help he or she can get. The tissues of micro preemies are extremely thin and friable (easily torn), and operating on a baby this fragile can be a daunting endeavor. Operating on a micro preemie's abdominal compartment is one thing (and most pediatric surgeons know that area quite well), but going into the mediastinum of a baby this small and delicate should give appropriate pause to any experienced pediatric surgeon.

The next day the baby was deemed stable, and there were no early signs of sepsis or cardiopulmonary compromise on this third day of life. I felt guardedly optimistic about this baby, but I wasn't going to stop my prayers. In fact, I stepped up prayers and lit a candle each night. I didn't want to be tested in any way.

I was never considered a selfish individual, but I was praying for the baby to get better but also for my own well-being. This could turn into a very bad scene very quickly. The baby remained stable, and the X-rays were virtually unchanged through this entire day and night.

On the fourth day of life, the baby was still stable by all parameters. The team appropriately discussed what the plan would be if things got worse and I needed to operate. This isn't a matter of allowing negativity into the energy and care of a compromised preemie. An experienced neonatal team, which includes the pediatric surgical team and the operating room personnel, must have that plan established and committed to. That way, if it needs to be employed, it will be done without hesitation, confusion, or delay.

That night as I settled in for my prayer lightings and healing endeavors, I thought that if we could just see clear improvement by the next morning, things may continue to get better. Then we might avoid an operation, and the baby would survive. I started the prayer session with the Lord's Prayer.

"Our Father who art in Heaven, Holy be your name. Thy Kingdom come, Thy will be done on earth as it is in Heaven. Give us this day our daily bread and forgive us our trespasses as we forgive those who trespass against us. Lead us not into temptation or 'do not bring us to the test,' but deliver us from evil, amen" (Matthew 6:9–13 ESV).

The words of the Lord's Prayer may change based on the Bible one is reading—King James Version (KJV), New International Version (NIV), or the English Standard Version (ESV) among others. Or it can vary depending on the branch of Christianity one follows. Frankly, I use whichever diction comes to mind. I don't hold myself to either version.

Why should I? I'm not reading or speaking Aramaic, Hebrew, Greek, or Latin. All versions are meant to convey the same meaning. When I was first learning the Rosary and committing it to memory by use of the internet, I realized that the words could be interchanged depending on what version I was watching. I found this refreshing, and in no way did I have an issue with it.

That line "Do not bring us to the test" stuck in my mind. Do not bring us to the test. I really didn't want to be taken to task or bought to the test. I wanted a save that didn't require me to have to go into the mediastinum of that tiny micro preemie. I prayed fervently that things would be great the next day and that I wouldn't need to worry. I've learned from the scriptures and from my life's path that God will give you what you need and not necessarily what you think you want.

The next morning I got an emergency call from the NICU. I was informed that a recent X-ray showed massive extension of gas and opacity through the baby's mediastinum and that the baby was deteriorating. The physiologic parameters were plummeting in commensurate fashion too. Some seemed to believe this baby's time on earth would be very short.

The director of our NICU, an excellent and very experienced neonatologist, looked at me with compassion. He expressed to me that nobody had ever had to operate on the mediastinum of a very ill 512-gram micro preemie such as this, ever in his long career. We both knew the baby needed an emergency operation if she had any chance of survival, but we also knew that the operation could end in a surgical death.

We spoke to the parents about the gravity of the situation. They had been prepared to hear the worst but hoped and prayed for the best outcome. Admittedly, the baby's chances of survival seemed slim— maybe less than a 10 percent chance of survival with an operation. The presumptive diagnosis was and had to be a perforated trachea and or carina or esophagus—presumptive because there was just no good way to tell without actually doing the operation. I knew the situation was grim. I had never been faced with this kind of situation in my entire career.

I defined the situation as follows to the NICU team and parents: The baby is septic, and apparently has a perforation of the airway and or esophagus. If I don't operate, the baby will not survive. That was 100 percent true. If I did operate, the baby would most likely die, and I told them the baby had less than a 10 percent chance of survival assuming I could even find the area to be repaired. Those chances were just considering the surgical/anatomic aspects of the case (i.e., surviving the surgery). Then we would have to deal with infection, which was certainly daunting.

The baby must be given a chance, and I believed that to the core of my core. If it is God's will that she survives, then at this stage it would require a major operation. I didn't want it that way. I told the parents that I had been praying for their baby since we had first met. I also reminded them that I had asked them to pray for their baby, and they indeed had done so. The team, the parents, and I were being bought to the test.

The operating room was notified, and the NICU was cordoned off to accommodate a sterile operating area. I asked my friend and colleague Jim to assist me as he had thoracic surgical training and experience as I did but on adults. Our pediatric surgical physician's assistant, Stacey was also going to scrub up and give us a hand as well.

As the team came together and the baby was prepped and draped, the pediatric anesthesiologist was very concerned (as he should have been) that the baby would most likely not survive. I totally understood how he felt, but I had to try. I believed the baby would become more stable from a respiratory standpoint once I had the chest and mediastinum open.

I asked for God's guiding hand to literally help me find the area I needed to repair and get the job done the right way, and the rest was then on His will. I also asked Saint Anthony very directly to help me find the area of concern so that I could repair it. All my prayers are in my heart and in my head. I never pray for show. I don't believe that's what prayer is about. You can quietly urge others to take up prayer, but do not make a show of it. That's not what it's all about. The prayer is for the recipient and between you and God. It's not about you and not about people who are in a position to watch you.

As the baby was finally prepped and draped and I was ready to start, I asked for the scalpel. I spontaneously and emotionally became one with our Creator. I was moving by the Spirit. I was taken over by supernatural forces. God's hand was upon me. Nothing else was perceptible to me. The room we were in could have been engulfed in flames, and I would not have been aware of it.

As I made my incision on the baby's right chest and entered her right thorax. I gently retracted her ribs so as not to fracture them. I then gently retracted the right lung upward so I could visualize the mediastinal pleura. A baby this small and premature has extremely delicate lung tissue. If you retract it just a little too forcefully, it can cause a hemorrhage inside the lung proper that could kill the baby.

So far the baby was completely stable, and her condition unchanged. I announced to anesthesia that I was about to open up an extremely distended and super pressurized mediastinal pleura. The pleura, in fact, looked like a piece of bubble wrap with a single large tense bubble that was harboring a purulent fluid. I used my scalpel to create a very small hole in this extremely tense bubble. As I did so, it was accompanied by a loud sharp pop just as if I had indeed popped a piece of squeezed bubble wrap.

My team all gasped. I thought the baby would remain stable at this point in the operation, and she did just that. Anesthesia and I were ready for a potential drop in ventilator pressure and volume as I was releasing back pressure on the apparent leak. The oscillating vent helped here very much, but as I knew from previous operations in the NICU, when a baby is on an oscillator, everything vibrates in a pulse wave because of the nature of the ventilation. I've gotten used to it over the years, but it would have been nice if the baby wasn't vibrating as I was working.

Now I was aspirating a copious volume of purulent, mucoid fluid that was clearly from an airway origin. In other words, it was from an airway leak or tear. I wondered how in God's name I would find the perforation amidst this slimy mess. I extended the incision in the mediastinal pleura upward and a bit downward. I knew that any significant blood vessels couldn't be or shouldn't be where I would cut with my Stevens scissors. As I did this, I saw mucus shooting out at me with each pulse of the ventilator. I could smell the anesthetic gas. As I went, I prayed for clarity and direction.

"Dear Lord, get me there. Saint Anthony, help me find the perforation please." I knew I couldn't be very far off now. I followed a flow of mucoid pus with a neonatal suction catheter, and as I did, the trail led me directly to the opening I was so desperately searching for. The perforation was actually right at the carina. The carina is the cartilaginous ridge that defines the bifurcation or forking of the trachea into right and left main stem bronchi.

I was amazed at how fast it had all unfolded. From making the incision to defining the perforation deep in this preemie's mediastinum took less than ten minutes. Now how was I going to repair this unclean jagged tear? I gently cut back tattered tissue and used 7-0 PDS, which is an absorbable monofilament suture. That means the suture slides easily and doesn't have braided strands where bacteria can hide. It's like a very thin fishing line. An 11-0 is roughly the caliber of a human hair, so a 7-0 is thicker but still very delicate.

You would never use a 7-0 on a skin laceration in an ER setting. It's way too thin and would not withstand the stretch and shear forces needed to keep skin edges together. Surgeons know to use absorbable suture on the airway. If not, the suture material will linger, give bacteria a place to grow, and cause abscess and even stone formation down the road because the airway is generally not sterile.

I used small pledgets made of AlloDerm to bolster the repair. It was difficult to create a seal in the cartilaginous carina of such a tiny patient. I've used AlloDerm on several occasions as stated in a previous chapter, and it's very resistant to infection. I tested the seal under gentle pressure, left a chest tube (a drain), irrigated the chest and mediastinum, said the Hail Mary, and closed up.

The entire operation took a little less than an hour. I actually didn't know what hit me. I stepped away from the table soaked in sweat and the top of my head burning hot from the overhead heaters. I made sure anesthesia was okay, and I peeled off my gown, mask, hat, and gloves. I looked around to regain my orientation. Our NICU director looked at me and smiled. I smiled back and went to sit down.

I had been controlled by the Holy Spirit! I had just done something that most observers thought was impossible under those circumstances and did it up in the NICU with lesser lighting, a bed that didn't tilt left or right, a vibrating micro preemie for a patient, and a very hot radiant heater on top of my head. The OR is made for this, and patient care units generally are not. That's true most anywhere you go in the United States and Canada. I knew how the operation would begin, but I had little idea of how it would proceed and finish.

In reality, everything happened as it was supposed to. I had little to do with how it all came down. Much like my record-breaking discus throw in 1978, I was oblivious to what was happening. For that moment I was the instrument, and the Holy Spirit was the current running through me. The energy in a situation like that is altogether different than what we are accustomed to day in and day out. Just prior to me scrubbing my hands for this case, I put a new stick of gum in my mouth. After the case, less than an hour later, that piece of gum had completely disintegrated in my mouth. Gum doesn't generally do that in an hour.

The operation was a success against all odds. I prayed for the full recovery of the baby every day and night. The operation was one thing, but now we had a 512-gram micro preemie with mediastinal and thoracic contamination, a repaired carina with sutures and pledgets, and an antibiotics regimen.

The baby was fighting for her life. Sewing cartilage together is not like sewing other tissue together that has a rich blood supply. Cartilage is relatively avascular (i.e., sparse blood supply). Thus, the subsequent healing can be difficult to achieve.

Micro preemies are prone to infectious complications that full-term babies or children generally are not. If you treat micro preemies with antibiotics for a known bacterial infection, they can at times succumb to fungal sepsis. Fungal sepsis is a very well-known killer of preemies, especially micro preemies. All these potentially deadly complications were now looming near our baby; however, God got us this far, and I believed God would finish it and see us through. Against all odds and only by the grace of God, the baby made a complete recovery. She was eventually discharged several months later after feeding and growing. The baby is now six years old. Praise Jesus!

Although Psalm 23 can be used in many instances of trial and tribulation, I believe it applied perfectly to the story of this baby. It applies to her as the patient and to me as her pediatric surgeon.

> The Lord is my shepherd: I shall not want. He makes me lie down in green pastures. He leads me besides still waters. He restores my soul. He leads me in the paths of righteousness for His names sake. Even though I walk through the valley of the shadow of death, I will fear no evil, for you are with me; your rod and your staff, they comfort me. You prepare a table for me in the presence of my enemies; you anoint my head with oil; my cup overflows. Surely goodness and mercy shall follow me all the days of my life, and I shall dwell in the house of the Lord forever. (Psalm 23, A Psalm or David ESV).

"And he told them a parable to the effect that they ought always to pray and not lose heart" (Luke 18:1 ESV).

Often you see small and big wires, new and old, cheap and expensive electrical cables. Alone they are useless, and until the current passes through them, there will be no light. The wire is you and me. The current is God. We have the power to let current pass through us and use us to produce the light of the world, or we can refuse to be used and allow the darkness to spread.[16]

"Jesus Looked at them and said, "With man it is impossible, but not with God. For all things are possible with God"" (Mark 10:27 ESV).

Dreams are almost always a symbolic expression of underlying spiritual truths, troubles, hopes, or prophecy. Some dreams are high-definition productions of emotion meant to leave an indelible message in your heart. The next chapter depicts a dream and visitation that certainly did that for me.

Chapter 18

The Most Frightening Place I've ever Been

After my usual prayer and meditation session, which typically began around eleven at night and could go until just after midnight, I prepared myself for bed. Nothing significant or consuming was on my mind other than the usual concern for my patients, family, friends, and humanity in general. I fell asleep with little difficulty this night.

My next moment of consciousness found me riding in a car as the front seat passenger in a large, light yellow, four-door sedan from the 1970s. I could not see the driver, but I was comfortable that I knew who he was. I never questioned where we were headed. It was very dark as we drove west on State Highway 22 coming out of Bridgewater, New Jersey. We pulled off the highway onto an access road that led to a two-lane country road. As we drove down this dark, lonely road, we came upon a long stretch of split-rail fencing that separated a large field from the road.

I recognized this place. We used to take our three small children there for the Fourth of July festivities. Every year the county held a huge celebration there that lasted from the morning until after the grand finale of the fireworks production. The days there were always long and action-packed with rides, restaurant stands, at least two bandstands, performers, a Revolutionary War reenactment, games of chance, and then of course, the annual Fourth of July fireworks display when the sun set. The planners always went all out. Short of the displays in New York City and Disney World, this was second to none. The event was so well attended that if you parked your car early in the morning, you had a good hour or more wait to finally get your car out of that huge grassy field at the end of the night.

Here we were at night driving up to that very same place. Why would we come here on an extraordinarily dark night? The driver pulled through the entrance and onto a cracked stone access road. I could feel and hear the stones crunching under our tires as the sound split the silence of the night. As we drove farther down this long road, I could vaguely see an old faded red barn about a hundred yards off in the distance. It seemed to get darker and darker the farther we went down this road toward the barn.

As we approached the barn, my driver turned our car to the right onto a small gravel parking lot. Our headlights illuminated the barn as they swept from left to right. Surrounding the transiently illuminated barn was complete darkness. My driver parked and turned off the engine of the car. I noticed that as our headlights went out, I could see nothing, not even my hand in front of my face.

I opened up my passenger side door and stepped out of the car onto the cracked stone. Apparently, I was supposed to be taken to this dark, cold, damp field to bear witness to something. As I took three steps away from the car, I was quickly overwhelmed by a foreboding sense of utter dread. I realized there was no sky, no stars, no moon—nothing.

The silence was as disturbing as the darkness that surrounded me. As I stood there, my senses adjusted to the stark blackness of the field that lie all around me, enough so that I could perceive a vast space that had no end. As my awareness became heightened, I knew for sure that I was not alone. I could feel the presence of people in that field. There seemed to be thousands of people out there, but they weren't standing or moving. They were lying down. It struck me that the place had the feel of a vast cemetery at night.

As I wanted to know more, the driver turned on the headlights without turning on the engine of the car as if he were reading my mind. A bright diverging path of light cut through the blackness to illuminate a corridor of this field as far as my eyes could see. I saw many hundreds if not thousands of people lying on the ground, each one on a towel that was on moist and tightly packed dirt. There was no grass at all and no trees. They were all lying on their left side, and all wore the clothing they had worn at the time of their passing. Some were in business suits, shirts, and ties. Others were in hospital gowns, while others were dressed for a night out on the town. They all seemed to be about twelve feet apart from one another.

They were certainly alive but just barely, subsisting with not more than a flicker of life in them. They had no ability to communicate with one another at all. They knew fully well that where they were was real and totally devoid of all light and that they were sentenced to be there. They were in an abyss of total darkness. They were essentially locked inside of their consciousness while in a frightening, endless dark void; however, they were aware that thousands were also there yet unreachable.

The overwhelming feeling and emotion was one of hopelessness for all eternity. I could feel their incessant longing to either be saved from this terrible fate or expire completely and permanently. With our headlights cutting a path of contrast across an expanse of this terrible place, these poor souls became immediately aware that we were there and that my presence, as a bearer of light, was causing a heightened sense of contrast for them and their fate just as the headlights did with their hopeless, dark surroundings.

They knew well that we came from where they had once been. They also knew that this terrible fate they suffered was brought on by the actions of their own dark hearts. They knew we were only there to bear witness to them and their fate and not liberate them. Our presence intensified their dread, anguish, and frustration, which compounded their feelings of hopelessness. I could feel their lament and their panic swelling.

To know we were there and that they would again be left in state was unbearable for them. Deep inside, each one of them yearned, longed, and suffered to be released into the light. They did not want to be left there to suffer any further as they had done for so long, in their terrifying and silent realm, which was completely devoid of light.

With literally no light to perceive, they were suspended in a dark suffocating state of reality that was completely without God. No God meant no light! At that point, I realized there were actually millions in that endless dark field.

A sense of horror and hopeless dread penetrated me to the core. I had seen enough! I needed to leave this place as fast as possible. Fear and panic ran through me because I could feel that each and every soul there was focusing directly on my presence. I could feel them slowly closing in on me emotionally.

I immediately hurled myself toward the car, and for that split second as I reached for the door handle, I wondered if the door wouldn't open to receive me. Was I taken on a one-way trip? Would I also now be locked there like all the others? I flung the door open, and as I jumped into the car in a panic, I ordered the driver to get us out of there right now! He turned the engine over, put the car in gear, and we spun gravel and cracked stone as we flew out of the scariest place I'd ever been!

As we made it back to the highway, I thanked God profusely for allowing my successful exit from that horrible place. Route 22 in the middle of the night seemed like heaven to me at that moment. I wondered what could have caused those poor unfortunate souls to have been banished there. Was this God's doing, or was it of their own accord?

I could now see streetlights, stars, and the moon! I was surely back in the world I had come from. The relief I felt was immeasurable! I could expand my lungs with fresh air and breathe again. I could again see all the light, colors, and contrasts I was so used to, although it was at night. With the realization of finally being delivered out from that place and escaping by highway, I immediately found myself sitting up in my bed, heart pounding and drenched in sweat.

I sat there for nearly an hour, my head spinning and reflecting on what had just happened. What in God's name was that all about? What was that place, and why was I taken there? Who was the driver, and why was it apparently an alternate dimension of a familiar park where so many in this world gather for fun and festivities? That intense experience stayed with me for a very long time. As I write this chapter, I can relive it all over again, and with little effort, I can bring back all those horrible feelings of dread. I would subsequently meditate on the experience and pray on it. I would pray for all those souls I left behind. What I had experienced was no dream. I was taken there for a reason.

About a year and a half later, I read a book by Vassula Ryden, whom many consider a modern-day prophet. While watching her videos, I learned that she had been taken to purgatory to bear witness to the myriad of souls who suffer there. It was abundantly clear to me that we were in the same place. She even described all the nearly lifeless people lying on their left sides. I now know beyond a doubt that purgatory is a real dimension where countless souls suffer and want to be released back into the love and light of God once again. God doesn't put them there. They put themselves there out of a sense of worthlessness, shame, and guilt! Praying for them even if you think you don't know them will help release them as your prayers are a gift of God's love and light.

There are many prayers you can read and incorporate into your daily devotions, especially for the souls in purgatory. Many can be found on the internet. So much of life is about being called upon to do for others what they cannot do or could not have done for themselves. This applies to the living and those who have passed before us. Use your heart to give them the gift of God's love and light.

"The people who sat in darkness have seen a great light, and upon those who sat in the region and shadow of death, light has dawned" (Matthew 4:16 ESV).

Now when these things begin to take place, straighten up and raise your heads, because your redemption is drawing near. (Luke 21:28 ESV).

Eternal rest grant unto them, O Lord; And let perpetual light shine upon them. May they rest in peace. Amen.[17]

Soul families are real, my friends. The next three chapters show us how even a mundane encounter can lead to a fantastic metaphysical voyage that was always waiting for you. This routine surgical consult completely changed my life forever. And so it is!

Chapter 19

Jorge

In August 2011, I got a consult on a fourteen-year-old male in our PICU. His primary diagnosis was acute myelogenous leukemia (AML). He had already been through state-of-the-art treatment measures, including a bone marrow transplant. Our oncologists were very concerned because Jorge had developed multiple lumps all over his trunk limbs and face. There was no way they could know if these lesions were metastatic recurrence or infectious. Jorge was presently neutropenic and very ill. Jorge's oncologist, called me and asked if I could biopsy representative lesions and send specimens for tissue culture and permanent section.

I was concerned over the thought of making multiple incisions on this child while he was neutropenic. I knew he would have serious issues with healing. If the lesions were metastatic, it would mean that Jorge would only receive comfort care. That's a declaration of no further treatment, just comfort measures until the terminal process ran its full course. If the lesions were infectious, then there were real treatment options, and comfort care would not be one of them.

I remember meeting Jorge's family in his PICU room for the first time. They certainly had that old familiar and terrible look. The look is a combination of shear exhaustion, terror, exasperation, and numbness mixed with flickers of hope. I can remember how polite and thankful they were for anyone who could possibly bring them hope and change. I explained the risks and potential benefits of the surgery. The surgery was scheduled for the next morning. They thanked me profusely and asked me to pray for their son. I told them he had already been placed on my prayer list and that I would be doing a personal healing lighting for him that very night.

I have had many such consults in my time as a pediatric surgeon. In many respects, this one was no different than the others, but in another respect, it was one of a kind. There was something very special about Jorge and his face. I felt as though I had met him before. I felt the same way regarding his parents. They were completely familiar to me. It was as though I had known them for many years. I can also remember having tremendous empathy for Jorge's little brother Victor Jr., who was eight years old at the time.

The next morning I took Jorge to the operating room. I had prayed the night before, and I was confident we were dealing with infection and not recurrent leukemia. Our immediate results didn't confirm that Jorge's lesions were *not* recurrent disease. The final diagnosis took several days.

Everyone rejoiced and thanked God for His grace and yet another chance to see Jorge healed. Now we were dealing with multiple incisions and no ability to heal. As I anticipated, all the incisions opened up and were eventually gaping open. Jorge had to return many times to the OR for local debridement and surgical wound care. By then it was October, and Jorge's wounds were clean but still open.

Part of my meditative work for healing includes spiritually taking the patient on a journey to my healing mountain. I would astral travel to where the patients were on the physical plane and then take them with me into the third world. The third world is a dimension of healing, a dimension where I can interact with God and the patient on a more spiritual level. Each night I would surround myself with the love and healing energy of the Holy Spirit through prayer and energy cleansing. Only when I was devoid of all negativity would I make my spiritual flight to the particular patient's location.

For Jorge, when at home, I would see his house and enter through the front door. I would go to his room where he was waiting for me. I would take him by the hand and ask him if he were ready. He always gave me a bright and beautiful smile and said, "Yes, of course." Up we would fly through the roof and into the night sky. Up, up, up we would go.

There were many thousands of stars to see in the clear night sky. As we approached our destination, we could see a tiny speck of bright light from below. That was the bright light from the meadow where a large oak tree stood at the junction of the light and the dark. Down we flew as the light got brighter and larger. We often would land on a large branch of a very large and wide oak tree. We'd sit there a while and take in the beauty of the meadow just ahead. We would always gaze back into the dark forest to underscore the contrast of light and dark.

The forest wasn't evil. It was just devoid of the beautiful dazzling light of the meadow. As we walked through the meadow, we could smell the tall grass that bent beneath our feet. We could see and hear bees fly by us and also see butterflies here and there. The light was so hot on our skin.

At the other end of the meadow was a rocky ledge that we had to climb. We always did. On the top of the climb was a plateau with the beginning of a road made of pure gold. Sometimes that road would move as we stood upon it, and sometimes we would walk it of our own accord. The road led to a huge white cloud that hung on top of the road. The cloud was the threshold between us and the land of the Holy Spirit.

Inside, the cloud was cool and white and perfectly silent. Sometimes we would just stay there and take in its splendor. As we moved through the cloud to the other side, we would find ourselves in a different terrain with different features and foliage. There were palm trees on the far side of the cloud but deciduous trees on the nearside. There was a stream we always saw running along the right side of the golden road.

Doorways would appear along this road and on the opposite side of the stream. They could be hundreds of feet apart from one another or only twenty feet between them. In each case, the doorways were completely different from one another. Some were dilapidated wooden doorways that you wouldn't think to pry open, and others were doors made of glass that had no apparent method of opening. Some were beautiful hardwood church doors with archways of carved granite.

Either way, only one door would offer us an opening. It was apparent that we did not control or choose which door we were supposed to take. When the right door would come up along the path, it would open for us. A foot bridge would appear and offer us a path over the stream. We needed to move quickly, or the doorway would close before we got through it.

When we did go through the door, we would find ourselves in a vestibule. We always had to reach to the right wall and turn on a light switch. Then a second set of inner doors would open and offer us entrance into the church or sanctuary room. At the back of that room, behind the altar, and through a doorway was a steep stairway that we would climb until we got to a very dark plateau room.

We would stand there in prayer until the back wall of that dark room would offer us a portal to the healing realm. We would jump through and find ourselves on a small side street in a busy city. A white box van would always pass from left to right first. Then we would cross to the other side of the street to go to a large hotel. That hotel was actually a spiritual portal. Our choice of entry was always either a glass revolving door or simply the front glass doors.

We would go inside, and the desk clerk would greet us with a smile. The concierge on the left would smile and acknowledge our passage through to the ballroom in the rear. The ballroom was a large empty room with doors numbered one through thirteen, but it only listed the odd numbers. We would always pick either number three or seven.

Beyond either door three or seven was a deck ramp that led to a shady sandscape with a canopy.

To the right via door seven was a path to the ocean where God's living waters were. The water was filled with ocean life that was there to bless you and rejoice in your arrival. There was also a beautiful sunny meadow up a sand dune where we would sit on a circular wicker mat and receive Holy Communion by breaking and sharing Holy bread and drinking sacred wine. If we went to the beach, we would bath in the healing waters and be surrounded by joyous ocean life, including dolphins, whales of all types, seals, and giant seahorses. They would bless us, and we would bless them. There is always a triple baptism in the living waters before we make our exit to the beach and up to the Holy meadow. As we left the waters for the meadow, a bright heavenly light would shine down upon us and dry us perfectly.

If we went to the left, we would climb a healing mountain as I have done a thousand times. We would always get halfway before we stopped and then turned to take in the spectacular view of the shimmering blue sea and white fluffy clouds just like I did all those times as a child while I had this same vision. We would enjoy the radiant heat of the bright sun on our skin. When we got to the top, we would stop to pray, praise God, and ask for healing.

We would have a triple baptism in a pool carved of stone. Then after the baptism there would be the same heavenly light that would engulf us from above, cleanse us, and perfectly dry us just as on the beach. Then I would anoint the person to be healed with anointing oil on the forehead, lips, heart, and abdomen. We would then praise and give glory to our Lord.

This spiritual healing went on for months. After my prayer and meditative healing sessions were concluded, I would give thanks to our Lord. I would then backtrack and return my charge to where he or she needed to be. It was then time for me to go to sleep.

Somewhere between the onset of my sleep and the alarm clock in the morning, I would have dreams of Jorge and others. In each dream that Jorge was in, I would see the same vision over and over again. I would be walking out of the hospital, and I would see Jorge's family pushing him in a wheelchair through a parking lot. He would look up and see me and offer me a big bright smile from ear to ear. He'd stick his arm straight up in the air, call me, and wave. "Dr. Gallucci! Dr. Gallucci! Hi! Hi!" It was as if he wanted to say, "Look at me! I'm going home! Thank you for helping me!" I saw this same vision over and over again for many nights. I wondered why it was always the same scene.

I lost contact with Jorge for about a month or so but never stopped praying for him or taking him to the third world for spiritual healing. One day just after Christmas, I asked Jorge's oncologist about him. I was concerned because I hadn't seen him or heard from him. The last I knew he was at home with nurses administering wound care to his slowly healing surgical incisions, one of which was on the bottom of his foot. Stan said he was doing well, all things considered, but the big miracle for this child, who everyone thought was on his deathbed, was that all his wounds had healed and that he was dancing at the oncology Christmas party.

In January, Jorge was admitted for a fever and a septic workup. Each time I went to see him, he had just been sedated for a painful procedure. I would sit with his parents, but Jorge was usually out of it, so the interaction was limited.

We all wanted to see him make his fifteenth birthday, which was on January 29. The pediatric floor threw him a party with cake and gifts. I was in surgery, so by the time I got there, he was exhausted. At his bedside his mom told him I was there, and I told him how proud of him I was. I wished him a happy birthday. He thanked me from a deep stupor.

One late afternoon after a long day, I was tired and hungry. I wanted very badly to just go home, eat dinner, and relax. Always think twice before you get upset when you are thrown off your usual travel path or when a slow driver is in front of you on the road. Your delay may very likely be happening for a good reason. Put your senses on high, and don't miss what may be coming your way.

I set out to leave the hospital on my typical route. The usual hallway was newly closed because of construction. I could go down an adjacent hallway and then cross over to another exit, but that hallway was being waxed and dried. I wasn't amused at this point. My last option was very out of the way. It would take me much longer, and I would have to exit through a door I almost never used. As I finally exited the hospital via the back steel doors, I checked my text messages. I was walking and texting and not paying attention to anything around me.

As I was looking down at my cell phone, I could hear in the distance a high-pitched voice. I thought nothing of it until I realized it was calling my name. "Dr. Gallucci! Dr. Gallucci! Hi! Hi! Dr. Gallucci!" I looked up in a state of confusion. When my eyes finally focused, I could see Jorge Garrido waving to me with his right arm straight up in the air and that beautiful bright smile on his face. His loving family was pushing him in a wheelchair through the parking lot.

I stood there in complete shock and awe at what I was seeing. It was the very same dream I had had so many times as I slept after my meditation sessions for Jorge's healing. I snapped out of my confused state and ran over to greet them. They were finally going home after a very long and frightening hospital stay. I told them to call me for any issues and to please stay in touch. We blessed each other and went our separate ways.

That was early February. Each time I saw the oncology team I would ask about Jorge, and I would get the update. He seemed to be holding on. Then one day in March, I sadly learned of Jorge's sudden passing. I felt as though a close relative had passed. It was very emotional for me. He also happened to pass on my youngest daughter's birthday, March 17. I learned from the oncology team that Jorge's mom had asked if I would go to the wake and funeral. I replied that I surely would.

By now I was trying to figure out a way to help the Garrido family. I tossed a few ideas around in my head, one of which was to set up a scholarship in Jorge's name. I knew nothing of how to achieve this goal. The day of the wake, I drove from the hospital to the funeral parlor a few blocks away. I got there early, parked, and went inside. I stood there, taking in the scene. I was early enough that there were only a few dozen people around. I went up to pay my respects to Jorge and his family. I was amazed at the poise and grace Little Victor, Jorge's younger brother, was showing. Victor was eight years old, and he had been very close to Jorge.

I sat in a chair and held back the tears. I went into deep thought and prayer. *Dear God in heaven, please help me help the Garrido family. I'll do anything in my power to do something for them that will be lasting and surely in Jorge's name.* After about thirty minutes of prayer, I felt it was time to leave. When I looked up, the place was packed. As I got to the parking lot, I could see my car was now blocked in by a sea of vehicles. I wasn't going anywhere soon. Okay, back into the funeral parlor I went. Now I had lost my seat, and there was none available.

Finally, a teen got up and left, leaving an empty chair for me. Nobody made a move toward it for several minutes, so I went for it. I sat down and became emotional again as I settled in for a long afternoon. I used the time I was given along with the energy of the room to pray to God for the ability to start a scholarship in Jorge's name.

Another teen immediately vacated the chair next to me, and a woman in a red dress with a red straw hat sat down. She nodded a silent hello to me, and I politely nodded back. I went back into my meditative state, asking God to help me find a way to create a scholarship for Jorge. I really believed the scholarship was the perfect idea, but I knew as much about creating a scholarship as I did about flying a jumbo jet—and that was nothing at all.

After a very short interval, the lady in the red straw hat said hello again. I opened my eyes and replied a hello back to her. I fixed my gaze on the front of the room and silently asked Jesus for help with the creation of a scholarship. This time my friend dressed in red touched my arm and said hello again. I politely said hello again as well. Inside I wasn't feeling amused by this. All I wanted was to feel connected to this family and have God help me help them. I wanted to be left alone. I had never been so serious in my entire life about getting something done.

I was a man on a mission, and this very nice and polite lady was distracting me. As I restarted my meditative state, she spoke to me once again. "Hello. How do you know the family?"

I turned to her and figured that if I engaged her, she might leave me alone once and for all. "Hi, I'm John Gallucci. I was Jorge's surgeon. I've come to know and love the family through the last seven months." She thanked me for caring for Jorge and loving the family. I once again returned to my meditation and petitioned God for help.

She then introduced herself to me, "I'm Eve Remsen-Sachs."

"Hi, Eve. How do you know the family?" I asked. She said she knew the kids and their parents because Jorge and Victor were excellent students and were enrolled in the Rutgers Future Scholars Program. She then told me she was one of the directors. I asked her what that program was all about. She explained it to me, but her next words nearly knocked me off my chair. She said, "I help people start new scholarships." My head lit up like a flash bulb on an old camera. I was speechless for a moment. Now the lady in the red straw hat had a name, a title, (directorship at Rutgers Future Scholars), and my full attention.

We spoke for quite a while regarding the scholarship program, and I shared with her my thoughts and wishes for starting a scholarship in Jorge's name. She looked at me as if she had known my intent all along. As the afternoon session was coming to a close, she asked me if I would be at the funeral the next day. I said I would. She then asked me if I was looking for a dog. *What?* I thought. *Am I looking for a dog?* My God, I was indeed looking for a dog. "Yes, I am looking for a dog. Why are you asking me this?"

I was recently separated, and now I'm in my own house with fifty-fifty custody of my three teenage kids. We had discussed getting a dog for quite some time. The issue had been heating up. My middle child, Arielle, had been bugging me for a wolf for many years. I would always say the same thing. "We aren't getting a wolf. Wolves are illegal. Don't ask me again for a wolf. A dog, okay!"

Dr. Sachs explained to me that Jorge had asked his parents to get him two huskies to raise and breed. Here was Victor Garrido Sr., a Peruvian immigrant in Piscataway, New Jersey, now going to breed huskies. So that's just what he did for his beloved son Jorge. Jorge and the Garrido family had purchased, raised, and bred Mya and Skylar.

The next day at the funeral on the steps of Saint John the Baptist Church, Dr. Eve said, "Here, look at this picture." It was a picture of Jorge holding one of the puppies in his backyard. The dogs were born on December 25, Christmas Day. The picture was taken on March 11, my mom's birthday. Jorge passed six days later on my daughter's birthday. Dr. Eve said, "Would you like him? He was Jorge's favorite of the litter!"

In a split second, I thought about everything that my kids and I had discussed. He was just beautiful. "Okay, I'll take him!" She said his name was Lucky. I said, "A male husky named Lucky? I was thinking something more exotic, something that smacked of the mountains, the snowy wilderness. Lucky? Well, okay. I'll take him, but my kids will want to change his name for sure."

It was only about four days later that we picked up Lucky at the Garrido home. On the way there, I told all three kids Jorge's story, all he went through, and how he begged his parents to raise huskies. The story certainly gave all three kids a moment of pause and reflection. They all thought about different names for the dog in the car on the way there. The discussion regarding dog names became quite spirited.

When we got there, it was a bittersweet reunion for the Garridos and me. My kids hit it off with Little Victor right away. Little Victor's energy and enthusiasm certainly broke the ice, and the energy of the moment quickly became light and joyous. Lucky had a sister named Icis. She was beautiful, and she and Lucky were inseparable. They asked us if we wanted both dogs. We were so close to taking both dogs, but I said no because I didn't believe I could care for two dogs with an empty house half the time. My girls cried because they didn't want to separate the pups. We all had lumps in our throats. We hugged and kissed the family and said we would be back for visits with Lucky.

On the way home, the kids fell in love with this dog immediately. As the fervor died down, my son Seth said, "Dad, can we not change the dog's name? Jorge named him. Therefore, he is Lucky." Everyone agreed. There would be no changing what was ordained by Jorge Garrido. We were blessed. We were blessed with our Lucky.

As each new day passed, Lucky became more and more of an authority in the house, the yard, and his cage. He was getting the hang of his new family and home. A few months later, we brought Lucky over to the Garrido's house for a play visit. At the time, Lucky saw his parents, Mya and Skylar, as well as Icis. They all ran and ran and had tons of fun, but I did notice that Mya, Lucky's mom, had gotten her hackles up and attacked Lucky in a fairly vicious way. She sounded as if she were going to tear his trachea out and be done with him. I said to Victor Sr., "Wow, what a nasty little monster!"

He looked at me and said, "Well, you know, Mya is different from Skylar."

"How so?"

He said, "Well, you see Mya is half gray wolf." I couldn't believe my ears. My daughter Arielle had bugged me for a wolf for many years. I knew Lucky was special and a spiritual gift, but over the ensuing year or so, I would learn just how profoundly true this would turn out to be. We had our Lucky, and Arielle had her wolf.

I've known for some time that all things happen for a reason, and it was abundantly clear that I was spiritually connected to the Garrido family.

It didn't take long for me to see that indeed Lucky was more than a dog. He was more than a pet. Lucky was a spiritual gift from a child and family that were connected to me for a very long time.

When I say that, I mean that we were connected from another time and place, another lifetime. As I've stated previously, I pray and meditate every night in my room at my meditation table. I also have an altar to my left where many candles are arranged. Each candle has a patient's name on it. The candles are used to amplify the prayers I give to the heavens. The energy you put into your prayer launches it into the universe, and the universe responds in turn. If you do a lighting with prayers, the energy from the candle helps you focus, but it also amplifies the energy of the prayer. This is why churches and monasteries use candles. This is why in the Hebrew tradition of Shabbat prayers on Friday nights are done with candles. This is a tradition and technique used by healers, priests, and saints from all over the world for thousands of years.

Lucky was living with us for about six months or so, and he was the love of our lives. One night while performing a prayer lighting for several patients at the same time, I slipped into a meditative state and found myself walking up a beautiful grassy hill. I could feel the gentle breeze pushing me from behind and the sweet smell of flowers and the thick grass below my feet. As I walked up this green hill, I became aware of something closing in on me from behind and to my right. As I turned to see what it may be, I was stunned to see Lucky trailing me with his nose to the ground and his white fluffy tail straight up in the air. He looked like a wolf dog on a mission for sure. He passed me on the right easily with his quick gait, and as he did, I said, "Hey, Lucky! What are you doing here? Who invited you on this trip?" He looked up at me and gave me a quick glance. Then he put his head down and kept trotting along. He never stopped. Nor did he seem concerned with my concern that he was there with me.

He was searching for something as he went, going from side to side and covering much more ground than I could ever hope to cover as I walked. I knew there had to be some significance to why he showed up in this alternate dimension of prayer and healing. I accomplished my meditation and my prayers, and then I went to bed. The next morning I looked at him and said, "I saw you last night on that grassy hill." He wagged his tail. For the next few nights, Lucky would show up in my meditation.

About a week or so later, I got a phone call from my friend and next-door neighbor Jane Casale, who is a psychic and medium. She said that a boy appeared to her and that he wanted her to get a message to me. She didn't know who he was. I hadn't discussed Jorge with her at all up to that point. She described him as a thin teen with a dark complexion, straight black hair, and a big bright smile. He came to say the following to me: "Thank you for trying so hard to save my life. Thank you for the prayers and all our travels to the healing places. Thank you for treating my family so well. Thank you for loving us the way you do. You see, I'm much older than you may think. I've lived many lifetimes. It was my time to leave. Please tell my parents that I'm doing very well and that I'm with Popi, a grandmother, and an uncle. Dr. Gallucci, you will play a very important role for my little brother Victor." He then said that he was so happy that I loved Lucky so much. "He is a gift from me to you. Tell my Mom, Dad, and Victor that I love them and that I will always be with them. We will all be very close in the future."

If you think that psychics and mediums can't be true Christians or followers of our Creator, think again. Padre Pio was a devout Catholic Franciscan, a healer, and a psychic medium. This is well documented. I knew the Garridos would be emotional over what I had to tell them. They were so very thankful to hear from their beloved Jorge. Now I understood that everything that had taken place was meant to be and that I was forever connected to this beautiful family.

I had only just begun as a powerful spiritual healer, and Lucky was given to me as an animal spirit guide. Healers and prayer warriors are often attacked spiritually by the dark forces that plague this world. We all are at times; however, those who function as healers are under forceful attack, and their efforts are frequently sabotaged.

Spirit guides come in all shapes, sizes, and species as mentioned in the chapter on animal spirit guides. Jorge gave me Lucky right on cue for my spiritual healing journeys. He was in place to guide me just as animal spirit guides can give advice to and teach shamans. Lucky is also a protector. Whenever Lucky shows up in my meditative travels, he is never there to play with me or interact with me. He is clearly there to guide me and protect me from attack and dark energy.

Spiritual healers can take on sickness and illness while healing those afflicted, and so do animal spirit guides in the flesh. I can remember very vividly dark energy besieging me several times after a cleansing or a smudging of a home or office space. After the cleansing/clearing activity was over, I would become very ill. Sometimes it was a pounding headache, and at other times it was unbelievable nausea that put me on my couch in the fetal position, unable to move or think straight. Lucky would walk over to me, sniff me, put the top of his head on me, and press it into me. He would hold his position for a few minutes and then fall onto the floor as if he had been shot. As he became ill, I became better. This is a classic example of an energy transfer. You can pull dark energy out of a subject or impart healing energy. They typical regimen would be the pulling or extraction of negative energy followed by a back fill with healing energy. It is quite effective and usually has dramatic results.

Lucky's sister Icis had been adopted by friends and neighbors of the Garrido family well after we took Lucky. We were admittedly so very close to taking her along with Lucky to keep the siblings together. From time to time, we would all look back and wonder if we did the right thing by passing on Icis. Was this beautiful family down the street meant to have Icis and not the Gallucci family?

On the second anniversary of Jorge's passing, I was once again anticipating being at the church for the anniversary Mass, and then I would go back to the house for a gathering. That was my plan all along, and I was looking forward to it. Instead of attending the Mass that day, I was called in to help with a life-and-death surgical emergency. I had to perform a lifesaving emergency operation and miss the Mass and the house gathering. Of all the millions of kids I could have been called for who needed a lifesaving operation, at that very day and moment, the patient was actually Jorge's friend, the teen who had adopted Icis. I would never second-guess our decision ever again.

When I traveled to San Jose in 2014 with my daughter Arielle, who was participating in the woman's National Ice Hockey Championships, I had the opportunity to drive thirty minutes north to spend the day at the national shrine of Saint Francis of Assisi in San Francisco. There I learned of the story of the wolf of Gubbio. I never knew the story of Saint Francis and the wolf of Gubbio. I wondered why I often saw his picture or statue with a wolf. I knew that among other things, he was the patron saint of animals, but I figured that was the reason he appeared with a wolf. When I read the story, I was deeply touched. When I showed Bernadette, the art director of the shrine, a picture of Lucky, she looked at me and said, "Ah, you have your own Gubbio, I see!" When I went home to New Jersey, I never looked at Lucky the same way again. Lucky is certainly my Gubbio.

Recently, my dear friend Renee saw me at the local farmers' market where she worked in town (see the chapter on Renee). Renee is profoundly spiritual and has tremendous intuitive ability. Renee has visions and dreams that are prophetic in nature and very often meant for those around her. This is something that occurs more and more in these times. "And it shall come to pass afterward, that I will pour out my Spirit on all flesh; your sons and your daughters shall prophesy, your old men shall dream dreams, and your young men shall see visions" (Joel 2:28; Acts 2:17).

There is certainly an awakening and an ascension process occurring that is positively affecting the entire globe. Renee told me that she was spiritually drawn to an area in my bedroom at my home. She had never been inside my home. She went on to tell me that there was a candleholder on my bureau in my room with a picture in it. I said, "Yes, there is. What's up with that?" She said she didn't know; however, it kept popping up, and she knew its appearance was for me to figure out.

Okay, so after my visit to the farmers' market, I went home and went up to my room. There was the stained glass candleholder as she had seen. I just stared at it as if to say, "Okay, there it is. It's been there a long time. Like several years." There was a picture rolled up inside it that I had placed there shortly after Jorge's passing. *Oh, my God, Jorge's passing!* It was a picture of the Garrido family with Jorge, and they were photographed for the Rutgers Future Scholars Program. I was being told to look at that picture. It must be Jorge telling Renee to tell me to look at his picture. Why? I got it! It was almost that time of year. The Rutgers Future Scholars Program would soon select scholarship recipients, and there was a beautiful program and ceremony at Rutgers University about to happen in the next few months.

I never got together with Eve Remsen-Sachs to create that scholarship, yet I was so intent on doing so. Separation, divorce, and life as a pediatric surgeon can very easily bury anyone under a world of stress and distraction. Several years had passed, and I just got so swept up in my busy life that I forgot all about it. Was Jorge gently reminding me to get my butt in gear and get this thing done? Yes, he was!

As I grabbed my cell phone to call the Garridos to say hello and to move forward with this agenda, I got a text from Selmira, Jorge's mom, at that very moment. We see each other several times a year and seldom text unless there's an event upcoming. So to get a text from her at that very moment was unreal. She texted me just after I had put two and two together regarding Renee's vision and Jorge's message to me about the scholarship. I told her what had just taken place. There's no way it was a coincidence. It's all about synchronicity.

The anniversary of Jorge's passing was a week away. There at the house was Eve Remsen-Sachs and Aramis Gutiérrez, the director and inceptor of the Rutgers Future Scholars Program. I was so thrilled to see them both. We all had a blessed gathering and discussed how to move forward. I left the Garrido's home that day feeling enlightened and so very blessed. Over the next two months, we came together as a team to make my dream of the Jorge Garrido Scholarship come true.

Over a subsequent lunch meeting at the Rutgers Club, I had the distinct pleasure to work with Dr. Eve Remsen-Sachs and Ms. Lavinia M. Boxill, vice president for Development Rutgers University Foundation. Things were really moving along nicely, and Jorge was absolutely behind this whole thing. Thank God for that, or it may not have happened when it did. My plan to create the Jorge Garrido Scholarship was finally materializing.

Dr. Eve and Lavinia guided the endeavor so that the scholarship would be awarded to a Rutgers future scholar who was actively enrolled at Rutgers University and pursuing a career in the medical field. The recipients are generally students who have a disadvantaged socioeconomic background. I was in a dream. I was floating on a cloud.

On June 10, 2016, the Rutgers Future Scholars Program would commence at the Nicholas Music Center on campus. The Garrido family would be there, and Little Victor would introduce me to the attendees and say a few words on the relationship that the family, Jorge, and I shared. I was then given the privilege of introducing for the first time the Jorge Garrido Scholarship. I then had the honor of introducing and calling up the recipient of the Jorge Garrido Scholarship, Ms. Tiffany Angeles.

This was a very special moment for me, the Garrido family, and Jorge Garrido himself. No one had any doubt in that Jorge was there with us on that beautiful day. To make it all even more amazing, we learned that Tiffany, the recipient of the scholarship, had pledged long ago to devote her life to becoming a pediatric surgeon.

I can tell you with certainty that an act of love and charity is contagious and addicting. I fulfilled one of my greatest dreams that day, and it's clear that Jorge had a hand in making it happen. The entire story of Jorge Garrido and John Gerard Gallucci could have been very different than what actually took place. I could have done my consult on Jorge back in the summer of 2011 and used only my brain and hands as most physicians and surgeons are trained to normally do. If so, it would have been the end of our story together. However, after my initial surgeon's assessment, I let my heart lead the way. I aligned myself with the greatest power in the universe, the divine power of love.

When you open your heart to your brothers and sisters and go the extra mile, you change people's lives. As more and more people on this planet make a knowing choice to do things that are loving and charitable, they will emit their love and light. As this *ascension play* of literally living at a higher frequency (more closely aligned with the energy of love as opposed to the lower energy of fear) grows and expands, the overall net state of human existence will become one of light from dark. There will be no more fear, just love.

As I have stated, acts of love, kindness, and charity are contagious and addicting. The inductive effect that occurs in people is usually immense, and the ripples go on and on and on forever. This, my dear friends, is how we change the world. Remember John Gerard Gallucci is merely the template and space holder in this book. The whole point of the book and the message in each of these stories is actually all about *you*, the reader! Just place your name where mine is!

Together we will create the kingdom of God here on earth as it is in heaven by one act of love, kindness, and charity at a time. Give thanks and praise to the Lord every day for what you have. Give your heart and your love to your brothers and sisters, and watch your world become enlightened and enriched in ways you could never imagine.

God bless you, Jorge Garrido!

"When the Spirit of truth comes, he will guide you into all the truth, for he will not speak on his own authority, but whatever he hears he will speak, and he will declare to you the things that are to come" (John 16:13 ESV).

By this all people will know that you are my disciples, if you have love for one another. (John 13:35 ESV).

"For the Kingdom of God is not eating and drinking, but righteousness and peace and joy in the Holy Spirit" (Romans 14:17 ESV).

Jorge and Victor Jr.

Feel the love expressed for Jorge in the words of his very own family in the following segment. God bless the Garrido family.

Chapter 20

The Garrido Family

We are the Garrido family—Victor, Selmira, Jorge, and Victor Jr.

Our story begins in March of 2010, when our son Jorge at thirteen years of age was diagnosed with leukemia. That was the toughest news and saddest times that we went through in our lives. That news certainly broke us down emotionally. Our Tito (Jorge's nickname in the family) was always a very happy kid and met everyone he encountered with love and affection. Jorge always left an impression on those he met. Many people will tell you that Jorge touched their hearts. Many say that meeting Jorge was a blessing and that Jorge actually changed their lives. Undoubtedly, Jorge was a very special kid, brave and strong. He took the news of his condition with ease and grace. He did and said everything he could to ease the pain and suffering that he saw us going through. He constantly told us that things would be okay. "Popi and Momi, don't worry or suffer. Everything will be fine, and I will beat cancer. You'll see! God didn't choose you, Dad, Mom, or Vic. He chose me because I am strong and I can fight cancer!"

Jorge was admitted to the hospital in New Brunswick, New Jersey. This was very close to our home. The staff, nurses, and doctors showered us all with attention, care, and support. They handled us as a family with true love and affection. This is certainly what we needed as it greatly helped us through as we watched our Tito deal with the pain and illness that biopsies and chemotherapy brought. There were times when we didn't know how any of us would survive. Jorge was in so much pain at times. The medications he received to help his pain would sedate him and help him sleep much of the day. There was a time when he developed lumps all over his body. The oncology team needed to know if the lumps were cancer or infections. That's when we met Dr. John Gallucci.

Dr. Gallucci is the chief of pediatric surgery at the hospital. He met us in Jorge's PICU (pediatric intensive care unit) room to make his evaluation. He was very kind and polite and very gentle with Jorge. Dr. Gallucci was very determined to help Jorge any way he could, but he was very worried that making multiple incisions on Jorge when he was so very ill and neutropenic (immunocompromised) could mean that Jorge would not heal at all and that he may suffer life-threatening sepsis (infection). In other words, having little to no healing ability and undergoing multiple incisions and biopsies could kill Jorge given his extremely fragile state. We, the oncology team, and Dr. Gallucci along with Jorge all made a decision. We had to have the answers. Jorge would endure the biopsies. Before the surgery Dr. Gallucci told us that he was going to light a candle at home for Jorge and that he was going to pray for Jorge's healing. He told us he would do his very best as a surgeon and as an individual who believed in God. God would hear our prayers, and they would reach Him because strong prayers offered up in numbers by many and from the heart always reach God.

The results came back, and we were all so happy to hear that the lumps on Jorge were not cancer. That meant they could be treated. There wouldn't have been much anyone could have done if it had been cancer. He had already had a bone marrow transplant. We were stunned that there were no signs of cancer anywhere in our Jorge. We know that our prayers along with Dr. Gallucci's prayers were answered. We know that God works in our lives day in and day out. We may not understand the things that happen, but God is there for us and guides us through good and terrible times. God brings people together who don't even know one another to create greater things. We were so grateful to Dr. Gallucci for sharing with us his willingness to not only operate on our Jorge but also pray for him. We never heard of a doctor who prays for the patients, or at least none that tell you so. Dr. Gallucci explained to us that every single person is sent into this world with a purpose and a mission.

Our Tito's mission was to unify many of us through love and faith in God through tough and terrible times. People came from all over to be like angels to us in such sad and difficult times. They offered care, affection, food, support, insight, friendship, prayers, and love. One of Tito's nurses named Ellen showed us great love and heart when she offered us her bone marrow for the transplant. We thank from our hearts the entire staff at the hospital for offering us their hearts. They also took our little Victor, who was then eight years old, in as their own. During countless days at the hospital and many sleepless nights, they played with Victor and gave him their friendship and love. Victor was one of the staff for many months.

Dr. Gallucci, Ellen, and many others were bought into our lives by God and Jesus. It was their affection, love, and expert care that got us all through those terrible days. They are our friends and are still by our side today. For two long and terrifying years, we would go home very hopeful but also have setbacks when Jorge was readmitted for fever or other symptoms. Through it all, Jorge remained strong and positive and told us, "Mom, Dad, don't worry please. I'll win this fight." It was not long after the transplant that Jorge developed stomach pain. When the doctors checked him out, they found he had cancer in his stomach. Our happiness over the transplant hadn't lasted very long. We had a choice to make—stay in the hospital and continue the chemo or go home with pain medication and oxygen. Tito made the decision at that point to go home and spend the rest of his days with his family. It was at home that we celebrated Tito's fifteenth birthday. To our amazement, he danced at his party and had a great time with his friends and family. He was home where he so desperately wanted to be.

Even though Jorge was so very ill for so long he said he wanted a pet. He wanted Siberian Huskies. So, we went and got him and Victor a male and a female Husky. The male is Skylar and the female Maya. As time went on our huskies had four puppies: Rocky, Icis, Daisy and Lucky. Lucky was Tito's favorite of the litter. He was strong and playful and loving. Tito gave them their names. Jorge was so very happy to see the birth of the puppies. We took pictures of Jorge holding the puppies in our yard on March 11, 2012. They were about ten or eleven weeks old. The puppies were born on Christmas Day, December 25, 2011. On March 16, Tito seemed to be okay. He didn't seem to be doing badly. The next day, March 17, God called Jorge home to him in heaven. Jorge (Tito) Garrido had completed his mission on earth. He came to touch hearts, show love, and bring people together through his faith in God.

For all of us, it was a horrible day filled with suffering, tears, and much pain to accept his death, which left a huge hole in our hearts. With all the faith in the world, we prayed to God for strength and for us to accept God's will and decisions without question. We will never forget Jorge's words of faith and wisdom. "Popi, Momi, don't suffer. I will be with our Father now. Everything is going to be fine. Just take care of my brother. I will always be with you all." It was with those words that we knew we had to be strong for our Victor to live. Jorge mandated it to us. *Take care of my brother.*

The darkest moments seemed to be over. There was only the future and Jorge's words to us. We understood from Dr. Eve Sachs that Dr. Gallucci was actually looking for a dog. We were so happy to hear that, and a few days later, Dr. Gallucci and his kids came to our home. They adopted Lucky. His kids wanted to change the name of the dog before they got here, not knowing about how he had been named. After coming and spending time with us and hearing the story, they all agreed that Jorge had named his favorite puppy Lucky, and that was that! His name would not be changed. Since then, Lucky has been inseparable from Dr. Gallucci and the kids. Dr. Gallucci has a very special relationship and connection with Lucky. He calls Lucky his spiritual gift from Jorge. They even went and got Lucky a friend named Rina.

Dr. Gallucci and many other people have expressed to us that Jorge had touched their hearts and changed their lives. To say that they will never forget him is an understatement. Jorge literally is always with them. They see him as their angel. We now have our own guardian angel— our loved and never forgotten Jorge, who will live forever in our hearts.

Thank you, son, for all the love that you have brought to us, for your lessons that you have taught us, and for taking care of us from the sky next to our Father.

We love you so much, Tito!

—Your parents and brother

The Garrido family

The beautiful words of Dr. Eve Remsen-Sachs say so much in the following passage. Dr. Eve, you are an angel clearly doing God's work. The Holy Spirit moved and spoke through you right on cue, and I am forever grateful.

Chapter 21

From Dr. Eve

"God works in mysterious ways. His wonders to produce." There was a family named Angeles that was struck with double tragedies. Their baby son was born with a cancer that destroyed his left eye. A few years later, the mother in the family was diagnosed with breast cancer. Struggling to cope with these tragedies, the daughter Tiffany pledged to God that if her younger brother and her mother were allowed to survive, she would devote her life to healing. God answered her prayers, and she is now living up to that pledge by earning top grades in college as a premed student. But this most difficult of majors requires both financial support and an encouraging role model and mentor. Into her life comes a guardian angel sent from God in the form of Dr. John Gerard Gallucci, who was seeking a way to honor and assuage the heartbreaking loss of one of his beloved younger patients named Jorge.

Dr. Gallucci is now providing scholarship support, guidance, and internship opportunities to his adopted future colleague Tiffany, who's will is to become a pediatric surgeon in honor of both Jorge and Dr.

Gallucci. "We know that all things work together for good for those who love God, who are called according to his purpose" (Romans 8:28 KJV).

Much Love,
Eve Remsen-Sachs

Lavinia Boxill and Dr. Eve Remsen Sachs

Invite the Holy Spirit into your hearts. Begin each day by wrapping yourselves in God's love. The next chapter shows us how we may begin each day by doing exactly that!

Chapter 22

Morning Prayers and Worship

I set the energy and tone of each day by dedicating prayers and intent as I leave my home and travel to work. I find the solitude of my car the perfect place to pray, say the Rosary, and commune with God. When I get to work, I'm ready for anything. It sure creates a good aura of positive energy in and around me as opposed to what any morning radio talk show would do to me.

Each prayer may be found with slightly different diction depending on the source.

(I make a daily dedication to a cause and/or people as I get in my car.)

The Lord's Prayer

Our Father in heaven, Holy be Thy name. Thy kingdom come, Thy will be done as on earth as it is in Heaven. Give us this day our daily bread, and forgive us our trespasses as we forgive those who trespass against us. Lead us not into temptation but deliver us from evil. Amen.

The Hail Mary

Hail Mary full of grace, the Lord is with thee. Blessed are thou amongst woman, and blessed is the fruit of thy womb, Jesus. Holy Mary, mother of God, pray for us sinners now and at the hour of our death. Amen.

The Holy Rosary

You may refer to various Rosary guides, or learn this routine from the internet. You can learn and keep your cadence and order of prayers with Rosary beads, but I do not hold Rosary beads while driving. I have it all in my heart and mind. Learn the Holy Rosary so you can say it anywhere with or without beads. If it's in your heart, this will be easy. There are many versions of the Holy Rosary on YouTube.

The Apostles' Creed

I believe in God the Father almighty, Creator of Heaven and earth. I believe in Jesus Christ, His only Son, our Lord, who was conceived by the power of the Holy Spirit, born of the Virgin Mary, suffered under Pontius Pilate, was crucified, died, and was buried. He descended into the dead. On the third day, He rose again, ascended into Heaven, and is seated at the right hand of God the Father almighty. He will come again to judge the living and the dead. I believe in the Holy Spirit, the Holy Catholic Church, the communion of saints, the forgiveness of sins, the resurrection of the body, and life everlasting. Amen.

Glory Be

Glory be to the Father, the Son, and the Holy Spirit. As it was in the beginning is now and forever shall be world without end. Amen.

The Fatima Prayer

O, my Jesus, forgive us our sins, save us from the fires of hell. Lead all souls to Heaven, especially those most in need of Your mercy.

Hail Holy Queen

Hail Holy Queen, mother of mercy, our life, our sweetness, and our hope. To Thee do we cry, poor banished children of Eve. To Thee do we send up our sighs, mourning, and weeping in this valley of tears. Turn then, most gracious Advocate, Thine Eyes or Mercy toward us, and after this our exile, show unto us the Blessed Fruit of Thy Womb, Jesus. O clement! O loving! O sweet Virgin Mary! Pray for us, O Holy Mother of God, that we may be made worthy of the promises of Christ.

The Days of the Week of the Holy Rosary

Monday: "The Joyful Mysteries." The Annunciation. The visitation. The nativity. The presentation of the baby Jesus in the Temple. The finding of boy Jesus in the Temple.

Tuesday: "The Sorrowful Mysteries." The agony in the garden. The scourging at the pillar. The crowning of thorns. The carrying of the cross. The crucifixion.

Wednesday: "The Glorious Mysteries." The resurrection. The Ascension. The Decent of the Holy Spirit upon the apostles. The Assumption. The Coronation.

Thursday: "The Luminous Mysteries." The baptism of Jesus at the Jordan River by John the Baptiste. The wedding at Cana. The proclamation of the Kingdom of God. The transfiguration. The establishment of the Eucharist.

Friday: "The Sorrowful Mysteries."

Saturday: "The Joyful Mysteries."

Sunday: "The Glorious Mysteries."

A Healer's Prayer

Oh, Lord, cleanse me. Holy Spirit, fall afresh on me and purify my heart, my mind, my body, my soul. May my spirit carry only love and healing energy. Jesus, forgive me my sins as I forgive others. I ask God to help me assist and heal my brothers and sisters. Holy Spirit, fill this space and fall afresh on me now. May the power of Jesus and the Christ light change me, mold me, use me, heal me, anoint me, bless me. Make me an instrument of your peace and love, oh Holy Master, for I give my life up to God and the Holy Spirit so that I may serve my brothers and sisters in Jesus's name. Amen.

—John Gerard Gallucci, MD FACS (7-21-2012)

The Prayer of Saint Francis of Assisi (Prayer of Peace)

Oh Lord, make me a channel of Your peace. Where there is hatred, let me sow love. Where there is injury, pardon. Where there is doubt, I'll bring faith. Where there is despair, I'll bring hope. Where there is darkness, light and sadness, joy. Oh, divine Master, grant that I may seek not to be consoled as to console, to be understood as to understand, to be loved as to love. For it is in giving that we receive. It is in pardoning that we are pardoned, and it is in dying that we are born to eternal life.

Speaking with God for Intent

Tell the Lord *exactly* what is in your heart and mind. Do not short-circuit this. Do not expect to live or pray by default. State your concerns and needs regarding any issue you are compelled to address. Lay it all on the line. Be direct and purposeful. Go for what you want, and say what you mean.

The Jesus Prayer

Lord Jesus Christ, Son of God, have mercy on me, a sinner.

(Repeat this as a mantra as often as you can.)

The Jesus Prayer for Healers

Lord Jesus Christ, Son of God, have mercy on me, a sinner. Let those whom I touch be touched by Jesus. May they receive it, and let them be healed.

(Adaptation by John Gerard Gallucci, MD FACS)

Closure

May the grace of the heavens fall afresh on me now, and may I receive it. May this truly be a blessed day.

(Make the sign of the cross.) Amen.

"The Lord is my strength and my shield; my heart trusted in Him, and I am helped: therefore my heart greatly rejoiceth; and with my song I will praise Him" (Psalm 28:7 KJV).

"The law of his God is in his heart; none of his steps shall slide" (Psalm 37:31 KJV).

"Trust in Him at all times people, pour out your heart before Him: God is a refuge for us" (Psalm 62:8 KJV).

"A good man out of the good treasure of his heart bringeth forth that which is good; and an evil man out of the evil treasure of his heart bringeth forth that which is evil: for of the abundance of the heart his mouth speaketh" (Luke 6:45 KJV).

While we sleep, we literally travel to different dimensions. If you set the spiritual tone of each day in the morning, you should see the benefit of setting the spiritual tone before sleep. Connect with God prior to letting go and traveling into that beautiful place called sleep. Stay wrapped in God's love morning, noon, and night. The following chapter shows how you can set your course for sleep and the wondrous places God will take you.

Chapter 23

Prayer, Worship, and Meditation

Every night prior to going to bed, I sit at my meditation table in my bedroom. I light a candle and often light either some sage or incense. Before the invention of candles, small oil lamps called votive lamps were used in ancient temples and home shrines as the faithful addressed their prayers to the deities of old.[18] I have two antique votive lamps on my table, but I don't light them. I use them as receptacles for negative energy. After I place the negative energy in the lamp, I then wave it over the flame of my candle to purify it with fire. The lamps are both brass. Candles made of beeswax were used in Egypt and Crete as early as 3000 BCE.[19]

I reflect upon the day and all the things that occurred. I do some deep breathing and settle in on what will be the topic of meditation for that night. Much like going to a spiritual bookstore where the book choose me—I don't choose them—the night's topic will surely come to me. I say some lead-up prayers and go to my spiritual safe house. Only after I'm safely inside that safe house do I begin my meditative journey.

I simply ask our Lord where He needs me. I'll get a clear visual of where I'm supposed to be. I may be escorting the spirit of a very sick child to my healing mountain in the third world, or I may see a dry dirt road, a jungle trail, or a filthy third world city street. It could be somewhere in the Middle East where many people are suffering from the ravages of war, or it could be Africa or India where many don't have enough to eat or live in inadequate shelters. For that matter, it could anywhere God leads me.

Often I will travel deep into the meditative dimensions, and as I do, I become completely unaware of my physical surroundings. I will find myself walking along any of the aforementioned settings and eventually come upon a group of children who are poorly clothed and have no food or clean water. They see me and rush for me, their hands outstretched and mouths agape with a combination of despair and hope all at once.

My heart breaks for them. I bless them and anoint them and lead them to a green pasture with a beautiful flowing stream. We sit down in cool thick green grass in the shade of a large tree and share the cool fresh waters of the stream. We then break bread and/or eat fruits growing nearby and give thanks to our Lord for the reprieve from suffering.

They all know that they needn't return to the devastation and suffering they came from. They can stay there in that beautiful oasis as long as they wish. We talk of the even more beautiful places to come and the joy that awaits them. They all understand that their journey is a progression and evolution from dark to light, from suffering and oppression to peace and love and joy.

After I'm sure that they have direction and understanding about where they will go next, I will bless them by placing the peace and love of the Holy Spirit upon them and reassure them of how much they are loved by God and the universe. They bless me in like fashion, and I move on.

A meditative journey like that will appear to take about twenty to thirty minutes, but when my consciousness returns to me as I sit at my meditation table, I will see that sixty to ninety minutes have gone by. The point here is that time is not a constant, especially when moving from one dimension to another. Yes, we are all capable of this. There is no time passage in the spirit world. When my journey is completed, I praise the Lord and thank Jesus for the opportunity to spiritually help others.

God will use the love energy and spread it all over this dark and parched world. As previously stated, the greatest power in the universe is love. The opposite of love is fear. If you just think of the world as a repository for either love or fear, then you can see how adding loads of love for your brothers and sisters will tip the balance of the energies toward love.

It is said that charity begins at home. Well, sit and meditate at home. But generate as much love, hope, and light as you can, and spread it all over the world. I have a globe that sits near my meditation table. When I feel the time is right, I'll put it in front of me, pray, meditate, and transfer energy to the globe, a facsimile of the world. I finish by seeing the entire world purified by Holy spiritual fire. The purple flame permeates the world and burns off only negativity and evil. It's a gift and a blessing from the Heavens to do this just as the grace of God is a gift. Thirst for it. Practice it. Live it, and you will change the world. Then it's time for bed.

Each morning as I leave my house for work, the dedication of that day will come to me. This was covered in detail in the previous chapter. I say the full Rosary every morning in the solitude of my car. There is a prescribed Rosary for each day of the week. I have it all memorized. I even know where I should be on my drive and what part of the Rosary I should be at. I also say all the associated Rosary prayers. I find myself about three or four miles away from work when I start my freelance praying and supplications. My intent for healings is said at this point. It can go on for a bit. Many people's issues and needs are addressed. After this segment of the morning prayers, I'll finish up the last mile or so by reciting a modified version of the Jesus Prayer. I call it the Jesus Prayer for Healers. "Lord Jesus Christ, Son of God, have mercy on me, a sinner. Let those whom I touch be touched by Jesus May they receive it, and let them be healed."

I'll say this prayer over and over again until I park my car. Orthodox Christian monks will say the Jesus Prayer as a ceaseless mantra throughout the entire day. I pray for each child I operate on and for those I do not operate on. Never underestimate the laying on of hands. When I do rounds and examine children, I am praying for them the whole time. If I see a patient I really don't need to formally examine, I will still touch their heads or put my hand on their shoulders in a reassuring way; however, I'm also praying for them.

Mostly every day I will go to the hospital chapel when it is quiet, and I'll sit and pray. Then I'll just sit in quiet observance of our Lord. When I do this, I feel a real transference of the energy of Holy intent. I bring the problems of the pediatric surgery service to God, and quite frankly, I lay those on Him. This really only takes about ten or fifteen minutes. It's gotten so that if I don't make it to the chapel, I feel a little cheated and a bit empty.

So I start each and every day with the full Rosary followed by the Jesus Prayer for Healers in my car on the way to work. It sure beats listening to talk radio, which is designed to rev you up, spin you around and sell you something.

When I get to work, I'm spiritually and emotionally ready for anything. The chapel visit spans the midday and brings specific issues to the forefront. At night I do meditative traveling. I know it has changed my life in a very powerful way, and I also believe it is helping to change the world that so desperately needs changing.

I suggest starting a daily prayer regimen of your very own. Write your own prayer too. Do you really believe you have more important things to do with your life? Cut down on TV, radio, and social media, and throw yourself into a life of prayer.

Everything starts from prayer. Without asking God for love, we cannot possess love, and we are less able to give it to others. Just as people today speak so much about the poor but still do not know them, we, too, cannot talk so much about prayer and yet not know how to pray.[20]

"He who has my commandments and keeps them, it is he who loves me. And he who loves me will be loved by My Father, and I will love him and manifest myself to him" (John 14:21 ESV).

"Let the words of my mouth, and the meditation of my heart, be acceptable in thy sight, O Lord, my strength and my redeemer" (Psalm 19:14 ESV).

"Wait on the Lord: be of good courage, and He shall strengthen thine heart: wait, I say, on the Lord" (Psalm 27:14 KJV).

Healing the world

The next chapter will show you how not everyone is meant to be healed physically. No matter what you do or how genuine, spiritual, and energetic your effort may be, there is a purpose for every happenstance under heaven. Sometimes God's plan and purpose is beyond our anticipation or comprehension. Read on for my first face-to-face supernatural encounter with Saint Jude (the patron saint of hopeless cases) and our Lord Jesus Christ.

Chapter 24

The Infant Who Changed My Life

I was consulted on a beautiful, full-term five-month-old male who had been admitted to our PICU with massive head trauma. The history of this child's present condition left us all deeply saddened; however, the story of what may or may not have happened certainly wasn't ours to judge. I was consulted on day seven of his PICU stay for what appeared to be an acute abdomen. This is a term used when there is a suspected intra-abdominal catastrophe that requires immediate surgery. I agreed with the attending PICU that the boy needed emergency surgery.

When I opened this child's abdomen in the operating room, I found nearly two-thirds of his small bowel so necrotic it had liquefied. He ended up with a third of his small bowel intact, his entire colon, and a proximal ileostomy (a bag to drain his feces). Ultimately, his intra-abdominal injuries could be overcome in the long term. His neurologic injury was severe. Little William may or may not make a neurologic recovery. We just didn't know.

I became very involved with this child and had many lengthy discussions with his mom and dad. I quickly prayed for him and did meditative sessions for him in the chapel and at my home, and I also placed him in our prayer group. Many saw my little brother's case as hopeless. I understood this perspective well, so when I prayed for him, I intentionally evoked Saint Jude. Among other things, Saint Jude is the patron saint of hopeless cases.

The ongoing neurologic assessments showed that William's condition was worsening. His prognosis was dismal. There eventually came a point when his parents were considering taking him off life support. His parents had reached their threshold, and they didn't want him to suffer any further.

Silently, in my heart I believed there had to be a way, a spiritual answer to his healing. One night while in a meditation specifically meant for healing William, I took him spiritually into the third world. It's another dimension just as real if not more real than this one and previously discussed regarding Jorge Garrido and others. For those who go there, it's a place where healing occurs through connection with God.

I took little William in my arms, and away we went into this beautiful dimension of healing. First, we flew through the night sky to a place where there was a portal, that beautiful oak tree that sat on the margin of a dark forest and a bright sunny meadow. I could see the bright speck of light from the meadow high above in the night sky. As we got closer, I could see the oak tree. We settled in under the tree and walked from the darkness of the forest edge into the blinding bright light of the meadow. As I carried him, I could smell the tall grass and feel the radiant heat all over my body. On the other end of the meadow, there was a hill that led to the road made of pure gold. As I walked upon this road, it began to move as an airport transportation walkway would.

Up ahead was that familiar white cloud, and we were headed straight for it. As we entered this cloud, I could feel the cool moisture of the cloud, and I could only see what was in front of me. It was peaceful and completely quiet in this cloud. I was well aware that this cloud was the threshold of the realm of the Holy Spirit. As we emerged from the other end of the cloud, still on the golden road, I knew we were in that sweet realm devoid of all negativity and evil. There was no fear, only love.

Along this road was the familiar stream to the right. As we moved along, I waited for our portal to appear, our special doorway. Each doorway was different, and some would display a characteristic that would clearly preclude our passage while the right one would invite us through. Our doorway finally appeared. It was just what I was expecting. It was heavy and made of dark hardwood like oak or mahogany. It was also set in a heavy stone threshold. This door was inviting and stood plumb and square as we approached. We stepped off the golden road onto a small footbridge traversing the stream. As we did, the door opened for us. I stepped into a beautifully appointed vestibule with coffered walls and marble floors. The inner doors opened for us, inviting us into the church itself. We walked up the side aisle and entered the sacristy behind the altar. There we climbed the familiar steep stairway up to a room that was completely dark. This was the next level of ascension en route to our destination.

As we stood there waiting reverently in anticipatory silence, the back wall of this room revealed a portal to our busy city street in the healing realm. I quickly stepped through the portal onto the sidewalk with the baby in my arms. I gingerly crossed the street as I always did but had to wait for the white van to pass as it always did when I took this route. On the other side of the street, there stood our hotel. This time I chose to enter by the automatic glass doors in the front and not the revolving doors. Then we went into the main lobby.

The concierge looked up and acknowledged me as he always did. The desk clerk did the same. They knew me and were anticipating my arrival. They knew my route. I passed between the concierge desk and the front desk on my way to an entrance to the rear ballroom. I entered the empty ballroom and saw six doorways from left to right numbered only with odd numbers. I always chose doorway number three or seven.

This time I chose number three. I went through the door and ended up on the ramp made of wood decking. It was a gentle down ramp onto a sandy beach. Straight ahead led to the base of my steep mountain. To the right there was a sandy walk to the beach. The ocean there contained the living waters of God's realm. All the creatures in that ocean anticipated our arrival, and when we entered the water, they approached us and expressed their great joy. They were healers by their own right, and all engaged in a joyous decree of love and welcome.

To the left of the mountain base was a rocky climb to a set of stairs made of pure white granite. The stairs were about two feet high by four feet wide. These steps ascended very steeply up the side of this beautiful healing mountain where souls interfaced with God, the saints, and the Holy Spirit.

This was an ancient place that souls from many worlds had traversed for healing throughout the millennia. As I climbed the steps with William in my arms, I could see the beautiful blue sea shimmering all around us. I could see the perfect white clouds above us in the crystal blue sky. The sun was a bright yellow-white round ball imparting energy to us as we ascended. At about the halfway point, I turned to the sea to enjoy this breathtaking sight.

As I continued my ascent, I eventually climbed above the clouds. As I approached the summit, I could see the stone altar and the white columned building behind it. I stood there at the very top, fully aware that I was as high as any mortal could go spiritually.

We had reached the summit that many sought as they petitioned God for the healing of their brothers and sisters. I stepped up to the altar and raised the baby over my head and began to pray. I began to pour my heart and soul out to our Lord and Master for the healing of this beautiful child. I wept as I begged God for the healing of William, my brother, his child.

Dear Lord, surely you have said, "Ask and it will be given to you, seek and you will find, knock and it will be opened to you" (Matthew 7:7 NIV).

I said, "Holy Master, my Holy Father, who imbued life into me, all in this universe, and beyond, please heal this child. If there were a child so deserving of your healing Holy powers, it is this one! Show your power and majesty to all, my Lord. All is possible for you, dear Holy Master!

Although all my energy had been totally focused on looking straight over the altar with my back to the sea, I was compelled to turn away from the altar at that very moment and look back out over the sea again. As I turned, I could see a tiny speck in the sky far off in the distance. I watched it get closer and closer. Eventually, I could see that it was a man dressed in ancient clothing, floating closer and closer to us. At this point I turned to fully address this approaching ancient male figure. As he drew nearer, I could now see that this was in fact Saint Jude himself. He was alive and well, and he had come specifically to address us.

As Saint Jude approached, he smiled at us. I could clearly see he was wearing a tan robe with dark purple borders and was holding his staff in his right hand. After he established in my heart who he was, he gave his approval of where we were and of our agenda. Saint Jude then gestured for me to look over my right shoulder. I hesitated as I wasn't completely sure of what he was telling me to do, so he gestured again with an upward nod of his head for me to look over my right shoulder. Saint Jude exuded peace, love, and kindness as he hovered there a few feet off the ground.

As I turned and looked over my shoulder, I could see a white cloud floating high over the stone altar. As the cloud slowly descended, it stopped for a moment and then began to ascend again to reveal a life-size crucifix emanating from within it. As the cloud dispersed up into the heavens from which it came, the crucifix gently descended until the base was about twelve feet off the ground, I could see there was a man on the cross.

I now had turned fully around to face what was obviously an event I could never have anticipated. The energy that ran through me was immense and nearly overwhelming. As the crucifix hovered just off the ground, I could see that the man on the cross was alive. I looked into His eyes as He stared directly into mine. Jesus Christ, my Lord and Master, had descended to me in response to my emotional petition.

Jesus Christ floated down off the cross and stood about eight feet from me. I immediately fell to my knees while holding the baby and began to weep uncontrollably. Through my tears I held the baby up to Him with outstretched arms and begged Him for healing. "My Lord and Master, I beg you for the healing of this child."

Jesus looked directly into my eyes and gestured for me to stand up. I quickly stood up in the presence of My Lord and Master, Jesus Christ. He looked at me and said, "You are a faithful follower." I was stunned at the words He spoke to me, and I immediately became paralyzed with a combination of inspiration and awe.

Jesus was beautiful. He was truly alive and well. He looked perfect. His hair was dark brown and came down to His shoulders, and He had a well-groomed beard. He wore a light tan robe with a soft rope around His waist and dark sandals.

Jesus gestured for me to hand Him the baby. I handed Jesus the baby as He had requested. He held the baby up with His left hand holding the back of the baby's head, His right hand supporting the baby from below. Jesus looked deeply into the baby's eyes. As Jesus was doing so, I fell to my knees again and begged him for the life and healing of this beautiful child, "My Holy Master, I beg you to please heal this child."

Jesus looked lovingly at me and gestured once again for me to rise. As I stood, He handed me the baby and said, "*You* heal him with the *love* you have for him." Jesus Christ personally gave me His directive and decree face-to-face with a firm yet gentle and loving tone of expectancy.

The words Jesus spoke to me sent a wave of excitation and resolve through my soul. His words were vintage Jesus of Nazareth, Jesus of the gospel. He challenged me to do what He did while He was here on earth. Jesus Christ directly charged me and challenged me to heal my brothers and sisters with the love I had for them. My heart and mind were racing with excitement. When Jesus was certain that I had gotten the message, He smiled at me and floated up and gently disappeared into the cloud He had descended from.

My face-to-face encounter with Saint Jude and Jesus Christ had come to a close. It was abundantly clear to me that this event could *never* be over. In my petition of love and healing for this baby, Saint Jude and Jesus Christ saw fit to descend to me alive and well. They issued their directive to me personally. How could an event like this ever be over? It never will be over.

Although this was certainly the most spectacular event in my entire life, it is abundantly clear that I am by no means the only one that this kind of encounter has happened to. I have been meditating on and praying to Jesus and the saints for many years—in fact, since I was a very small child. Now Jesus and His Holy associate Saint Jude (the patron saint of hopeless cases) descended to me and issued their loving decree.

I've read accounts of this happening here and there all over the world. In no way did I anticipate this. Nor could I have ever appropriately prepared for this. I came away from this Holy encounter knowing fully that no matter where I was, no matter the circumstance, no matter how desperate the situation, Jesus Christ and the saints were watching and waiting for us to seek them and thirst for them with all our hearts, minds, bodies, and souls.

When we do so, we metaphorically turn their heads and their hearts enough that mountains can be moved. When this Holy encounter was done, I spiritually returned the baby to his PICU bed. I could see the digital displays on his monitors and could hear the soft sounds of his ventilator. I said good night and put my hand on his head lovingly. I spoke to him and told him that Jesus and Saint Jude were there for us and that all would be well one way or another. "Have no fear, my little brother!" I said.

I returned immediately to my room at home. I found myself in my meditation chair, and I was wide awake. No, I had not been asleep, and this was no dream. Those who meditate will understand. I sat back with an exhale that punctuated my return to our three-dimensional present. I gazed into my prayer candle and burst into tears. I sat there sobbing for quite a while. They were tears of joy, and I had a completely fresh view of the world.

I said some completion prayers and gave profuse thanks to God, our Father, Jesus Christ, the Holy Mother, and the saints. I would never ever doubt that Jesus and the saints were real, alive, and well. My life and my world had changed forever. I now had a Holy agenda. I was resolute. Tomorrow I would ramp up my prayers, and I was sure I could help save him from an early demise. No matter how difficult, no matter how uncertain his future may be, I had my duty. I was going to see this through. I would heal him with the love I had for him.

The next morning I had a very big day at work. I thought the right thing to do was to see him in the PICU early—perhaps sixty forty-five in the morning—before my day started. As I drove to the hospital, I imagined all that was ahead for me and him. I couldn't wait to get to the PICU. As I walked down the quiet hallways, my excitement grew greater and greater. I had butterflies in my stomach.

As I rounded the corner and passed through the PICU doors, I looked up at the staff. A double team of nurses and several residents just stared at me. There wasn't a sound. They had all been emotionally involved with this case, but they all knew I had thrown my heart and soul into the fight for this baby's life. I stopped and looked into his PICU room. The room was empty and clean. It was completely turned over for the next patient.

Where is William? Not a sound came from the staff. All eyes were trained on me. *What? What is going on? Where is he?* His nurse softly explained to me that he had been transferred out of our hospital to an outside hospice facility in the middle of the night. The word got back to the PICU staff that he had been taken off ventilator support and was pronounced dead by early morning.

I was so stunned that all I could do was say, "Okay. Thank you." I turned and walked away. My world had just been rocked. I was blown away. I felt every emotion one can possibly feel given the series of events that had occurred over the last week and culminating in last night's unforgettable, unbelievable voyage.

Why would Saint Jude and Jesus Christ appear to me? Why would they speak to me face-to-face, and why would Jesus take the baby from me, look deeply into His eyes, and offer His charge to me as He did? Jesus had issued me a personal directive. "*You* heal him with the *love* you have for him." I had experienced the most incredible occurrence of my entire life. I got to work with a heart and agenda as big as the heavens only to find out the baby had passed in the middle of the night.

My mind was reeling with confusion. I didn't have any doubt about God though. I didn't doubt last night. I had confusion over what the underlying message was. Why would this happen? What kind of sad, unfortunate ending to such an incredible story was this? I pondered this incessantly for the next several days, thinking about how I might not get over this tragedy for a very long time. How could I second-guess Jesus Christ? I wouldn't! What did all of this mean? How could I move forward as a pediatric surgeon and a spiritual healer? Well, as the saying goes, "All in God's time." Everything happens for a reason, and I am not running the universe. God is. As it turned out, I didn't have long to wait for my answer.

"Everyone who drinks this water will be thirsty again, but whoever drinks the water I give them will never thirst. Indeed, the water I give them will become in them a spring welling up to eternal life" (John 4:13–14 ESV).

"He sent them to preach the Kingdom of God and to heal the sick" (Luke 9:2 ESV).

"Again Jesus spoke to them, saying, I am the light of the world. Whoever follows me will not walk in darkness, but will have the light of life" (John 8:12 ESV).

"As long as I am in the world, I am the light of the world" (John 9:5 ESV).

"Jesus said to him, 'I am the way, and the truth, and the life; no one comes to the Father but through me'" (John 14:6 NASB).

"For God so loved the world, that he gave his only Son, that whoever believes in Him should not perish but have eternal life" (John 3:16 ESV).

The following picture is from the first page of my Grandfather's bible. It was given to him as a very thoughtful spiritual gift by his grade school teacher Marguerite Wharton in Newark, New Jersey when he was ten years old. She thought enough of him that although the bible was a family heirloom from her grandfather she gifted it to him all the same.

Grandpa's Bible. A gift from 1916.

Dear Thomas,

*My grandfather gave me this bible and I know that he is glad
that I am giving it to you. I hope you will read it especially the
four gospels which tell the story of Jesus The most wonderful
life that has ever been lived. I hope that you and I will try to be
like him and to be able to meet him some day face to face.*

*With love and best wishes
Your friend,
Marguerite Wharton
December 1916*

The previously outlined supernatural occurrence gave me great pause and threw me into a deeply reflective state. As I posed the question "Why would this happen?" the next story literally gave me my answers, and no, I didn't have long to wait. It all happened the very next week. The next story can be considered a love story. It depicts the love between a family (but especially a grandfather and his granddaughter) and the love a pediatric surgeon can have for his dying patient. Remember love is the greatest power in the universe. Become as one with it and move mountains!

Chapter 25

I Heal Her with the Love I Have for Her

I thought I would be licking my wounds over the saga of little William, our five-month-old, for a very long time. In no way could I understand why Jesus and Saint Jude would have descended to me and personally given me a directive on how to heal my brothers and sisters only to result in a deceased baby. I had put my heart, mind, body, and soul into healing that child. I literally did everything I could possibly do to bring about and evoke healing. I prayed fervently. I meditated with great ease, clarity, and success. I used all my skills as a pediatric surgeon successfully. I even evoked and met Saint Jude and Jesus Christ. None of it made any obvious sense to me.

I tried my best to look at this from every conceivable angle. I prayed on it. I meditated on it. I evoked the saints on it. I clearly understand, however, that my will isn't necessarily God's will. This is absolutely one of the most difficult concepts for any human being to digest, no matter who you are or where you are on this planet.

I talked to Jesus about it. I finally concluded that something big was about to happen, but apparently, I had to wait quietly for God's timing. I really believed that for something so confusing to be rectified sensibly, an equally amazing event had to be coming. I was being prepared for something that would put everything into its proper perspective. This event would answer all my questions and erase all doubt forever about who God and Jesus were and the role they play in all our lives.

August 20, 2012, was like any other Monday. I got up, got ready for work, had some coffee, got my kids off to school, and hugged Lucky. Off to work I went. There was nothing unusual about the way the day started or how it progressed. Or so I thought.

As the long day ended, I finally went home. I was on call for emergencies, but it was time to settle in for some dinner. Just as I finished dinner and started to relax, a call from the hospital came in. It was the director of the pediatric intensive care unit (PICU).

I had been involved one way or another with patient care and surgery since medical school. I graduated in 1990. For more than thirty years working in health care, I had never heard before the words I was about to hear. The PICU director said, "I have a teenager who is being transported to us as we speak from an outside hospital. She has an abdominal compartment syndrome. She is very near death. She has no sustainable prograde blood flow and is about to code. I'm asking you to meet the transport team in the OR, put her on the table, and cut her open immediately."

"I know what you're thinking," he said. "There is no time to come to the PICU. If you are to save her life, this is how it will have to be. If not, she will die for sure. She is intubated and has a nasogastric tube in place with intravenous fluids ongoing. Please, John, just take her straight away from the ambulance to the table."

I responded, "What? Are you serious?"

He said, "Trust me. Just do it … please!"

"Okay, I got it. I'll call the OR right now. What's their ETA?" He said they were less than twenty minutes out. I called the OR, and as destiny would have it, there was a team already there. They had just finished an add-on case. There were times after hours when you would need to wait an hour for a team to assemble. We were not a trauma center. I explained things to the team as I drove to the hospital.

I began to pray to God and Jesus for guidance. I asked them for their help. I ran into the locker room, changed as quickly as I could, and ran down to OR number one. The transport team was rolling her into the room straight from the ambulance. As I got close to her, I could see what looked like a typical patient with multisystem organ failure. She was intubated and had anasarca. Her whole body was purple, and her belly was as hard as a rock and very much distended. I also noticed that she had liquid feces actively running out of both nostrils.

This was a disaster case if there ever was one. I helped transfer her to the operating table. Her whole body was literally as stiff as a board. I asked anesthesia to place a second large bore NGT and put both on suction as soon as possible. I quick scrubbed up with my resident, and we went right back into the OR. I was gowning and gloving as my resident was pouring betadine on her. The towels and drapes went on, and I stood there, arranging the last few items I needed like my suction and Bovie cautery device.

The circulating nurse did a quick time-out, a required endeavor. As she finished, I was overcome with emotion. I knew very well the gravity of this situation and the slim chances of saving the patient. All in a second's time, I imagined this was somebody's precious child, somebody's sister, somebody's cousin, somebody's grandchild, somebody's future wife, and somebody's future mom. I asked for the scalpel. I took it in my hand. I looked to the heavens and felt tears rolling down my face and a lump in my throat. I evoked God. I evoked Jesus. I said to myself as if right on cue, "I heal you with the love I have for you!"

I was living the directive Jesus had Himself given me less than one week prior. I went into my trauma-emergency mode—steady, cool, precise, gentle where as needed. I went into a zone that surgeons know all too well. I was on automatic pilot. Her abdomen was as tight as a drum. It was extremely difficult to get into free abdominal space and not hit a piece of stuck and grossly distended bowel. She was fraught with old adhesions and scar tissue everywhere.

Whenever I find myself in similar circumstances regarding bowel obstructions, I wonder how anyone could have a functioning gastrointestinal tract up until a day before surgery and how it could become this bad and this hostile so quickly. She had apparently had several surgeries as an infant in another state. What was even more interesting was that she was apparently playing volleyball and eating less than twenty-four hours ago.

As I lysed a massive amount of adhesions, her bowel became untethered. Her small bowel was grossly dilated to the point of near perforation. She began to stabilize in a relative sense, but she was still gravely ill. She required massive fluid resuscitation on the table and intravenous medications to keep her blood pressure up. She slowly started to make urine, which was a good sign. Everything was eventually—and successfully—decompressed. When the operation was done, nearly seven hours had passed. It took that long to decompress her bowel and relieve her multiple points of obstruction. I saw no point in stopping halfway there.

If her precarious condition had worsened, I may have had to stop and close with a sterile plastic sheet, but that would have left huge dilation with persistent obstruction. It all seemed like I had made my initial incision just a few hours ago. That was how it often went when you were in that emergency zone and you knew of nothing else going on around you. It's the same as moving in the spirit. As incredibly sick as she was, she was alive! She certainly was alive with reasonable blood pressure (albeit with the help of several pressor agents) and a slowly increasing urine output.

Anyone middle-aged or older would probably not have survived the event. A young heart and other organs played a big role in her survival capacity. I was so thankful to God that we got her through the operation and were now transporting her to the PICU, where the director was waiting with his team. I knew in my heart of hearts that she was going to make it. After I gave my report to the PICU team and handed her off to them, I staggered my way to the family waiting room. I was soaked in sweat, and I looked like I had just done a very intense and messy emergency operation for nearly seven hours.

I took a seat facing the patient's grandmother. We were the only two people in that room. She saw the look on my face, a look that I was in no way attempting to hide. She said, "That bad, huh?"

I said "Well, yes. Your granddaughter came about as close to dying as one can, but she lived. She is in no way out of the woods. I believe she is going to make it, but being this sick, all bets are off. It's still too early to tell if she will develop pulmonary failure or slip into irreversible multisystem organ failure. That potential certainly looms heavily over her."

The grandmother looked at me and made a gasp and said, "Oh, my God! How? Why? I was speaking to her earlier today. Do you know her history? Angela is all I have! Her mother and father passed when she was an infant! That's my baby!"

I looked her deeply in the eyes. "No, I don't know anything about her."

The grandmother was the guardian for most of Angela's life. Angela had recently gotten very depressed because of a family tragedy. She loved her grandfather very much and lived for him. Five days prior to this terrible event, Angela's grandfather had passed away. This threw Angela into a serious depression with bouts of angry outbursts. She had even once stated that she didn't want to live anymore.

It would be quite a long time before I learned that Angela had an amazing metaphysical experience while on the operating table. Angela eventually conveyed to me that during this operation, when she was under anesthesia, she was sobbing and crying. Her recently passed grandfather approached her. Angela tells this story in the next chapter.

Angela was terribly sick in our PICU. She was on presser agents and intubated for more than a week. When she finally turned the corner and was stable enough to be extubated (have her breathing tube removed), I was so thrilled to finally meet her and hear her voice. She was awake. She didn't have much of a voice, but we briefly spoke. It was an awesome experience to say the least.

With each day, Angela got stronger and stronger. I learned more and more about her from her aunt and grandmother as the days passed. Angela was finally transferred out of the PICU to our pediatrics floor. That was a great day. She looked good, but I knew how terrible things were in her abdomen. She had acute chronic intestinal dilation, and apparently, she had experienced issues with eating and digestion since she had been an infant. Angela finally did well enough to be discharged from the hospital after about a month or so.

Approximately six weeks after her initial emergency surgery, Angela developed another small bowel obstruction. I knew this was from adhesions (scar tissue) that could develop inside the abdomen after surgery. This is ultimately what caused her original bowel obstruction to begin with. She certainly was at a high risk for it as there was a huge amount of inflammation and dilation when I was in there. Angela was readmitted for what looked to be a partial small bowel obstruction, but it soon progressed to a complete obstruction. We attempted to turn this around with nasogastric tube suctioning, but to no avail. It was irrefutable. Angela would eventually need to return to the operating room.

I had to open her up again and do whatever I must do to fix her obstruction. I knew it wasn't going to be a walk in the park. I also knew that I had pulled off a very difficult seven-hour or so operation with every chance to perforate her bowel, and yet I hadn't. This time I knew it was going to be almost impossible. I explained it all to Angela and her family. They were all very concerned, but I told them we really had no choice in the matter. Back to the operating room we went.

I got into her abdominal space without too much difficulty, but dealing with her extremely dense adhesions made the first operation seem like a walk in the park. This time things were much more difficult. I took down all her adhesions, but the toughest parts causing her multiple obstructions were not going to come apart without tearing. Her small bowel was entrapped in a very tight gnarled ball. This was not going to right itself on its own without surgery.

Alas, I had my first enterotomy (breaking into the bowel). There was a tear in her jejunum that was about ninety centimeters from the junction of her duodenum and jejunum. A second enterotomy was also unavoidable, but this one was at around 150 centimeters from the duodenal-jejunal junction. It was either go for the takedown (release of bowel obstruction), remove that portion straight away, or just leave an obstruction. Well, we had to go for it. That was the nature of this case.

I wasn't about to beat myself up over two enterotomies in a very hostile abdomen over what was nearly another seven hours of intense lysis of very dense adhesions. With this, I created what's known as a diverting ileostomy at about 150 centimeters from the duodenal-jejunal junction. I felt I needed to do this as her colon was very beat up from inflammation and massive lysis of adhesions. There was also one enterotomy on her colon that I repaired directly. I needed to protect this area so it had a chance to heal. A blowout or leak from any part of her bowel after I closed her would be a disaster. Finally, I had everything unfurled and her obstruction clears. I ultimately decided to close the upper enterotomy and pray that with prolonged nasogastric decompression and TPN (IV nutrition), this would heal, and we could avoid short bowel syndrome.

This decision was certainly controversial, and I knew it. Some surgeons would have made the stoma at ninety centimeters and repaired the break at 150 centimeters. I knew doing so would leave her with a high output stoma and totally dependent on IV nutrition possibly for months. This was *not* something that anyone takes lightly. There were many factors that went into my decisions that day. I couldn't see her not developing profound short bowel syndrome if I had created a diverting small bowel stoma as high in her GI tract as ninety centimeters.

As Angela slowly got better, I kept my prayers up for her in a very big way. She had such a difficult time eating. She would vomit so often that she had no will to eat. Her stoma, although at 150 centimeters, would still go into high-output mode. Angela was a very difficult puzzle with pieces thrown all over. Putting her back together—physically, physiologically, and emotionally—would take a very long time. Angela now slipped into the dreaded short bowel syndrome, even after I made her stoma sixty centimeters downstream from where it could have been. If I had not created the anastomosis (sewing the bowel together) at about ninety centimeters, she would have had very profound short bowel syndrome. This is where one doesn't have enough reasonably functioning small bowel to adequately digest and absorb what he or she ingests. As this person eats and drinks, his or her gastrointestinal tract acts like it is too short, and everything the individual take in shoots right out of him or her into the bag. If untreated with long-term central venous access and total parenteral nutrition (TPN), this person will dehydrate, become malnourished, and ultimately go into renal failure because of severe acute and chronic dehydration. Ultimately, this individual will die if not supported thoroughly through this process.

I imagined that Angela's bowel had endured such an insult with the first abdominal compartment syndrome. The microstructure of her bowel could be damaged beyond repair. Would it regenerate and function again or not? If so, great. If not, this would spell ultimate disaster. People with short bowel syndrome that you can't turn around can be sustained on nutrition via the intravenous route, but this will only get the patient so far. Ultimately, this will lead to liver failure and death unless the patient successfully receives a small bowel and liver transplant.

This is going all the way down the line with this issue, but that's what I was worried about if we couldn't turn her around. I knew Angela only had a foot or so of small bowel to bring back into circuit when I eventually would close her stoma (put the two ends of the intestine together and remove the bag). If I had three or four feet of small bowel to reconnect, then I wouldn't be so worried. But I only had a foot or so. That might not be enough length to turn things around.

Prayer mode was as high as it had even been for her. I was using lots of different techniques to bring about healing through the Holy Spirit. Angela was enrolled in a large prayer group. I stepped up my meditative healing sessions with Saint Jude and Jesus. I evoked other friends of mine who were very ill themselves and asked them to pray for Angela.

I use many types of visual and meditative imagery while healing the sick. I would see the crystal cord of white light emanating from the I Am presence through the Holy Christ self. In Ecclesiastes, it is known as the silver cord (Ecclesiastes 12:6 NIV). Through this umbilical cord flows a cascading stream of God's love and light. Some refer to it as God's life stream. I use this often and call upon it for its miraculous healing powers.

Recruiting infirmed individuals who are themselves willing and capable of prayer for the healing of others is a very strong healing modality. Their acts of faith and their intention to consciously heal others who are ill are very powerful. The healing energy is maximized when it's generated from acts as selfless as praying for others when you yourself are seriously infirmed. "Let the sick lay hands on you"[21]

Once again, I was doing everything I possibly could to heal Angela with the love I have for her. She had all the usual complications that a patient with short bowel syndrome could have. She had several line infections that brought her right back to sepsis and dehydration.

She came to see me one day in an office follow-up as an outpatient, and I expected to see a teenage girl who was doing reasonably well. Yes, she was on TPN, and yes, she had an ileostomy bag; however, things should have been reasonably stable. If not, they would have called me and said something was wrong. But when she showed up, she looked gray and weak as if she were about to pass out. I admitted her to the hospital immediately and did a complete workup. I also got gastroenterology to see her.

Angela was a very difficult case. I also learned that she was not eating what she claimed she was. At this time Angela was self-destructive. I called all the appropriate services to help her through this. What else could go wrong for her? It appeared as though bad energy had settled in on her and her family and wouldn't let go. Even her beloved dog had apparently jumped a fence and gotten his leg caught, and he subsequently hung upside down for many hours. He was nearly dead when the neighbors found him. They saved his life.

Angela got better with a lot of TLC and lots of nurturing health care professionals all doing what they could for her. This ongoing issue of dehydration and sepsis in a recurring cycle delayed the closing of her stomas for several months. Finally, we had a day picked to take Angela back to the operating room and close her stomas. It was a do-or-die scenario for several big reasons. Angela couldn't deal with a bag, especially one that leaked frequently. Angela also needed to get off the TPN and restore her ability to eat and drink and sustain her life without artificial means.

All I could think of was that foot or so of terminal ileum. It had better be ready to work very hard to bring her out of her short bowel syndrome. The day before we went to the OR, Angela came into the hospital for a tune-up prior to what could be another long and difficult surgery. However, while in the hospital, she developed a very serious and profuse upper gastrointestinal hemorrhage. I watched as the gastroenterologist scoped her and cauterized a large bleeding duodenal ulcer.

If they failed to stop her hemorrhage with their endoscopy or if they perforated her bowel, that would have meant me taking her to the operating room and doing a huge operation on her abdomen to stop the bleeding. If I was met with all the previous adhesions and scar tissue I had experienced twice already, then the issue would become seriously life-threatening as it would potentially take me hours to successfully reach the area that was bleeding.

To say that Angela and her situation caused me distress and anxiety would be an understatement. Through Angela and her illness, I learned to apply the following simple realization: The beginning of anxiety is the end of faith, and the beginning of faith is the end of anxiety (George Miller, 1805–98), director of orphanages in Bristol, England.[22]

By the grace of God, GI had indeed found the bleeding ulcer and successfully cauterized it without perforating an already thinned-out duodenal wall. However, once again we were delayed months before closing her stoma. When Angela was ready, I had a contrast study done through her mucus fistula to assess her distal ileum (downstream remaining small bowel) and colon as a prelude to her stoma closure. I wanted to make totally sure there were no strictures or issues that may need to be addressed before I closed her stoma, thereby creating a fully continuous gastrointestinal tract.

That contrast study revealed that Angela had much more small bowel beyond her mucous fistula than what we had recognized during the previous surgery. This was a game changer. It was hugely important to her ultimate well-being. I saw it as a miracle. I had left about eleven inches or so of distal ileum the last time I closed her abdomen. Angela desperately needed more bowel length than that to alleviate her short bowel syndrome. A multitude prayed for it, and apparently, we got it. I wouldn't know for sure until I went in.

Finally, the day was upon us. Angela would go to the OR in a stable state for an exploratory procedure and stoma closures. I had to make sure not to cause any harm in what had always been a very hostile abdomen. I had to take down her ileostomy and the mucous fistula and trim and prepare both ends. I would sew them together and have it heal without another bowel obstruction, leak, or infection. For weeks prior to this final operation, I used all the spiritual know-how I could muster up.

My dad used to recant to me a famous old saying, "There are no atheist is a foxhole." I understood how this saying would come to mind during moments of extreme challenge. I'm also reminded of another quote: "I never behold the Heavens filled with stars that I do not feel I am looking in the face of God. I can see how it might be possible for a man to look down on earth and be an atheist, but I cannot conceive how he could look up into the Heavens and say there is no God" (Abraham Lincoln, 1809–65).[23] "The Heavens declare the Glory of God and the sky above proclaims His handiwork" (Psalm 19:1 NIV).

Angela had to get out of short bowel syndrome. This operation had to work. There would be no more operations for Angela Scott. Let the final healing begin. "God, please help me heal Angela. Jesus, surely, you have said, 'Ask and it shall be given. Seek and ye shall find. Knock and the door will be opened' (Matthew 7:7 NIV). Yeshua, my Master! Yeshua, my brother! Yeshua, my Savior and Redeemer, truly you have said to me face-to-face, 'you heal her with the *love* you have for her.'"

When I finally went in, I found what I consider to be a miracle. I found almost no adhesions at all anywhere and nearly two additional feet of distal ileum that was not accounted for at all after her second operation. In other words, she had a foot or so of terminal ileum to eventually bring back into circuit after the second operation, but I found nearly three times that much (eighty-three centimeters) ready to connect. I was quietly stunned.

Small premature infants will grow bowel in length and caliber over many months, but it doesn't happen with seventeen-year-olds. I gave thanks and praise to our Lord for helping us. How else could this have happened? The stoma was closed. Angela made a great recovery and was discharged about a week later. "God does creative miracles! He makes physical things out of things that do not exist."[24]

I have no doubt in my heart and mind that Angela is a miracle child of destiny and fate. She came through hell for many years as only few have. She persevered through darkness and ultimately walked into the light. Angela was on a trajectory for an early exit from this world with negative energy all around her.

Jesus Christ and Saint Jude had everything to do with the healing of Angela Scott. I was given the opportunity to heal her with the greatest power in the universe. I helped heal her with the *love* I had for her. Now I understood my directive from Jesus.

Today she is doing very well, and her home life with her family is better than ever. Angela and I are friends, and we stay in touch via social media very often. We will be dear friends and inextricably tied to each other forever, I believe we always have been.

The story of Angela Scott is another unbelievable example of how God works miracles and speaks volumes to this world through weak instruments and everyday people. This summer Angela spent several days with me, my daughters Arielle and Gemma, and our two dogs Lucky and Rina on the Jersey Shore. We had a blast. When we would go out to dinner, I would watch Angela devour her food. For the first time in her life, Angela could eat freely and enjoy what she was eating. I'd get teary-eyed and have to stop and let it all sink in. Thinking back to that phone call from our PICU director and the first time I ever laid my eyes on Angela as she was rushed into OR one, I knew I was witnessing a miracle before my eyes. People walking by on the sidewalk of Cookman Avenue would have no clue about the miracle that was taking place under the red umbrella at Bonney Read Restaurant in Asbury Park, New Jersey.

God does create miracles! He said, "Let there be light," and light became into being (Genesis 1:3 NIV).

"To another the working of miracles, to another prophecy, to another the ability to distinguish between spirits, to another various kinds of tongues, to another the interpretation of tongues" (1 Corinthians 12:10 ESV).

While God also bore witness by signs and wonders and various miracles and by gifts of the Holy Spirit distributed according to His will? (Hebrews 2:4 ESV).

Jesus looked at them and said, "With man this is impossible, but with God all things are possible." (Mark 10:27 ESV).

Angela in Ocean Grove, New Jersey with me, Lucky and Rina

Office hours with Angela

The next segment is precious and God-given. Angela is my superstar! She tells us of her experience while in a perioperative coma.

Chapter 26

From Angela

I never thought that God was real until I woke up from an induced coma nearly two weeks after I very nearly died. August 20, 2012, was absolute hell for my family, apparently. My grandmother, whom I live with, spoke to the emergency room doctor the night of my transfer to the hospital where my emergency surgery would be performed. He told her, "Your baby has a 10 percent chance of living." Everyone was hysterically crying because an hour or so prior, I told my grandmother that I would see her at the hospital and that I loved her very much. Emotions in my family were running very high because I had just lost my grandfather. He was the love of my life. I love my family very much, but my connection to him had been very strong for my whole life. Grandpa was my strength, my rock. I could go to him with any issue, and he would make me feel better. My mom and dad had passed when I was a baby.

My condition had rapidly deteriorated to the point that I was apparently transferred from the first hospital straight to the operating room of the second hospital directly from the ambulance with no time to go to the pediatric intensive care unit. Dr. Gallucci had been notified and was there in the OR with his team waiting for my arrival. He subsequently told me that I was the single sickest patient he had ever seen in his entire career who lived. I barely made it through a very difficult and lengthy surgery. I was so unstable that I was placed in a medically induced coma and kept on a ventilator (breathing machine) to reduce the stress on my system. While I was in my coma, I had many dreams. Some I just don't remember well enough to retell the story. I do remember very clearly that my grandpa came to me. He said to me, "Angela, my sweetheart, why are you crying? Why are you so sad?" I told him that I missed him and loved him so very much and that I just didn't know if I could live without him. He told me that I had to live! He said that he had died so that I could live! I was also told that because of the prayers said for me and God's strength and will, I live today. Yes, I sometimes still doubt His existence, but then I remember that God put me on this earth to tell a story. John Gallucci is telling you his story with God, and I am part of it.

I pray that even if you don't believe in God, please keep an open heart and mind and believe that miracles are from God, that they do happen, and that I am one of those miracles.

Much love,
Angela Scott

Spiritual people do recognize one another and for all the right reasons. The following story tells the saga of little Pedro. Against all odds, he overcame multiple life-threatening congenital malformations one after the other. Faith, prayer, forgiveness, and the Holy Spirit helped overcome many formidable obstacles that could easily have ended a very young beautiful life.

Chapter 27

Pedro

A call from the maternal fetal medicine (MFM) doctors came in. They told me about a woman who had a fetus that most likely had esophageal atresia and possibly duodenal atresia too. She was about thirty weeks into her pregnancy, and they were going to come and see me for an antenatal consult.

This is part of what I do. I see parents who are expecting a baby who will most likely need major surgery shortly after birth because of major birth anomalies (malformations). Sometimes surgery is needed the day they are born. Other times the surgery can wait for a day or so, and other times it can wait for months depending on the urgency of the situation and weather the malformations can potentially cause a sudden life-threatening issue.

All the information I had been given told me that this baby was a male and most likely had an esophagus that was not continuous (not connected to the stomach) and that the distal (downstream) esophagus was connected to the trachea and not the upper portion of the esophagus. This is a completely fatal condition if not surgically corrected by a pediatric surgeon right away. This malformation doesn't kill the babies actively. It totally prevents them from eating, and the secretions of the GI tract may end up in their lungs.

Also, it looked as though the baby could also have a duodenal atresia. The duodenum is the first portion of the small bowel just beyond the stomach. The word *atresia* connotes an incomplete growth and development of any given body part. An intestinal atresia means that the bowel has either a congenital (from birth) obstruction inside it or that it hasn't connected to the bowel downstream. This essentially means an intestinal obstruction. Gastrointestinal tract obstruction—if not fixed— is incompatible with continued life regardless of your age.

This baby had an atresia of the esophagus with a life-threatening abnormal connection to the trachea (airway) and an atresia of the first portion of the small bowel. He had a double whammy. I counseled the parents on the flow of events and how things should generally go.

On the day of delivery, we were all ready to go. The baby was delivered and taken to the neonatal intensive care unit. I was there on the spot to make our surgical assessment. It was absolutely true that this baby had an esophageal atresia and an abnormal connection of the downstream (distal) esophagus to the trachea, a fistula.

It wasn't completely obvious at this time if he had a duodenal atresia too. We just couldn't say for sure. This diagnosis would be clearer in a few hours as gas going down the GI tract from the trachea could give a clearer picture. What was certain and not expected was that little Pedro had an imperforate anus as well. This is an atresia of the anus. Yes, that's right. He was a baby born without an anus. This is something that is diagnosed on physical exam of the newborn. It wasn't until we got radiographic studies several days after the initial surgery that we truly knew he had a triple deformity. That meant there were three gastrointestinal atresias. Each one would be uniformly fatal if not corrected with surgery. Pedro had all three. This is all part of what is known as the VACTERL syndrome. This is a congenital syndrome where malformations are typically seen in some or all of the following body systems:

V signals vertebral.

A signals anus.

C signals cardiac.

TE signals tracheoesophageal

RL signals radial/limb and/or renal.

Generally, in a child with the VACTERL syndrome, the anomalies can be very severe and certainly life-threatening. If the abnormalities are isolated, the baby has a much greater chance of a good outcome. If there are major anomalies in conjunction with genetic abnormalities, then things can be very difficult, and the outcome can be dismal at best.

The first point of repair was Pedro's esophageal atresia with its usual tracheoesophageal fistula (abnormal connection to the airway). I needed to separate the distal esophagus (the portion coming from the stomach up into the chest) from the trachea as the first order of business and repair the trachea. A repaired trachea makes it much easier for anesthesia to properly ventilate the baby through the rest of the operation, and it removes the chance of dreaded gastric reflux into the lungs which in and of itself can be life-threatening. Then I would dissect out the upper esophageal segment that connects to the hypopharynx (back of the throat), open it up, and sew it perfectly to the distal esophagus that had been congenitally connected to the trachea. When all is done, you have created a working esophagus where there was none and taken the lower esophageal segment off of its anomalous connection to the trachea.

This is all done through an incision on the baby's right chest wall and between the ribs. This is a huge lifesaving reconstruction done through a roughly one-and-a-half- to two-inch incision. A chest tube is left in place for drainage, and then the case is done. This depiction is certainly an oversimplification. The baby won't eat for a good week or so, and radiographic contrast studies are done prior to feeding to look for leaks in the area where both open ends of the esophagus were sewn together.

In Pedro's case, when this portion of the surgery was done, I then had to reposition the baby, prep again, drape the patient, and begin the next phase. The next phase was to open the lower abdomen and pull out a piece of distal colon (large bowel) and make a diverting colostomy and a mucous fistula as the first step of several in repairing his imperforate anus.

In this case, a diverting colostomy would mean finding the farthest distal portion of colon, cutting it in half, bringing it outside of the abdominal wall, and sewing it there so that the patient can pass feces into a bag. This essentially allows passage of fecal material out of the body so the patient can eventually feed and grow. For Pedro, this relieved a second congenital GI obstruction. The distal end of the colon that led to a blind pouch in the pelvis was bought out as a second stoma (open bowel) that was known as a mucous fistula. These babies can have an abnormal connection from the rectum (blind end) to the bladder, urethra, or vagina in females. You want to allow feces, urine, and mucous to escape so the open end of this piece of bowel is fashioned into its own stoma.

After a week or so, a radiologic study is done through this mucous fistula under pressure to see if there actually is an abnormal connection from the blind-ending rectum to either the genitourinary tract (the urethra, bladder, or the vagina). After all was said and done, I repaired the esophageal atresia with its abnormal connection to the trachea, and I relieved the imperforate anus obstruction during this operation. The anal atresia was temporized with the stomas described until the abnormal anatomy was fully studied. Then a final anorectal reconstruction would be done to create a new anus.

After the subsequent anal reconstruction heals, then the diverting colostomy is reversed, and the baby finally has a continuous GI tract.

Not so fast in Pedro's case. It took a few days to study the duodenum to determine if I indeed needed to do an intestinal bypass around the potentially atretic duodenum. Pedro did indeed have a duodenal atresia. Thus, I did an intestinal bypass when I thought the timing was right. It took about three months in total to create and completely repair a continuous GI tract for Pedro.

I can sense when an individual is spiritual in nature and usually without uttering a single word. I found this out about Pedro's mom Ana Maria right away. It's almost like sensing or reading people from a similar ethnic background or religious sect. You can feel it in one another. I thought this was true about Ana Maria when Pedro was still an inpatient in the NICU. I didn't say anything regarding what I could feel. When they came to the office for the first postoperative visit, it all came out like a swiftly flowing river.

Ana Maria sensed in me a profound spiritual nature, and she knew I was a firm believer in God and His ways. She quickly revealed to me that she had come under heavy spiritual attack. She was certain this darkness willed Pedro to either die around his birth or sustain significant birth trauma and/or defects that would make life for Pedro and his family very difficult to say the least. We all spoke of how forgiveness could help us avert spiritual catastrophes even if the attack seemed unredeemable.

When I learned about this information, it came as no surprise at all. I could feel it from the first encounter in my office. Now that it was all on the table, I asked Pedro's mother and her husband, Pedro Sr., if it would be okay if I put little Pedro on a prayer list. All the members of my prayer group were very spiritual and knew the intricacies of spiritual warfare well. This group prayed in concert (all at once), and they also coordinated so that there was always somebody praying for the recipients 24-7.

While all this was going on, I also came to know Pedro's paternal grandmother. We had several deeply spiritual conversations during office visits. As long as we were all on the same page, then it was perfect, and we certainly were in agreement.

One day at an office visit just before Pedro's last surgery to close his diverting colostomy, Grandma bought in a gift for me. She had attended a book signing at Barnes & Noble in Springfield, New Jersey, on Route 22. She had seen a living prophet and author named Vassula Ryden. She bought me a copy of Vassula's first book, *Heaven Is Real, but So Is Hell.* I was so deeply touched by her beautiful gesture.[25]

As I read, I couldn't believe what I was learning. So many of the things that had happened to Vassula had also happened to me. From early on I could see things others could not. I could feel emotions others could or would not. I had sinister ugly hands trying to grab me and kill me as a small child while I was lying in bed. As an adult, I was taken to a very scary place in a dream. Vassula had also been witness to a very similar place. In my perception, I was taken to purgatory. How could this be a coincidence? It was no coincidence at all.

Vassula's first book was a lead-up to her signature piece. The first book was inspired by the second actually. The second book was Vassula's transcription of the dictated words of Jesus, the Virgin Mary, Archangel Michael, and God our Father Himself.

In Vassula's second book, *True Life in God,*[26] she essentially takes dictation from God for more than twenty years. This book is meant to be a very strong message to humanity. It calls for repentance and unification of the body of Christ. The body of Christ is essentially all Christendom.

When we hold ourselves to God's standards and we treat others as if God were truly inside of each and every one of us, then the earth will be transformed. What made this amazing relationship with Pedro and his family possible was that we all had the scales removed from our eyes and we had eyes to see God's light in one another. We also had the ears to hear one another and the stories that we would subsequently convey.

I believe that most people in general would never have heard or picked up on what it was that Ana Maria was saying to me. I certainly did so. I engaged as such. I saw and heard with my heart. She saw and heard with her heart. This takes a certain level of grace. Grace is a gift from God. You can't order up Grace. Nor can you will it into place. This notion that grace is a gift is long recognized in theological writings.

Although it is true that grace is a gift, I absolutely believe that you can conduct yourself in a way that will turn God's head and thereby bring about grace from the heavens. When Grace is upon you, then you are one of the droplets of holiness that will coalesce with others to bring about the kingdom we are all waiting for.

If you feel the call of God's grace, then live it, acknowledge it, and nourish that feeling! What can we do to turn God's head our way? For starters, remove your doubt and see God in all living things. To do this, you must earnestly believe that it is true because it *is* true.

Pedro is more than five years old now. After his complex surgical reconstruction, another potentially life-threatening issue came up. It looked as if this family couldn't catch a break. Little Pedro had a few subtle neurologic issues that required a neurology consult that in turn led to an MRI of his brain.

The presumptive diagnosis was leukodystrophy. This is a degenerative disease of the brain, specifically the white matter. It is progressive in nature and generally has a worse outcome the earlier the diagnosis is made. It's usually taken as a death sentence. If the young patient continues to make milestones and keeps progressing in health and neurological development, then the diagnosis most likely is not leukodystrophy.

With this news and a sobbing mother in front of me, I assured her that we were given the opportunity once again to ramp up our prayers and see this through. The neurologist and neurosurgeons didn't say that it was definitively leukodystrophy. They said it could be. The only way to tell was to watch and observe his neurologic development or lack of. Not knowing if your young child will live or die and having to wait years for the answer would be pure torture for anyone as the parents are called to keep watching and waiting.

I am ecstatic to report that Pedro is doing very well and apparently is making progress where it is essential and needed to prove he will be okay. God is good. Sickness and disease are works of the devil, and Jesus came and "disarmed principalities and powers, He made a public spectacle of them, triumphing over them" (Colossians 2:15. ESV).

"When you are in Christ, you can expect to be healed" (Mark 16:17–18 ESV).

"Just know that what was good for people then is good for us now, because Jesus is the same yesterday, today and forever" (Hebrews 13:8 ESV).

The point of this segment of the book is to make clear what our roles can potentially be here on earth as opposed to what they are all too often. Open your hearts to the challenges of your brothers and sisters. This surely includes your own family members. Never forget your own children in the process. Give of yourselves no matter the issue, no matter where on the globe it may be, no matter other people's races or religions or lack thereof. Open your hearts to your brothers and sisters. After all, we are one big family connected by the same God, the same Creator!

When you let your heart lead the way, you will see the world with the eyes of God and not with the eyes of the ego. "Ask the Lord how often you have been telling your children that you love them, out loud, in words, with your own mouth. Don't assume you know; your perception of the truth may be inaccurate."[27]

God bless Pedro and his beautiful family. May the grace of God be upon you all today and all the days of your lives.

"Jesus went about Galilee, teaching in the synagogues and preaching the Gospel of the Kingdom, and healing all kinds of sickness and all kinds of disease among the people" (Matthew 4:23 ESV).

"For verily I say unto you, that whosoever shall say unto this mountain, be thou removed, and be thou cast into the sea; and shall not doubt in his heart, but shall believe that those things which he saith shall come to pass; he shall have whatsoever he saith" (Mark 11:23 KJV).

"If my brother hurts me, I will tell him that he hurt me. Then if he asks for forgiveness, I will forgive him. If he continues to hurt me and asks for forgiveness each time, I will forgive him every time" (Luke 17:3–4 ESV).[28]

Pedro's first day of school

Loved ones who have passed can help facilitate our overcoming extremely difficult life lessons here on earth. The next chapter shows us in a very dramatic way how that can be. This story is all about connecting with God's river of love and light from the other side to facilitate true healing of the heart, mind, body, and spirit. Yelena's story is as fantastic and metaphysical as a story can be. The spirit world may at times appear to conspire either for or against you. Align yourselves with the love of God, and God's purpose will prevail and ultimately be in your favor in spite of how things may look at the onset.

Chapter 28

Yelena

Although the book of Ecclesiastes suggests that everything is "meaningless under the sun," I don't believe it should be interpreted that the things that occur have no value. I believe that in and of themselves, worldly things ultimately just don't matter in the long run. However, life's challenges and what we make of them absolutely have meaning, and the lessons we learn stay with us for our eternity. It's all about spiritual growth.

It was apparent to me as a child that if people ran into the same roadblocks and suffered the same defeats and challenges over and over again, it had to mean they hadn't passed some spiritual test of sorts. They just hadn't learned a certain lesson that was notably and purposefully encoded into their lives. These challenges may not be observable to others and very often may not be realized by the recipient of the challenge itself.

The Colon family was about to have their fifth child. Apparently, this baby was diagnosed with autosomal recessive polycystic kidney disease (ARPKD). This is a genetic disorder characterized by the growth of cysts in the kidneys and liver that can cause a myriad of severe physiologic issues. Every so often there's the need to perform nephrectomies (kidney removal) right up in our NICU in order to save a baby's life. This occurs when a baby with ARPKD no longer has adequate renal function and has kidneys that get so large because of urinary entrapment that they stop movement of the diaphragm. Thus, the baby can't be reasonably ventilated. If the kidneys are of no use and only a detriment, causing at times severe hypertension and sepsis, then we surgically remove them and implant a peritoneal dialysis catheter at the same time so that we can maintain that baby on dialysis.

These babies would need to feed and grow for about two years in order to go on a renal transplant list. As it turned out, Mom and Dad had an eight-year-old who was healthy and did not have ARPKD, but they apparently had lost three other children to the same disease. The latest loss happened only two years ago. When baby Yelena was born, she immediately found herself in a fight for her life regarding her worsening renal failure. Nephrology was very deeply involved and reminded me that it was in fact the same family that had lost three previous children to the same disease. Eventually, we had to remove Yelena's kidneys and place a dialysis catheter in her abdomen.

This healed, and she did reasonably well for several weeks. She then had big issues with her GI function and suffered several catheter failures and even a bowel obstruction. By now she was also developing liver failure, which could be a significant issue in ARPKD. After several surgeries Yelena developed another bowel obstruction and again needed to go to the operating room. This operation left her with a diverting small bowel stoma. Her intestinal contents would now drain into a bag on her abdomen. This is always a difficult situation when you have a working stoma in a child who is dependent upon peritoneal dialysis and now a central line for TPN (nutrition by vein) because of short bowel syndrome.

The stoma tends to increase the risk for both catheters becoming infected by bacteria typically surrounding a stoma. Through Yelena's time in our unit (several months), her mother never left her side. She remained undeterred that this child would live. Her father was very supportive of his wife and child but tended to see what could be another life lost.

Yelena's life was now resting on another operation to reconnect her intestines so that she no longer needed nutrition by vein. The nutrition by vein was certainly worsening her liver failure. One situation was being compounded by another. If she had any chance of surviving to transplantation, I had to reconstitute her GI tract and sooner rather than later. Surgery was set for the next several days.

I had devised a plan that would include several different types of intestinal bypasses if the need presented itself. I knew her abdominal cavity would be very difficult. She had four surgeries thus far. There would be lots a scaring and adhesion formation. It is also known that with each subsequent abdominal exploration, the ensuing inflammation would render the abdominal lining less effective as a dialysis membrane.

Yelena's liver was also enlarging and now occupying most of her abdominal cavity. Yelena's life depended upon peritoneal dialysis completely. We were between a rock and a very hard place in a very big way. The day prior to the surgery, Yelena became septic. Her line was infected again. The surgery was postponed until after I would return from an eight-day workshop in spiritual healing. The parents understood. Nobody would undertake such a big elective operation in a patient who was septic.

I went off to Elm Ridge, New York. Elm Ridge is a small gated community near Buffalo, New York. There are several hubs in this country that are considered spiritual and metaphysical centers of historic excellence. The town was founded in 1868 and is the home of the Elm Ridge Council. I went to Elm Ridge as part of the ongoing evolution in me regarding healing my brothers and sisters. I went purely for the spiritual healing workshop. My dear friend and next-door neighbor Jane Casale told me she knew I was a healer from the moment she met me. Jane is a fabulous artist, a businesswoman, but as previously stated also a psychic and a medium. There have always seemed to be many friends and people in my life with metaphysical capabilities. That was just how it was. It was true for my grandparents and at least one aunt. Jane suggested I travel to Elm Ridge with her and an entourage so that I could further my abilities as a healer. I am profoundly spiritual to say the least so, I was excited to begin an eight-day workshop in spiritual healing. The teacher and master of the course was a man named Theodore. I looked him up and saw that he was in fact a healer, an ordained minister, and the director of their school of healing and prophecy.

I was very excited to take part in this workshop and was immediately amazed at what we as a class were achieving. We did all types of spirit-based exercises and incorporated many extremely interesting lectures into what we were learning. Not only was I having lots of fun, but I met some very interesting people in my class too, including many mediums, psychics, and Reiki masters.

Each day had us learning something new about how we as human beings are constructed spiritually and how that translates energetically and physically. There was so much to learn about who we are and why we are here. I had invested decades into learning the scientific/medical aspects of life, but now I was learning the spiritual/energetic basis for all that I had already come to know via traditional medical doctrine. Add all of this to my deeply spiritual nature, and I was thrilled at the chance to advance my healing abilities.

We are so much more than what most realize. As part of the course, we learned that the veil between our third-dimensional physical world and it's inherently low-vibratory nature and the spirit world can be very thin. In fact, Elm Ridge is a place that absolutely demonstrates just how thin this veil can be. We learned concepts that elucidated the anatomy of what we are spiritually and energetically and how that effects what we are physically.

These issues and imbalances in our ethereal/energy bodies will and certainly do have direct affects upon us physically, physiologically, and psycho-emotionally. Often disease processes have their origins not in the physical realm but in the spiritual realm and have their basis in either energy imbalances or deficiencies.

During one of the many exercises we did, we would choose partners, close our eyes, and use our hearts to see into our partners' heart space. Imagine that there was a carnation at the center of a person's chest deep inside. Concentrate on its energy and what you see with your heart, not your physical eyes. My partner for this exercise was a woman I had not been partnered up with yet. Her name was Melissa Wren. I sensed a vast intelligence within her. I could feel it flowing from her. As we began, I had my doubts about being able to see anything at all, but I was excited to try. All of a sudden, I could clearly see my partner's heart flower. It was a big beautiful white carnation at the center of the inside of her chest. As I watched it with my heart's eye, I could see it spreading and unfolding to fill her entire chest. Then something incredible happened. It began to snow inside her chest. Baby blue snowflakes were falling. It snowed hard enough that eventually the big white carnation in her chest was completely covered in baby blue snow. It was the most beautiful and extraordinary thing I had seen in a very long time.

When the exercise was finished, we were supposed to tell our partner what we had experienced. She went on to tell me that she had three sons. Her sons were the loves of her life, and she was filled with the love she has for them and them for her. It was obvious to both of us that there was something very real about what had just happened. Her big heart flower was covered with baby blue snow symbolic of her three sons and their love also covering her heart.

The whole course was basically one spiritual metaphysical occurrence after the next. As we went through this amazing workshop, each day we learned more and more about one another but also about ourselves. One of the women in the class called to me while we were on a break and said, "John, I have something to tell you! I'm a medium and a psychic." This was no surprise in Elm Ridge. She went on to tell me that I, in fact, had come back (reincarnated) to help humanity. She told me that I was a healer and that much of what I was about went well beyond my role as a pediatric surgeon. She said I hadn't really hit my full stride yet as a healer. She assured me that I didn't *need* to reincarnate, that I had chosen to. I had done it all through many lifetimes and could have stayed in the spirit world. I had earned that right. However, I chose to come back and help my brothers and sisters in their quest to connect with God.

During another fascinating exercise, we had to bring a notebook into the woods. We had to identify three trees while in the woods. We could pick them, or they could pick us. Whatever happened, we would need to come back and report to the class our experiences in the woods, specifically with the trees.

Off into the woods I went. I could see elm trees and conifers, and interestingly, I couldn't find a single oak tree. I thought that was a little strange, but it wasn't a big deal. I looked and thought and tried so hard to pull something spiritual or metaphysical out of this jaunt through the woods. I thought about reporting how the mosquitoes had slaughtered me because I had forgotten my repellant. I saw a small hemlock and jotted down some thoughts about how it could survive being only two feet high and far below the forest canopy. How would it ever reach the sun? Perhaps it had tenacity and perseverance.

The next tree I was attracted to was a large elm tree. I tried as hard as I could to feel something from this tree, but not much was jumping out at me. The last tree I was called to was a white birch. Now I had a story to tell here. I knew that most white birches in the New York and New Jersey area had suffered a viral blight back in the late 1980s. It killed most if not all of them. We had a beautiful white birch on our front lawn where I grew up. My dad and I both missed that tree. It was his favorite. I was amazed that I found one – it was a big deal for me.

I felt that this tree had persevered through the blight. It was the last of the Mohicans. It had to survive to keep its species alive! Well, that was all I could think of. It seemed a bit sappy (no pun intended), but I was striking out here on this "tree in the woods" thing. I figured I would talk to this tree and let it know how special I thought it was. I stood there talking to this white birch in hopes of it somehow talking back. I got nothing. I was polite and then thanked it for its attention.

As I started back to our campus, one of my classmates scared the daylights out of me. Bonnie was just off the trail I was walking on, and I didn't see her as she was also doing the same exercise. She blurted out, "Hey, John." She had caught me totally off guard. She said, "Hey, wow, I heard the conversation you had with that tree."

I nervously laughed and said, "Yeah, well, it was more a monologue, I guess. I was speaking *to* it."

She said, "No, I stood here and watched a two-way conversation between you and that tree!"

"You did?" I stood there, just looking at her. I remembered where I was. I wasn't in New Jersey anymore. I was in the forest in Elm Ridge, New York. The veil was very thin in this place. Apparently, it had large holes in it too. I believed her, but I had heard nothing. I smiled, gave a polite acknowledgment, and headed back to class.

When we were all back in class, we arranged our chairs in a circle. There were about fourteen of us. Each class member was meant to tell of their experiences in the woods with the trees. Each one had something amazing to say. As I was the last one to speak, I felt more and more like a loser as each story told was more interesting than the next.

When it was my turn, I apologized to the class because nothing so spectacular had occurred with me. I told them of the white birch I had seen. I told the story of the blight and how I thought it was amazing that I had found a white birch at all. I spoke of strength, tenacity, perseverance, and the last of the Mohicans. At the end of my story, the instructor leaned toward me and asked, "Are you *sure* there was nothing else to tell?" I said that I had felt a bit remedial, but no, there wasn't anything else I had to say.

He chuckled and nodded his head over this. He said, "Tonight I want you to think about it. Tomorrow you can tell us all about it." I smiled and said I would.

As the class was dispersing the only other guy in the class, a fellow from Long Island named Mike, asked me if I wanted to go to the Elm Ridge bookstore with him. He went on to say that it wasn't the tourist bookstore but the one that the residents of Elm Ridge would go to. It was only open for limited hours. I actually didn't feel like going, but something told me I needed to take him up on this offer. This was the first time in six days that Michael and I had said anything to each other, so I accepted.

Off we went across the campus to the bookstore. We made small talk, and I had mentioned to him that whenever I went to a metaphysical bookstore or a Barnes & Noble, the book always picked me. I didn't ever pick the book. He laughed and said, "Yep, I know how it is." Once in the store, he went his way, and I went mine. After more than half an hour in that very tiny store, I felt nothing. Was this another strikeout? Mike walked over to me and asked, "Well, anything speaking to you? Has a book picked you?" I turned around and looked up at him. I was about to say no, but as I glanced at him, I saw across the room right over the top of his head a bright lime green book on the top shelf. I said, "Uh, wait a minute. That book!" He turned around to look. "See that one up on the top shelf against the wall?" I went over to it. It was a small book about six inches high by five inches wide. I had to jump and poke it with my finger to knock it off the top shelf. As I did so, it fell off the shelf and into my arms.

The book was titled *When a Child Dies.* I stood there with my jaw wide open in amazement. He said, "Well, is it something for you like you suspected?" I showed him the cover. He knew what I did for a living. He said, "Well, John, you nailed it. Oops, I mean it nailed you! The book called you, didn't it?"

"Yep, it sure did."

"You gonna buy it?"

"Ha! How can I not?"

As we walked back to our respective hotels, I said, "See ya tomorrow," and then I went to the cafeteria for a bite to eat. I was enjoying a very laid-back, relaxing, and fun time in Elm Ridge, and I had none of the work stress that had me so wound up back at home. As I sat there in that peaceful café, I still felt irked by my strikeout regarding the tree exercise. How could everyone in that class have had a truly metaphysical experience and not me? It bugged me big time.

As I sat there waiting for my food, I pulled out my cell phone and went to a search of trees. Cell coverage wasn't great up there, but it was working now. I looked up elms and hemlocks and white birch. As I went back over my experience and looked at the pictures of the trees on the internet, I came across the very tree that I had been talking to in the woods. I thought it was a white birch. I knew it wasn't really white like the one my dad had on our lawn. It was more of a gray color. "Okay," I said to myself. "The squirrels are jet-black up here, and in New Jersey, they were silver gray. So a white birch looked gray up here. So what?"

Then I began to read. The tree that chose me and spoke to me was not a white birch but a silver birch. *What? A silver birch?* I thought I'd had a fairly good education and understanding of trees. How could I have never heard of this tree called a silver birch? Now I really felt like a loser because the story I had told in class was all about the white birch. Not only was the story apparently just my lame attempt to be creative and not a metaphysical occurrence at all, but I had even gotten the tree wrong! What would I say to the class tomorrow? Why did Theodore lean toward me and give me that look as if I were missing something? Did he know that I was only telling a creative story because nothing else had happened? Ugh! Oh, well, it was what it was. *Get over it, John.*

As I sat there enjoying the food in that cafeteria, I figured, "Well, let's look through this little green book *When a Child Dies.* If Michael had not asked me to go with him to the bookstore, this little green book could not have chosen me as its owner and reader. I couldn't help but think of Yelena's family back at the hospital as I pondered the title.

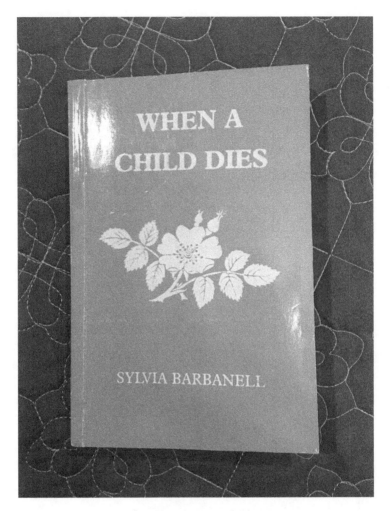

The little green book

I had indeed already taken the opportunity to tell my class about her story and the upcoming surgery I needed to do when I returned home. That surgery was clearly a do-or-die scenario. My heart and mind was filled with Yelena and her family. Of all the books in this bookstore, could this one be the source of help I needed for Yelena and her family? I read through the first few pages. Then I noticed that there was a full-page foreword at the very beginning of the book. The following is that foreword:

To Those Who Mourn Their Children

Do not weep because you think you have forever lost the fairest flower in your garden. The truth is that the flower has been transplanted into a far more beauteous garden where it sheds a greater perfume and is lovelier and more beautiful than ever it could be on earth. It has been spared many of earth's sadnesses and sorrows. It has been spared many cruelties and many blights. Your child will never know much that has darkened your own life. Rejoice that freedom has come to a young soul who will never be distressed by the many miseries that afflict your world. Do not grieve for the child; grieve if you will for your own loss, for you will miss the little radiant face, the childish prattle, the diminutive figure. But though your physical eyes cannot see, and your physical ears cannot hear, your child is ever present. If you stop shedding tears that create a mist in front of your eyes, you will see the truth that in God's great Kingdom there is no death and all continue to live in far better conditions in a world which is richer and sweeter than anything you have ever dreamed. Do not sorrow for the child. Know that an all-loving God has given angels to protect her or him and the child will, in fullness of time, be reunited with you.[29]

My fork slowly fell from my hand as I was reading this amazing foreword, which was directed specifically toward a special group of people and me. That group was bereaved parents. This *was* about Yelena and her parents. I was being offered help with a very difficult situation. But who was offering the help? After reading this amazingly beautiful and insightful passage that brought tears to my eyes, I gazed down at the author, Indian Spirit Sage Silver Birch! Silver birch? This ascended master spirit whom

I had never heard of in my life was there. He understood the issue and attempted to speak to me by attracting me to the silver birch tree in the forest—the silver birch tree that I had no idea existed. Through Michael's offer to go to the other bookstore and my acceptance and then finding that tiny green book above his head across the room, Silver Birch was leading me to this book and the foreword written by him in spirit. This *is* how the spirit world often works in our three-dimensional paradigm. The spirit world moves us in the right direction even in spite of our denials, disbelief, and outright recalcitrance.

The next day in class, it was my turn to update everyone on what I had learned. I was squirming in my seat as Theodore called upon me to tell my story. He looked at me with a knowing expectancy. He knew all along there was more. When I told the story and delivered the final punch line of the foreword and revealed who the author was, the class gave an excited gasp.

It was truly an amazing happenstance that turned what I thought was a strikeout into a home run! Our instructor went on to explain to us all that Silver Birch was well known up in that area of New York State. He then went on as a healer and medium and explained to us that Yelena's soul was in fact the same loving soul that had incarnated four times into that family with a lesson for her parents, specifically her loving mother. The lesson she was charged with teaching her mother was the lesson of letting go. This was her fourth incarnation in an attempt to help her mother learn this lesson.

With the help of Silver Birch and me after my time in this spiritual healing workshop, this would be Yelena's fourth and final incarnation. Yelena's soul would now undoubtedly move on to either a well-earned rest or help with other issues. Yelena is part of that family forever.

Theodore explained that Yelena's soul would often be there in the ICU room but not necessarily in the body as it was very often too painful for her there. This beautiful soul remained with Yelena and her parents until she knew her mom would read the Spanish translation of Silver Birch's work, which I had prepared for her.

When her mom read the words, she just sat there as still as she could, holding the paper. She looked at me and then looked at Yelena and then looked at the paper. She wept tears for Yelena and tears for her lost children. She thanked me profusely as she wept. She then began sobbing and thanked Yelena over and over, professing her deep and undying love for her.

Later that very night, Yelena's sweet soul passed back into the spirit world. She had finally completed her earthly mission, which had been ordained in heaven. She came with great love and compassion—no matter how difficult it was for her to reincarnate over and over again into a very sickly baby's body. Her mother would no longer suffer out of her inability to let go.

Showing love for your brothers and sisters in the face of tremendous adversity and pain is one of the greatest gifts of all. Everything in this world really does happen for a reason, and the reasons are usually based in the spirit world but best learned in the physical realm.

While in Elm Ridge, I could easily sense that spiritual eyes were upon me. I felt them morning, noon, and night. I would stay up most nights until about four in the morning, holding meditative prayer vigils for those who were suffering from varied diseases and conditions. I could feel the spirit world conspiring with me. I got very little sleep, but I was so moved by the spirit that it didn't bother me or deter me. I was really in my element, and I loved every bit of it.

The night that we students would perform at the Healing Union on the grounds of the Elm Ridge Council, I felt nervous and uptight. I really couldn't tell you why that was the case. Here I am—a top doctor in pediatric surgery for many years. I take babies apart and put them back together and hand them back to their parents, and here I was getting uptight over performing spiritual healing sessions at the Healing Union.

Well, maybe it's just my personality to feel a bit unsettled if I'm doing anything on behalf of others for the first time. I just want it to be right. Their expectations were high, so I felt I had to make no mistakes. I had to be perfect for them. I place lots of pressure on myself. I always have.

Class adjourned at about four that afternoon, and that left about three hours before we had to show up at the temple. Busloads of people were supposed to show up for one-on-one healing sessions. I got a bite to eat, and then I felt I should nap so that I could be on top of my game come seven o'clock. I went to my room, set my alarm, and turned on the fan I had rented for ten dollars. There were no air conditioners in our 150-year-old hotel, and it was easily ninety-five degrees with thick humidity.

I got down to just a pair of shorts and laid down on the bed with the fan directly on me. As I pondered what this evening would be like, I felt the sweat running off me. I was lying there with my legs and arms slightly apart to cool myself off. As I cooled down, I slowly drifted off to sleep. My left hand was hanging off the mattress as was my right.

At some point as I lay there regenerating my brain and body, an amazing thing happened. I went to sleep with a feeling of trepidation in my mind. As I slept, someone took hold of my left hand and squeezed it gently but firmly. It clearly woke me up. This person was clearly trying to get my attention by waking me but not frightening me. I lay there completely awake at this point, but both my eyes were shut. Someone was obviously holding my left hand. I knew my door was locked and bolted. I had also slid a chair in front of the door. I also knew I wasn't in New Jersey anymore.

There I was in as vulnerable a state as one could ever be. I was where the veil was fenestrated, where spirit and body move in and out of the other's realms. I knew it was comical, but I just had to look. So like in a cartoon, I opened my left eye and kept my right eye tightly closed. I certainly had never seen or experienced before what I was about to witness.

I was staring at a rainbow spirit in humanoid form. It was at least six feet or more tall and had all the colors of the rainbow. The spirit's rays were oriented horizontally. It had no skin or hair on its head. I could see through it, but the colors were magnificent all the same. I closed my left eye again, and as I did, it pumped my hand as if to say, "Hey, I'm here to help you!" With that, I opened both eyes, and there it was standing and still holding my hand. I wasn't afraid. I was calm and completely amazed as I gazed at this guiding spirit that was clearly there for me.

As I blinked my eyes, the spirit's spectrum of colors changed from horizontal to vertical, and with that, it shot up through the ceiling. In a flash it completely disappeared. I didn't jump up. Nor was I energized. I slowly got off my bed and stood where the spirit had stood. I looked around the room and got back on my bed. I rolled over to my right and felt a calm and peace that I had never felt before ever in my life. I quickly fell asleep until my alarm woke me.

I had no trepidation or nervousness at all after my encounter with the rainbow spirit. The healing sessions at the Healing Union went well. We saw and helped several hundred people that night. I suspected I was being watched closely, and this encounter proved me right. The universe was certainly conspiring with me in my plight to be the best healer I could be.

As our class proceeded through the last day of the workshop, I was very sad to see it end. It was clearly one of the most incredible and worthy things I had ever undertaken. The things I learned were immeasurable, and the people I met will be in my heart and mind forever.

Theodore was walking up the same road I was on. We greeted each other, and I expressed my gratitude to him for leading such an amazing workshop. He smiled and thanked me in return. He then asked me, "What made you come here?" I was a little taken aback by his question. I took it at face value. I answered, "I was very interested in your spiritual healing workshop as my friend and neighbor Jane suggested that I come here with her."

He looked at me, a bit puzzled. He said, "Do you have any idea who or what empowers you?"

Again, I was a little taken aback by what he was driving at. "I'm not sure what you mean," I said. "I'm a follower of Jesus Christ. I've met Jesus and Saint Jude in meditation. They both addressed me, and Jesus gave me a charge to heal my brothers and sisters with the love I have for them."

He acknowledged that as I had previously discussed it with him. He then said, "You have been around for a very long time. You bring with you the spiritual empowerment of ancient Egypt, ancient Greece, and the saints." I was stunned but not entirely surprised by what he said. I told him that I had always had an unexplained fascination and affinity with ancient Egyptian architecture and culture as well as that of ancient Greece. My visions of the healing mountain in the sea with an altar and a columned building certainly seemed to be from the Greco-Roman era. That spectacular ancient place of healing that I take the sick and infirmed to I have apparently known spiritually for thousands of years.

As for the saints, I explained that I had met several while in meditation. Saint Francis of Assisi came to my aid in a dream. He sent his dogs to help run off an evil demonic intruder. I had been drawn to my back deck late on a dark night. I sensed an evil presence coming from the dark woods in my yard. As I watched the tree and bush line, I could make out a dark figure wearing a long black robe with a hood standing in the shadows. This figure floated along the ground slowly. Its head was down, so I couldn't see its face.

As it approached my house, it methodically stopped as if to study and choose the best way of entry. It proceeded to move up my side yard between my house and the neighbors'. It was clearly aware of me as it slowly passed and raised its head to expose its hideously decayed face to me. The demon's face had features from both a pig and human. I felt horror as I saw the face of evil, but I had inner resolve that I would decisively win this apparent showdown.

As it passed through the side yard, it ended up at the front of my home. I quickly ran through my house to look out the front picture window. There it was looking up and studying my home, figuring out a way to gain access. As it drew nearer and nearer, a large band of dogs came rushing from down a city street. There had to be at least a dozen of them. They were on a very aggressive hunt, running everywhere with a look in their eye that said that if they caught whatever they were hunting, they would tear it to small pieces.

With the rush of the dogs, this hideous demon threw itself on all fours and leaped like a toad as fast as it could from my property. Eventually, it disappeared out of sight. The dogs were all over my property, sniffing and growling as they went. They took up chase after the demon. The lead dog was a large white lab-golden retriever mix. He ran as fast as he could up to my window and acknowledged me face-to-face, letting me know that they had the situation in hand and all would be safe for me and my family. Then he ran off to join his canine posse. As the last dog dashed out of sight, Saint Francis whispered in my left ear, "Be at peace, my brother."

After this occurrence I obtained a brass statue of Saint Francis and put him on my altar. I also was drawn to visit the national shrine of Saint Francis of Assisi while I was in San Francisco. I now have a beautiful marble statue of Saint Francis on a stone pedestal in my yard. I've studied his life and read several books about him and his work. Let me make myself abundantly clear on this, I do not pray to statues. They serve as a reminder and point of focus. Please don't misconstrue my use of icons and statues.

Saint Anthony of Padua is very near and dear to me. I first learned of Saint Anthony from my grandmother Angelina Giaimo. Grandma lived with us from 1978 until about 2001. She was as amazing and as loving as a grandmother could be. Whenever she knew we were looking for something, she would say, "Pray to Saint Anthony, and he will help you find what you're looking for." One night when I was in college, I was studying for a big exam I had to take the next day. I was outlining the chapter and rewriting parts of it that I knew needed to be committed to memory. I was tired, and it was about one in the morning. The study night was young. I pondered what I was studying, and as I did, my pen became unscrewed and fell apart. The spring inside it shot out across the room and quickly vanished from sight. Now I had to write by holding the skinny ink tube from the inside of the pen. There were no other pens available that worked in the entire house. This was back in the 1980s, and that was just how it was. I went on an exhaustive search for my pen spring. I crawled on my hands and knees, and I looked everywhere.

My grandma came into the dining room where I was studying, and she asked me what I was doing. I told her about my misfortune. She looked at me and said, "Pray to Saint Anthony, and you will find the spring."

I looked at her as if she were stupid. I said, "Are you kidding me? It's one in the morning. I have a huge test at eight o'clock, and you think if I pray to Saint Anthony, he is gonna help me find the spring to my pen? C'mon, Grandma! Stop messing with me. I need that spring!"

She looked at me as if *I* were stupid and said, "How many times have I told you this?"

I said, "Many."

She said, "Well?"

"Okay, okay, I'll try it just for you. Dear Saint Anthony, please help me find my pen spring."

As soon as the last word cleared my lips, my head turned to the left, and my eyes went directly to a crack between the dining room hutch and a side lamp table. There was a small beam of light that made it to the very end of that crack where the woodworking met the hardwood oak floor. I was staring directly at a shiny object. I got off my chair and got on all fours. I reached my arm into the crack and blindly advanced it to the object against the wall. My fingers fell upon a tiny object. I pulled it out of the crack, and there was my pen spring!

I stood up in complete amazement, holding up the prize. My grandma just looked at me and laughed in my face and said, "See! See! Don't ever doubt me or Saint Anthony ever again!" I can tell you with certainty that I never doubted again.

I evoke Saint Anthony all the time in the operating room, especially when we can't get an IV on a child at the beginning of a surgical case. No IV means no surgery. There have been times when three really good pediatric anesthesiologist can't get the IV placed, and I will say out loud, "Dear Saint Anthony, help me find an IV." And boom, there it is—like magic! One time I even amazed a medical student by showing him Saint Anthony's power. Here we were once again with a child nobody could get an IV on. Several pediatric anesthesiologists had failed along with a very good pediatric circulating nurse. I grabbed a new IV catheter, an alcohol swab, and a tourniquet. I specifically told the medical student to watch everything I did. I readied the catheter. I already had the leg prepped. I alerted the student to the fact that I was closing my eyes and that he should watch me. I gently lowered the catheter to the skin, made my stick, and advanced the catheter subcutaneously. I opened my eyes, and the IV was in the greater saphenous vein. There was good back flow too. *Voila!* He looked up at me and just stared. He had no words. I said, "See? Never doubt the power of Saint Anthony!" Our anesthesiologist just shook his head as if to say, "What a parlor trick!"

Well, ladies and gentlemen, nobody could get an IV, and now we have one. Plus I did it with my eyes closed! What happened between no IV and now? You can evoke Saint Anthony when in need of anything, not just small items. If you need solace or peace of mind, energy, strength, love, anything you search and long for, just ask Saint Anthony. Thank him when you find what you're looking for.

Saint Padre Pio is another incredible saint. He was a Franciscan who was born in 1887 and passed 1968 at eighty-one years of age. He was a psychic and a medium who could read people and also bilocate. Why should this be a surprise to anyone? Saint Padre Pio is proof that metaphysically capable people can be and are very close to and in service of our God. He also founded a hospital in San Giovanni Rotondo, Italy, where his monastery was.

I have a very close relationship with him now. He speaks to me in dreams and guides me in difficult situations. When I get very emotional over any given issue, Padre Pio intervenes for me. He shows up and helps me in healing and guiding others. I used to close my eyes and see what his room looked like in the monastery at San Giovanni Rotondo. I have never been there. I just saw what I saw when I closed my eyes. Then one day while I was researching him online, I saw a photo of his cell or room as it is today. It was on display as a museum piece. It was the same exact scene I had seen over and over again whenever I was meditating on him in his cell.

I'm not really surprised over this. When I have such close relationships with people, I can see their surroundings very often. Padre Pio hasn't appeared to me face-to-face as Saint Jude has. Padre Pio imbues me with his spirit. His energy infiltrates my heart and mind. I start to think as he would.

Padre Pio once said that there were two hearts—his heart and the sacred heart of Jesus. As he got closer and closer to Jesus over time, the two hearts became as one. When that happens, Jesus rests in your heart, and you rest in the sacred heart! You become inseparable. Therein lies the yearning of the hearts of every man on earth—communion with the body of Christ and joining of the sacred heart.

When I explained all this to Theodore, he looked at me and said, "No, I don't mean some of the saints. I mean all of them."

"All of them?"

He said, "All of them use you as a channel to reach people on earth." I was stunned and humbled to my core. All I could think was that I was just me. If what he said was true, then I had better start acting like it. Since that moment, my life has never been the same.

We ended the conversation by affirming how we enjoyed each other's presence and stating that we should stay in touch. How can anyone forget such a workshop and an exchange like that? I do my very best to get to know the saints. There are many. I pray to God in heaven that I may always offer the saints a conduit to my brothers and sisters here on earth.

"In God, whose word I praise, in God I trust; I shall not be afraid. What can flesh do to me?" (Psalm 56:4 NIV).

"Sing praises to the LORD, O you His saints, and give thanks to His Holy name" (Psalm 30:4 NIV).

"But the saints of the Most High shall receive the Kingdom and possess the Kingdom forever, forever and ever" (Daniel 7:18 NIV).

The next chapter is the story of Jahi McMath. When you are spiritually connected, you can't explain it, but you are called to action against all odds. The Holy Spirit will move mountains, and this next story is an incredible, unbelievable example of how God works in mysterious ways on behalf of those who hear His voice. Unimaginable things are achieved when you connect with God's purpose!

Chapter 29

Jahi

It was a Thursday, which meant it was one of my OR block days. I had five cases lined up for that day. After the third case, Anesthesia and I took a quick lunch break in the OR lounge as we usually did. I sat down and grabbed a sandwich and a cup of coffee.

The TV was on. It was a typical cable news segment. Story after story revealed nothing but bad news and tragedy just as all news outlets like to intentionally cater for our consumption. Their job is to keep the masses of people enshrouded in scripted negativity. As a teen, I used to wonder why every time I put on the news, it was the same exact agenda—house fires, murders, car accidents, and arrests. Throw in a rape or two, and you had programming fit for a proud news network executive.

Who wants to see this stuff? I thought. At that earlier stage of my life, I didn't realize why they did this, but I knew for sure it was intentional. You never saw a great story that was uplifting—*never.* So as I watched each horror story being programmed into my brain by the talking heads, I was snapped out of my stupor by yet another terrible story that I immediately became ensnared by.

My heart and mind were churning with emotion. Jahi McMath, a thirteen-year-old African American girl from Oakland, California, had gone to a hospital for the surgical treatment of sleep apnea. Post-operatively she was admitted to the pediatric intensive care unit. At some point that evening, Jahi began to hemorrhage. She apparently hemorrhaged so profusely that she went into cardiac arrest. She was resuscitated, intubated, and transfused. She was stabilized by the ICU team.

Within seventy-two hours of her surgery, hospital representatives had approached Jahi's mother Nailah with the bad news. "Your child is brain dead," they said. Her heart and lungs were resuscitated, but she experienced severe anoxia (depravation of oxygen to the brain). Thus, there is no hope for recovery. "We want you to understand that it's time to remove your child from life support. Jahi is dead. There is nothing further anyone can do."

God only knows what it must feel like when you are told something like this. The mother refuted this claim of death. Three neurologist independently examined Jahi, and all of them proclaimed she did indeed fit the criteria for brain death. In California, a death certificate is issued if one is declared brain dead.

The story hit me hard. Now that was a tragedy fit for any news network. Talk about a downer. The video cut to a snapshot of Jahi in school and a video of the mother crying followed by the hospital administrators giving a news briefing.

As a human being and an empath, my heart broke. A news story hadn't had an effect on me like this in a very long time, maybe never. I couldn't let this one go. Or should I say that it wouldn't let me go? As a pediatric surgeon, I felt a sick twisting deep in my gut. There but for the grace of God go any surgeon!

By the time you finish your surgical training (mine lasted eight years after medical school), you know full well that things usually go well and as planned, but that may not always be the case. This was every patients, parents, and surgeons' nightmare played out on national cable news.

As the network moved to other stories, I became filled with the overwhelming sense that I had to do something about this on behalf of Jahi and her family. What could I possibly do? She was in California, and I was three thousand miles away in New Jersey. What could I do? I did what came naturally for me. I began to pray! I prayed as fervently as anyone could possibly pray. I evoked the saints and Jesus Christ. I prayed during my cases. (Yes, I can multitask.) I prayed between cases. I prayed on rounds, and I prayed in my car on the way home. I informed my friend and spiritual healing mentor Sandra about Jahi and her story and how profoundly it had affected me. I expressed to her that I had to step up and change this. My God, how was I going to do this?

Each day I would pray for her, and each night I would hold a prayer lighting for Jahi and her family. So I made her a personal healing candle with her name on it in purple. It was a six-by-three-inch white pillar candle.

I took Jahi spiritually into the third world each night. Sometimes I took her alone, and there were times when I would take her in a group with several other children who were also in desperate need of healing. I would take her to the beach where we would bathe in the living waters and also be baptized. Then we would receive Holy Communion in that beautiful sunlit meadow just behind the dunes.

Other times we would journey up my healing mountain where the altar and columned building stands. This is the very same place of healing that Saint Jude and Jesus appeared to me. There we would pray together, baptize, and anoint. Prayer and spiritual indulgence is surely amazing and so very crucial, but if I could only touch this child and pray over her in person!

This went on for about two weeks. I was following the story the best I could by television and the internet. I saw videos and news reports that mostly portrayed Jahi's mother as an unreasonable woman who was hostile to the system. I couldn't believe the ugly, cruel stance many in the media took on this issue. I, however, never lost hope or faith. For some reason, I was connected to this child. Why was I so moved by the plight of Jahi McMath?

About three weeks after I had first seen the story on TV, I got a phone call from the Chairman of surgery at our hospital. "John, I got a call from the hospital administration. We are assembling a surgical team to help an unfortunate child."

"Okay," I replied.

He said, "You, me and a third surgeon will be the operating team.

I thought it was strange that a consult was coming my way via the administration. Consults are either emergency issues by the ER, transfer service, the inpatient sector, or they are elective and come by way of the clinical office. "Okay, I said. What's the deal?"

"Apparently, there is a thirteen-year-old girl in Oakland, California, who had a complication after ENT surgery. California has issued her a death certificate on the basis of brain death, but the family refused to take her off life support. The courts have allowed the family to take this child out of California. They are apparently transferring her from Oakland to us here at our hospital.

"What? What did you just say to me? Who from where?" I couldn't believe my ears. I actually made him repeat his words. Then I made him promise he wasn't joking. This had to be a clear sign from God that something very big was happening. Could this be for real? Was this all a dream? What were the odds that I would sit and watch this story and become so emotionally engrossed in it? I immediately felt the call of the Holy Spirit as well as the duty and obligation to institute a constant regimen of prayer, meditation, and healing. If that wasn't enough, this very same child would be transferred three thousand miles to us, to me?

What in God's name was happening here? That night I talked to God as I always did. This time I had a profound understanding that this child was a spiritual VIP. What did all this mean? My heart and mind were in overdrive. The next day as I awaited Jahi's arrival, I became deeply aware of something. I was reminded that God speaks volumes to this imperfect and dark world through weak instruments. People of humble means are His voice. It's the people who aren't world leaders, corporate executives, rich or famous socialites, and certainly not TV doctors from the mainstream media. God shows His power and might through the small, the weak, and the meek. Jahi was that very person. Who was she? Compared to the big, fast-paced, expensive, corrupt, high-flying world, Jahi McMath was an innocent child, a scapegoat, a lamb of God. Jahi McMath was, in fact, God's perfectly chosen weak instrument.

We planned to operate on Jahi and place a PEG (percutaneous endoscopic gastrostomy) for feeding and perform a tracheostomy. She needed this so that we could sustain her on long-term life support. There were no other surgical issues at all. When she arrived, she was transported directly to the PICU. I went to meet her and her family. I didn't know or anticipate what the energy of that encounter would be. I took a deep breath, cleared my throat, opened the door, and entered her room.

There she was. I almost couldn't believe it. I held back the emotions that were threatening the professional nature of the moment. Everyone was very polite and to the point. I explained that the family would meet the rest of the team very soon and that the surgery would take place the next morning. Jahi's mother and family were very appreciative of our efforts and intent.

After leaving her room, I went directly to the hospital chapel to commune with our Lord. I was the only one in the chapel at that moment. "Lord Jesus Christ, I am your faithful follower. I present myself to you, my Lord, to ask you for your Holy guidance. I ask you for the wisdom, the strength, the knowledge, the stamina, the heart, the mind, the body, and the soul to correctly and perfectly achieve this task you have given us. Holy Father, let your will be done here on earth as it is in heaven." Then I sat there in quiet observation and contemplation of our Father.

That night at home as I meditated and prayed, I knew that Jesus was my guide and that this event was no mistake. I was humbled at the thought that I could be given a chance to do my part in what I knew was a very big spiritual event. It was crystal clear to me that I had to heal her with the love I have for her.

The next day each part of the surgery went perfectly. I accompanied Jahi with her transport team back up to her PICU room. Later that day I went to the chapel to pray and again sit in quiet observance of the Lord. I thanked God for the Holy Spirit that moved in the hospital administration so that they would see to it that Jahi had a chance at life. They cleared the way and helped carry out God's great plan.

The next day on rounds, I entered Jahi's room. I wanted her mom and stepdad to understand that we would do everything we could for Jahi medically, nutritionally, surgically, and spiritually. We had it covered from every aspect. Why else would she have come three thousand miles? I felt moved by the Holy Spirit. Thus, it was my moment to share with the family the Healer's Prayer that my friend and fellow prayer warrior Sandra prompted me to write several years prior. They were surprised but very accepting.

A Healer's Prayer

Oh, Lord, cleanse me. Holy Spirit, fall afresh on me and purify my heart, my mind, my body, my soul. May my spirit carry only love and healing energy. Jesus, forgive me my sins as I forgive others. I ask God to help me assist and heal my brothers and sisters. Holy Spirit, fill this space, and fall afresh on me now. May the power of Jesus and the Christ light change me, mold me, use me, heal me, anoint me, bless me. Make me an instrument of your peace and love, oh Lord and Master. For I give my life up to God and the Holy Spirit so that I may serve my brothers and sisters in Jesus's name. Amen.

The family was stunned and beyond appreciative. They were also amazed that a physician and surgeon would pray for them and with them—never mind that I had actually written that prayer and recited it for them in their daughter's room. I believe this moment took us all to a different place. It helped remove some of the fear and confusion that they had been plagued with for so many weeks.

Each day on rounds, I got to know Jahi and the family a little bit more than the day before. I explained to them that although I was the chief of pediatric surgery, I was also a spiritual healer. I showed them pictures of my altar at home and Jahi's personal candle along with many others. There came a point in time when I felt moved by the Spirit to share with them who I felt Jahi was.

I believed then as I do now that Jahi had been chosen by God for a very special purpose. I explained to them that God did indeed speak volumes to the world through meek and gentle instruments. We know that God needed voices in ancient days. The voices He used moved the people. They were often just ordinary people who turned hearts and minds toward God. Those voices were eventually known to be prophetic. A prophet is one who proclaims the will of God, points to future events, and turns the hearts and minds of the masses to God.

In today's world, it looks as though darkness is all around us and drowning out the light. Prophecy certainly suggests we may be in the end times (not the end of time though) when darkness makes its final push to win the great spiritual warfare being waged all around us. Turning the hearts and minds of people to God is an amazing and profound achievement, especially in these difficult times.

Understand that Jahi's case has been televised all over the world. Hundreds of millions of people have been moved by her plight. There are prayer groups all over the world praying to God on her behalf. If many hundreds of millions of people have prayed for Jahi once, they have done so many times just as I have.

This translates into billions of prayers worldwide generated by this beautiful child. I believe it is undeniable. Jahi is God's weak instrument that speaks volumes for the Lord. Jahi McMath from Oakland, California, in her weakness and silence has generated billions and billions of prayers. Jahi McMath is God's sleeping prophet.

Consider the prophetic burden-bearer. This is a term used to describe the role of the prophet priest whereby this person is primarily occupied by God, shouldering loads of sin or parts of those loads, leading to the redemption of those they serve. God seeks to bring people to repentance and redemption and not destroy them. The burden-bearer role of the prophet includes symbiotic prophetics, prophetic intercessions, and vicarious punishments or discomforts at times.[30]

The most pronounced example of this prophetic requirement is found in the ministry of the prophet Ezekiel. Many of his early object lessons included the Lord laying burdens upon him much like He did to the Aaronic priests the judgments earned by his people. In modern times this responsibility can mimic sickness, disease, catastrophe, extreme emotional distress, and psychological stress in prophets. These are only alleviated when the season of suffering has passed. They may also be eased when the suffering prophet spends time in intense spiritual prayer or supernatural warfare. Our Savior's entire earthly ministry consisted of this cumbersome service for the sake of our salvation. "The Lord has laid upon Him the iniquities of us all" (Isaiah 53:6 NIV). "This was to fulfill what was spoken through the prophet Isaiah: "He took up our infirmities and bore our diseases" (Matthew 8:17 NIV).

There came a time when Jahi was eventually released from the hospital and was set up elsewhere with a 24-7 ICU nurse. When she finally left our hospital for her next location, she was severely neurologically impaired but not brain dead. I would go there from time to time and pray over her and also perform Reiki and energy transfers on her. I'd do this in her presence and also remotely.

Jahi is absolutely God's sleeping prophet, and she will help change the world. As a matter of fact, she already has. Everything really does happen for a reason, and Jahi was transferred from California to our team in New Jersey three thousand miles away for all the right reasons. What happened, my dear friends, was no coincidence.

It doesn't matters why or how it all came to be. You can explain it all away with intelligent rationalization. What matters is that it happened just the way it did. This entire book is dedicated to helping you see the world with your heart, and when you do this, you see with the eyes of our Creator. As you walk through life and its darkness, just use your spiritual eyes, and let your heart lead the way.

Having the scales fall from your eyes and seeing as God does only occurs by the grace of God. Most do not see in this way. They think and see conventionally or by the will of their egos. Well, that's a shame, but it's understandable. Without seeing Jahi with the eyes of God, she would just be a girl who suffered a terrible perioperative hemorrhage and a severe anoxic brain injury.

Jahi is on the front lines of the great spiritual warfare that is raging on. The role Jahi plays is beyond most of our comprehension. *Regardless of the outcome for Jahi herself, she will selflessly help rewrite the books, and she will change the world in her silence without uttering a single word.*

As for her family, they have been persecuted nonstop for the love they have for Jahi and their belief that she is not brain dead. Jahi and her family in effect have taken up the cross through their unshakable belief in God, Jesus Christ, and what they truly believe in their hearts and minds. This tremendous love of theirs sustains them through their trials and tribulations all while three thousand miles from home. This is truly suffering and extreme hardship of biblical proportions.

Years have passed since Jahi's initial injury. Along the way I have personally witnessed her responding to her mother's commands on multiple occasions. Jahi had several admissions to the hospital regarding her feeding tube and its functionality. On the most recent admission Jahi was admitted to a nearby hospital. Jahi's condition deteriorated slowly over several weeks. A workup revealed that she had what appeared to be a dead or necrotic colon. This was a very serious and life-threatening turn of events. This diagnosis was correlated by blood work and an abdominal and pelvic CT scan. A physical exam in her case was unreliable. None of the physicians involved had ever seen a lactate level rise from four to more than twenty-two in a patient who didn't have significant tissue ischemia and/or necrosis somewhere either ostensibly or occultly. At this time, there appeared to be nothing else wrong with her. All other major body systems appeared to be working save for her known brain injury and ventilator requirements. However, the picture seemed to only get worse as the days went by.

The medical/surgical team had a huge decision to make. They believed if they did nothing, Jahi would pass from her dead colon. If they operated on her, she would be at an extremely high risk for sepsis and non-healing because of chronic corticosteroid administration. She certainly could pass as a result of the operation and in spite of all the best efforts to save her by an expert team. The team made a big decision to try to save Jahi's life by going in and removing her dead colon. When they went into her abdomen to remove her dead colon, what did they find? They found nothing wrong with anything in her abdomen—no dead colon or small bowel, no organ damage or necrosis anywhere. It was an open-and-close case. It was a negative laparotomy. Again, Jahi McMath defied reality. Jahi reminded me of a beloved prizefighter getting knocked down to the canvas over and over again only to rise to the prayers of loved ones. She came back to defy all odds. Jahi's story is a supreme example of an occurrence happening against all odds. She is surely God's sleeping prophet.

More than a week had passed since her surgery, and Jahi began to spontaneously bleed. She developed a hemorrhagic diathesis. She bled from her mucous membranes and then stopped. Jahi now seemed to be in liver failure. Treatment was administered, and no further bleeding was documented. After a few days, her hemoglobin dropped without any outward signs of bleeding. A scan showed there was blood in her abdomen. Doctors approached Nailah and told her that Jahi's condition was worsening and that she may not make it. With that, Jahi turned her head all the way in the direction of the doctor's voice spontaneously. It was obvious that as sick as she was, Jahi was in no way brain dead, but we knew that.

Jahi's case was an extremely difficult one as she stumped and confounded everyone who ever administered her care. A very courageous surgical team in conjunction with the family put their hearts and minds together. This was a do-or-die moment again. A decision was made to make one last-ditch effort to open Jahi's abdomen in the OR and to find and stop the bleeding. Off to the operating room they went. The family was eventually informed that the doctors couldn't control Jahi's condition. Jahi McMath, God's victim child, had passed during a heroic surgical attempt to save her life.

The news came like a swift blow to my gut. It was as if I were reliving my sister's passing. We all knew it was possible, and some truly believed it was inevitable, but when it happened, it left a lasting, surreal, irrevocable numbness in me.

Jahi had come to test our very imperfect health-care system. Jahi had come to challenge many who were sure in their supreme arrogance that they knew better. Jahi had come to protest those who would coldly dismiss her plight and that of her family just as countless others have been tossed to the curb from city to city over many decades. Jahi had come to rewrite the literature. Ultimately, Jahi came to generate billions of prayers in an age where humanity needed that the most. Jahi did just that without uttering a single word!

I know where I stand. I stand with Jahi and her family. I always will. God bless you, Jahi, and your family. May God bring you every success along your ongoing supernatural quest to change this world from dark to light!

"There are those who rebel against the light, who are not acquainted with its ways, and do not stay in its path" (Job 24:13 ESV).

"He will bring forth your righteousness as the light, and your justice as the noonday" (Psalm 37:6 NIV).

"Peace I leave with you, my peace I give unto you: not as the world giveth, give I unto you. Let not your heart be troubled, neither let it be afraid" (John 14:27 KJV).

"The light shines in the darkness, and the darkness has not overcome it" (John 1:5 NIV).

"Whoever loves his brother abides in the light, and in him there is no cause for stumbling" (1 John 2:10 NIV).

"I have said these things to you, that in me you may have peace. In the world you will have tribulation. But take heart; I have overcome the world" (John 16:33 ESV).

Jahi

Grandma Sandra, me, Nailah and Marvin Winkfield

The next segment is written by Nailah Winkfield, Jahi's loving mother. The love she has for her child comes from deep within her heart. No man-made power or system can overcome the love they have for each other.

Chapter 30

From Sister Nailah

I met Dr. Gallucci at a time when I was angry and scared of doctors and hospitals. I had just been traumatized for twenty-nine days, fighting with a hospital so that they wouldn't kill my daughter. When I arrived at the hospital where he worked, I met several doctors and staff members. They were all nice, but Dr. Gallucci stood out.

I had a connection with him that was deeper than anyone in that hospital. I remember when he told me he was a spiritual healer, and that touched my soul. I remember him talking about God and prayer, and that was the first time I had ever heard a doctor speak like that.

Dr. Gallucci had saved my daughter's life, and what he doesn't know is that he saved mine too. Every conversation I have ever had with him has always been encouraging. He always spoke to me at the right times. It's almost like he knew I was breaking, feeling suicidal, and feeling discouraged. *He knew!*

I thank God for him daily. He is a friend for life, and I am so blessed to know him.

—Nailah Winkfield

The next brief segment shows how one obvious action of intent can actually be a front or lead-in for another much more important purpose. My dad's attempt to connect me with his financial advisor for eighteen years finally occurred a month prior to my dad's passing. The relationship he finally facilitated was about much more than mere financial matters.

Chapter 31

My Dad and Brother Bill

My dad always tried to help me in every aspect of my life. He truly believed he had a good understanding of how things should be. He really was a life coach for me in many ways, and for that I was blessed and very thankful. He was and still is the best dad I could imagine. Sometimes, however, Dad would get in my face about certain things. Either we occasionally didn't agree, or I didn't have the time to pursue what he was addressing. I do remember that my dad wanted me to connect with a financial advisor for years. For most of his life, he hadn't done so. He knew very little about finances, money, or budgets, let alone investing for the future.

Dad was from an old-school immigrant family that worked very hard and basically lived a hand-to-mouth existence. If the pasta and wine were good, all was right with the world. They didn't have a lot of trust in doctors and certainly not bankers. All those years later, Dad found a financial advisor he knew he could inherently trust named Bill Ryan. Apparently, for nearly twenty years, Bill helped my dad greatly. Bill set Dad straight on many issues of investing and was also a very personable individual. The matchup worked well.

I'm embarrassed to admit it took nearly twenty years for me to finally meet Bill Ryan. I would hear from Dad that I should call Bill Ryan. I'd say, "Dad, okay. I'll call him." Bill would occasionally call me and leave a voice mail, and I think I called him several times to do the same. I always believed Bill would help me. I just needed to find the time.

My dad was a larger-than-life superhero of a man and as strong as a bull. As the years passed, he became very ill. At the age of seventy-seven, he had defeated kidney cancer. Then two years later, he had a seven-hour cardiac surgery that nearly killed him. Just as he was getting well enough to think about golf again, Dad developed leukemia.

He went through all the standard treatments. My brother Tom and I were there with him for all of it. I also included him in a prayer healing group as well and employed all my other healing modalities. Dad finally made it to remission. His leukemia was held in check. I thank the team at the Cancer Center that cared for my dad and treated him so well. I also thank God for hearing all the prayers and allowing remission. I do know that when healing takes place—whether medical, surgical, or spiritual—you're buying time. Let's face it. Nobody lives in this physical realm forever. It's not our forever dwelling.

About two years after his diagnosis and remission, Dad was now in recurrence. The family was hit hard. We all knew that nobody lived forever and that our dad, our rock and hero, was being told there was nothing that anyone could do. I remember the look on his face when his doctor told him in front of me that all his treatment options had been exhausted. My dad then asked him what was next. The doctor looked at him and said, "Mr. Gallucci, you'll need to get your affairs in order."

Dad asked in reply, "You mean that's it?"

"I'm afraid so."

Dad turned to me, smiled, shrugged his shoulders, and said, "Okay. How long?"

The doctor said, "Not long."

The doctor explained that it was not appropriate to just keep transfusing him. He was in a cycle of receiving a unit or two of packed red blood cells twice a week and still deteriorating. We all got our heads around this as best we could. My dad bounced back and forth a few times to the hospital for infections and some antibiotic administration. He tried to get everything he wanted to say off his chest while he still could. It was around that time that he looked at me and said, "Would you please make an appointment and go see Bill Ryan? Please! I've been asking you for so many years." Of all the things a man could say in his last days, this was certainly stunning to me.

I looked at him as if to say, "Really, Dad?"

He knew what I was thinking and said, "Yes! I'm not asking you anymore, John. Now I'm telling you."

"Okay, Dad. I promise." The next day I made my appointment. I went to see Bill Ryan a few days later on the first day of my vacation in early June of 2014.

The day of my appointment, I had a certain nervousness in my entire body. I had a lump in my throat and a twist in my gut. It was all about my dad. He tried for so many years to make this happen. As I rode the elevator, I almost wanted to turn around and not see Bill. I thought that if I didn't see Bill now, Dad would have to wait to die until I did. Ah, it was a wishful fantasy. Well, I wasn't turning around. I had all my financial papers with me, and I was finally going to meet Bill Ryan.

I was about to fulfill one of my dad's more persistent and meaningful wishes for me. I had imagined so many times what Bill would look like. His voice on all his voice mails suggested that he was easily older than I was and probably wore a suit and tie. When I walked into his office suite, I was amused to see a very youthful, in-shape guy who was easily younger than me and dressed casually. He was just the opposite of what I had imagined given his booming voice mails.

We made our greetings and talked about my dad for a bit. Then we touched upon my goals and where I was at the present time financially. All that took about twenty minutes. For the next three hours or so, Bill and I engaged in a conversation that included the meaning of life and topics like God, earth, heaven, and hell. We were both stunned. We spoke of prayer and healing and how the world in its darkness so profoundly and desperately needs people to turn to God and Jesus.

The entire conversation seemed to take thirty minutes, but it was actually closing time. From that moment on, Bill and I were brothers. We were spiritual brothers bought together by a man I considered the leader of the band. Dad was clearly charged with getting me together with this man named Bill Ryan.

My dad passed about six weeks later. The week he passed, he thanked me for finally seeing Bill. He asked me what I thought of him. I told my dad that Bill was one of the most important people in my life and that I was so sorry that it took so long for me to take the time to see him. Dad looked at me and lovingly pointed his finger at me and said, "See, I told you." And then he reminded me as he did so often in his last year or so to "remember who you are."

Dad knew Bill would help me financially, but he also knew deep in his soul that he was the man that had to bring Bill and me together for all the right reasons. Those reasons are much bigger than anyone's financial portfolio.

Since then, Bill has become an integral player in the Reiki Therapy Center. The center is my sanctuary dedicated to health, wellness, spiritual growth, and evolution. Bill is an intelligent individual who is an avid researcher and healer. Bill is also a very powerful prayer warrior.

Bill Ryan and I see this world together in the same fashion as spiritual brothers do. Bill has accentuated and certainly strengthened our growing spiritual center. He is clearly meant to be there with us. For all of us involved in its endeavor, we see the center as a relay station and amplifier of God's river of love and light. Spiritual warfare is real, my friends, and Bill Ryan is my prayer warrior brother-in-arms.

"The Spirit of truth, whom the world cannot receive, because it neither sees Him nor knows Him; but you know Him, for He dwells with you and will be in you" (John 14:17 NIV).

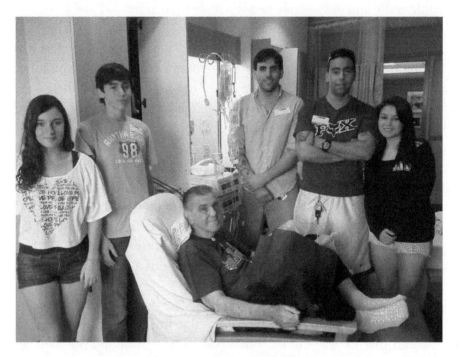

Gemma, Seth, Dad, Michael, Tommy and Arielle

Brother Bill is my brother in spiritual arms. God bless you, Dad, for putting us together. The next brief segment is in Bill's own words.

Chapter 32

From Brother Bill

Thomas Gallucci was a friend, coach, and client. I was a financial advisor just starting my career. Tom would bring motivational quotes to keep me on my path to success, knowing I had a long road ahead. The road I chose was Wall Street, which was not known for doing God's work.

Tom's vision was greater. It was never about his monetary goals or the ups and downs of the stock market, even though those topics were discussed. Mr. Gallucci knew his purpose was to connect me with his son John. For eighteen years, connections were attempted and missed. God's time line is perfect but not necessarily quick. Finally, a month or so before Tom's passing, John and I met. More than three hours later, we ended our first of many profoundly spiritual fellowships and conversations. We are part of God's spiritual army, and what can be more important than that?

John, God bless you and the work He is doing through you.

Jesus's supernatural army, which is led by the Holy Spirit, is being anointed and united.

Your brother in Christ,
Bill Ryan

The Reiki Center

Mere words cannot adequately express the deep meaning of the following chapter. Tragedy can strike like a bolt of lightning out of a clear blue sky. When it does, be strong, and look to God! Everything on this earth happens for a reason, even unthinkable and seemingly senseless calamity. Remember that we are eternal spirit beings living a temporary physical existence. We are all connected by God's river of love and light. When all seems to be lost, remember we do not die! We live on and are all around our loved ones until our glorious reunions!

Chapter 33

Anthony

It was almost high school ice hockey season, and tryouts were upon us. This season was my son Seth's junior year and Arielle's sophomore year. There were a few new faces out there, but one kid apparently was moving from the Carolinas and would try out. I knew we needed some firepower, and I heard this new guy was just that.

Anthony was a strong kid who played triple-A hockey and seemed to know the game well. It was clear that he could set up plays, fore-check, and back-check, but wow, this boy could shoot that puck. His shot was as good as any high-level junior player I'd ever seen. *Well, at least we have some firepower this season,* I thought. As the season unfolded, it was obvious to many that Anthony settled right in on this team, and he had some really good success with setting up plays and scoring goals.

My son naturally backed him up very well as a defenseman, and so did my daughter. Before long, it was apparent that Anthony and my daughter Arielle were getting to be close friends. Arielle would say to me, "Dad, I'm going for ice cream with Anthony."

"Okay, have a good time," I'd say. Anthony would come over, and they would watch TV or rent a movie. I'd met his parents many times at the games.

Anthony and Arielle shared a love for pickup trucks, animals, ice hockey, and country music. Oh, and the local diner on Route 22. It seemed as if they were always together, and they thoroughly enjoyed each other's company. After the first season, they were always together. I'd say, "Arielle, are you and Anthony dating?"

She would say, "No, just really good friends."

I'd say, "Arielle, it's okay if the answer is yes."

She would reply, "Dad! I told you. Just good friends."

"Okay, okay."

After the season was over, they all played on a spring/summer team together called the Penguins. The next high school season would be the last hurrah for Seth, Anthony, and several others. Most of those kids who had played since they were four or five would never suit up again. It was always an emotional and poignant moment regardless of the sport or the endeavor. It was a huge chapter that had consumed so much of our lives, but it also flavored our lives so sweetly. Now all that was coming to a close— at least for my son. Everything happens in God's time.

From the beginning it was obvious that whenever Anthony was on the ice with Arielle, he was her protector. Most guys on the opposition knew Arielle from years of travel hockey in the New York, New Jersey, and Pennsylvania areas. She either played on their teams or against them. Because of this, nobody who knew her tried to physically hurt her. Arielle was very tough, and she certainly wasn't a pushover at all. She was the first female to earn her varsity letter as a freshman on a boys' varsity team at our high school. Even so, there were always a few boys who were threatened by her presence on the ice, so they would take a cheap shot at her, and if Anthony was on the ice, it got ugly fast.

If he wasn't, he would line the offender up pretty well when he had a chance. That is absolutely ice hockey. If you begged for a beatdown, you'd usually get one.

The team had highs and lows, but eventually, they got inched out of the playoffs. Senior night at our rink was something I will personally never forget. As many parents everywhere do, I have watched our sons, daughters, and friends play hard for nearly fourteen years through fall, winter, spring, and summer and almost always right through major holidays like Thanksgiving and even Memorial Day. This was it. There wasn't a dry eye in the house. All those years of practices, private lessons, games, and tournaments were done.

Through it all, Anthony and Arielle were very close. Anthony's mom Laura at one point said to me, "Can't we get Anthony and Arielle together for real?"

I looked at her and said, "Yes, I would like that very much. I've always thought they were natural together."

Well, it apparently wasn't meant to be. Both families were saddened. The progression in Anthony and Arielle's relationship had come to an impasse. They just couldn't or wouldn't get together as boyfriend and girlfriend. At the team banquet at the end of the year, things were easy and fun, and there wasn't any friction at all between them. Both had significant others, respectively. It was what it was. They were good friends but not a couple.

During the awards segment of the banquet, it was Anthony's turn to get called up. The coach introduced him as he did for the others to a loud applause. "Congratulations, Anthony Mascia, on a great season, and congratulations for being the leading goal scorer and most valuable forward on our team. We will miss Anthony. He is a graduating senior, and Anthony will *not be with us next year.*" Those words gave me pause. I thought that was a strange choice of words to use. He didn't use those words for the other seniors. The evening came and went, and with that, the hockey and sports careers of most of the seniors were over.

The spring came and went, and it was time for graduation. It was a hot sunny day. The football field was full of graduates, and the bleachers were packed with well-wishing families. In that crowd of thousands, it would turn out that my ex-wife and I ended up sitting with Anthony's mom and dad. That was just fine with all of us as we seemed to hit it off well regardless of the relationship we all seemed to have anticipated that didn't happen. This certainly didn't mean we didn't like any other boyfriend or girlfriend they may have had in the interim.

Anthony and Arielle were still very dear friends and always seemed to be with each other. The autumn was now upon us, and we had heard after the fact that Anthony's grandmother had passed in September. This apparently hit Anthony very hard as he had been very close with her. My father was in fact battling leukemia, and on July 11, 2014, his fight with cancer was over. My dad was a larger-than-life figure for many people. It was a sad period for both families.

Several months had passed since graduation, and with Anthony no longer at high school, he and Arielle didn't see each other quite as often. They both had significant others, and life was busy for everyone. Even so, there was a strong bond between them, and at any given time, they would be out either getting ice cream or sitting at the local Sunset Diner on Route 22 in Green Brook, New Jersey. That was their hangout. They went there after hockey games with most of the team, but sometimes it was just the two of them. They often went after open hockey at the Rock Ice Rink, but they didn't need an excuse to go to the diner.

Anthony Mascia was a very significant part of my family through my daughter. He sat on my couch countless times with Arielle, watching TV or playing with my dog Lucky. Anthony was a family member.

October 9, 2014, was like any other Thursday for me. I got up, tended to my dogs, got ready for work, and headed out for the hospital. I usually had several cases lined up. It was about eleven in the morning, and I was on my third case, doing a hernia repair on a three-year-old when my cell phone rang in my back pocket. The circulating nurse asked me if I wanted her to answer it for me. I playfully acted out and said, "Is there no sacred time at all anymore? Can we please just not answer this phone just once while I'm operating?"

The circulating nurse dug in my pocket and pulled out my cell. She looked at it and said, "It's Arielle."

I said, "No, forget it. Whatever she wants can wait! She let it go to voice mail." The phone rang a second time, and I said, "Oh, wow, who is it now?" She said it was Arielle again. With that, my stomach went into a twist. I immediately felt that this wasn't the usual call to complain about something or request something from me like kids often did.

"Please answer it now!"

She did and said, "Arielle is crying and wants to talk to you right now."

"Okay." The nurse put the phone up to my ear. "Arielle?"

"Dad! Oh, my God, Dad! Anthony is dead! Anthony Mascia is dead!" Arielle was sobbing and screaming like I never heard ever before.

"Arielle, what are you saying to me? Who's dead?"

"Anthony! My Anthony!"

"No, no, Arielle. No way."

"Yes, Dad! There was a terrible accident on Route 22 early this morning!"

"Where did you hear this from?"

"Dad, it's true! The whole team got an email this morning from the manager."

I stood there in total shock and utter disbelief. My throat tightened up, and I couldn't speak. My eyes welled up, and I couldn't see. I was halfway through an operation. "Arielle, where are you?"

"I'm at school, Dad. The school is going to call us all in for a meeting with a counsellor."

"Okay, sweetheart. Do you want me to come and get you?"

"No, Dad. I need to stay here."

"Okay, sweetheart. I love you so much. I'll talk to you when you get home. If you need me, call me."

"Okay, Dad. I love you too."

With that, I turned my attention back to the room I was in, and you could hear a pin drop. I stood there and calmly recounted what I had just been told. All I heard was, "Oh, my God," from both the anesthesiologist and the scrub tech working with me. I finished the case and looked for the email on my cell phone. There it was—just as she had said.

Apparently, Anthony was at a red light on Route 22 just after eating at the diner with a friend. A tractor trailer plowed into him from behind at a high rate of speed. The impact smashed Anthony's pickup truck into the concrete divider and ruptured his gas tank. The truck exploded with Anthony in it. He never had a chance. The highway was closed for nearly six hours.

As I contemplated what had happened that day, I became completely overwhelmed with immense grief. I couldn't handle what I was told. I thought I would jump out of my skin or stop breathing or both. I tried to imagine what his parents and sister were feeling. As I write this, I can feel the pull of the vortex of extreme grief all over again. It never leaves me. It just goes dormant for stretches of time to this day. This was just too much to accept, too much to handle.

My daughter loved Anthony. Anyone who knew him loved him. I loved him. I couldn't think straight. My heart was broken, and I couldn't see any way it would ever be okay again. I did my best to calm myself down, and I began to pray for him and the family immediately.

That night I would sit at my prayer and meditation table and make Anthony a candle. I lit that candle and went into deep meditation. I had done this many hundreds of times before, but it was on behalf of someone (usually a child) who was alive but sick and in need of healing in one way or another. This time it was for a dear friend, an eighteen-year-old whom I had imagined would someday be my son-in-law, and he was now physically gone and in such a very disturbing way.

I was in uncharted waters. I had to have the answers. I couldn't let it go. I said the Rosary. I said every prayer I could think of. I said every healing prayer I had in several books from Padre Pio and Saint Francis of Assisi. I did this on behalf of Anthony, his family, and all who grieved for him. I was a total wreck, and it was just getting worse as I went. I had never wept and sobbed like this ever before, even when I had lost my sister, two young first cousins, several friends, and many older relatives over the years. This was something completely different. I likened it to a raging tsunami of extreme grief five hundred feet high and never-ending in its rampage.

As I sat there praying and fighting all sorts of feelings, including extreme anger, my cell rang. It was my dear friend Jane Casale. As previously stated, Jane is my neighbor but also a medium. She said she felt my turmoil and needed to call me. I told her that our dear friend had passed suddenly. I asked her if she could help me so that I may offer help to the family. She immediately went into her zone. She saw the accident and told me that Anthony was there with her to recount what had happened from his point of view.

Anthony went on to say that he was sitting there in his truck and talking to his bud through their respective open windows. Anthony's truck was on the right, and his friend's truck was in the left lane. They were just saying good night while they were stopped at the red light. It was about three thirty in the morning, and nobody was on the road—or so they thought. The next thing he knew, there was a great impact. He felt nothing, just impact. No pain. There was a second impact. He only felt pain for about two seconds.

At that point, someone shoved him from his right so forcefully that he flew out of his truck and onto the street. His truck had spun around so that the driver's side was on the street side, the passenger door faced toward the concrete divider, and his truck faced the wrong way on the highway. Anthony had no idea who had shoved him like that. All he knew was that when he stood up, he saw his truck burning and engulfed in flames, but it looked as if he were still inside. Anthony immediately protested over what he saw, but then there were two people with him who explained to him that he couldn't go back. *He wasn't supposed to go back*, and everything would be okay.

It took him the better part of that first day (in earth time) to come to grips with what had happened. He settled in with family members on the other side, including his beloved grandmother, who had recently passed and had left him so brokenhearted. There is no linear time on the other side, so what took all day for us here in the physical realm was an interval enough for him to settle in. He was with loving family members who knew him very well in a place he had originally come from. In fact, *he was home*. His message was that he was better than okay, but he was very worried over his family and friends.

At hearing this, I broke down in tears over and over. My friend had not been told of the accident. She knew nothing. She had been given the details by Anthony. I thanked her profusely and returned to my meditation and prayers. I cried and prayed myself to sleep in my chair in front of his candle. I woke up an hour later and went to bed.

I fell into a deep sleep. At around two thirty in the morning, I awoke to an extremely bright light shining through my window shade across from the foot of my bed. I realized that the room was dark, and there was no light coming through the other window about eight feet away on the same wall. As I looked at this light, it got brighter and brighter and eventually came right through the window and shades. It filled my room with an incredible brilliance that made me look away as it hurt my eyes to look directly at it. As it came closer and closer to me, the brilliant light changed into a ball of light that was slowly spinning. As it floated over my bed, I sat up straight to address it. It stopped directly in front of me. There I was face-to-face with this immensely bright light about three feet from my face. It then revealed itself to be a brilliant cluster of diamond-like crystals and was about four to five inches in diameter. It was slowly spinning and turning as it was emitting the most incredible brilliant light and love I had ever seen or felt before.

This spirit entity had heard and seen my lament. It had heard and felt my prayers. It knew my intent and knew how broken my heart was for Anthony and his family. I shouted angrily as I stared at it, "I want Anthony back!" I slammed my right fist down on my bed repeatedly. "Anthony's family wants him back! Arielle wants Anthony back!"

There was at that point a crystal-clear acknowledgment and reply from this cluster of heavenly brilliance. This, in fact, was Anthony! I had been given the privilege to see Anthony in his heavenly light energy form! One could say I was witness to the Merkaba within him. (Merkaba is the primal pattern that created all things and all universes seen and unseen. It is also taken as the vehicle that carries our God center to heaven.) I was witnessing Anthony's heavenly God center. It's the very essence of how we are made in the image and likeness of God. It is our God source. It is our brilliance. It is the very God light that we shine into this world yet are completely unaware of with our physical earthly eyes. With this revelation, I went into an ecstasy and was completely transfixed upon this heavenly light.

Anthony had given me a brief glimpse of what we *all* come from and what we all eventually return to. We are all a brilliant spark of God's love and light. God is love and light, and so are we. Anthony was from God, and he returned to God. He let me know that he was where he must be and that his family would be just fine. He acknowledged that he would always be Anthony Mascia, son, grandson, brother, and friend. He would always be very close to his family, and for that matter, he would never leave any of us. He also made it very clear to me that this wasn't over. One day Anthony would be back!

With that, he flared brightly and flew out through the window and was gone from my sight. I fell on my side and began to sob. I thanked God profusely for what had just happened. I thanked Anthony for his empathy, compassion, and love. It took me quite a while to get back to sleep. Who could sleep after that?

Since October 9, 2014, I have gotten closer to Anthony's family. His sister Nina was hoping to apply to medical school. I reached out to her so that she might spend time shadowing me at the hospital. Nina is a brilliant woman, and I knew she would make a great physician. I was thrilled when Nina asked me to write a letter of recommendation for her admission to medical school. I'm even more thrilled to say Nina will start medical school this fall.

I know Anthony will be right by her side through it all. I have a guiding angel in my sister Fran, and Nina has one in her brother Anthony. My dear friend and mentor Sandra and I are always there for Paul and Laura Mascia, and we will assist them in any way we can.

My family and I give the Mascia family our hearts and our love. I know Anthony is completely aware of this, and that makes me happy. Many believe that souls incarnate and do so as soul groups or soul families. I believe when you feel this kind of love and connection to others, they are certainly part of your eternal inner soul circle, even if they are only physically in your life for a relatively brief period.

Even though all things in this life do happen for a reason, this tragedy is beyond comprehension. Offering your heart, love, and friendship to others, especially in times of great tragedy, sorrow, and need, is what this world so desperately thirsts for! Do not shy away from those in need. Behold the words of Jesus from the gospel according to Mark as he recounted the two most important commandments. "And you shall love the Lord your God with all your heart and with all your soul and with all your mind and with all your strength. The second is this: You shall love your neighbor as yourself. There is no other commandment greater than these" (Mark 12:30–31).

God bless you, Anthony Mascia. I know you watch over your loving family and will do so until we are all reunited in God's kingdom once again.

Amen.

"Be gracious to me, oh Lord, for I am in distress; my eye is wasted from grief; my soul and my body also" (Psalm 31:9 NIV).

"Therefore you now have sorrow; but I will see you again and your heart will rejoice, and your joy no one will take from you" (John 16:22 NIV).

Anthony and Arielle

When the spirit world has a message for you it may come at times that seem strange, meddlesome or downright infuriating. This next chapter tells how I have come to recognize when a message is on its way from the other side. I no longer get upset. I no longer worry about not getting enough sleep. I now know to be accepting of it and to be profoundly thankful for the message and moment. Are you recognizing your moments?

Chapter 34

Insomnia—God's Workshop

I've learned over the last several years to expect a message from God if I go to bed completely exhausted yet can't fall asleep. We have all had the experience of feeling so tired, but after a few moments, we just know we aren't going fall asleep no matter what we do. Usually, this specific phenomenon takes me by surprise because I'm already exhausted. Usually, when I am that tired, I fall asleep, and that's that. If several hours go by and I'm still tossing and turning, I now just go with it and know better not to fight it. In the midst of a bout of insomnia, I now know a mystical and metaphysical message is most certainly on its way.

Daniel

About five years ago, I wanted to get into better shape than what I had allowed myself to fall into. I had been an athlete and a weight lifter most of my life, so I wasn't happy at all breaching the fifty-year mark and not being in the great shape I'd expected of myself. My career as a pediatric surgeon made staying in good shape possible but not probable.

As many of us know all too well, getting rid of unwanted fat and staying fit as we age can be an impossible task. I've tried it all—low-carb diets, no-carb diets, vegan diets, paleo diets, distilled water diets, and fasting. Some worked for a while, but nothing really did what I wanted. I'm not talking about a spiritual fast. That's a separate issue. Lately, I've gotten very good at spiritual fasting and will routinely do three to four twenty-four-hour fasts each week.

Usually, when I put my heart and mind to a task, I can get it done one way or another. On this particular night, I was exhausted and chronically frustrated about having extra pounds I certainly didn't need. The feelings were coming to a crescendo for me. After prayer lightings for some of my patients and some meditating on their healing, I then hit the prayers hard regarding my quest to lose some weight. I went to bed really exhausted.

Fifteen minutes after my head hit the pillow, I was still wide awake. Thirty minutes passed, and then sixty minutes went by. I was no closer to falling asleep than I had been while at work that day. My body and mind were very tired, but something was preventing me from turning off. Now nearly two hours had passed from the time when my head hit the pillow, and I was still wide awake.

I sat up and turned on my lights. I looked around, trying to decide if I would turn on the TV or grab a book. There on my nightstand was my Bible. I figured the Bible had to have something more useful for me than late-night TV. I placed the Bible on the bed in front of me and flipped through the pages like a dealer shuffling cards. Then I released my thumb so that the book opened where it would. I noticed that it opened to page one of the book of Daniel. I thought it was interesting that it landed on page one of any book.

For those who don't know, the book of Daniel is an apocalyptic writing of the Old Testament that deals with the events of the siege of Jerusalem by the Babylonians and subsequent destruction of the temple in or around the year 589 BC.

Daniel and his cohorts were taken prisoner and bought back to the kingdom of Nebuchadnezzar, ruler of Babylon. The king welcomed the capable and intelligent from Judea and saw to it that they were assimilated into his kingdom. Daniel and his three friends fell into good favor with the king. It was proclaimed that the four Judeans would share in the royal food and wine of the king's court. Upon hearing this, Daniel refused and proclaimed he would not be defiled with such an offer as they were still captives in a foreign land. They demanded the same food as the other captives.

The chief chamberlain explained to Daniel and the others that he was afraid that should the king see the Judeans looking thin and frail compared to the other young men, it could mean his head. Daniel then said to the guard, whom the chief chamberlain had appointed to oversee Daniel, Hananiah, Mishael, and Azariah, "Please test your servants for ten days: Give us nothing but vegetables to eat and water to drink. Then compare our appearance with that of the young men who eat the royal food, and treat your servants in accordance with what you see." So he agreed to this and tested them for ten days. At the end of the ten days, they looked healthier and better nourished than any of the young men who had eaten the royal food. So the guard took away their choice food and wine they were to drink and gave them vegetables instead (Daniel 1:12–15 NIV).

There I was, at nearly two thirty, sitting on my bed, completely stunned by what had just happened. God works in our lives every day and night.

I grew frustrated and saddened with my inability to lose my gut in my early fifties. I prayed on it and tried many methods to achieve my goal, but to no avail. I felt the issue coming to a head emotionally, so I went to bed and talked to God about my concerns. I should have fallen asleep, but I didn't. I became annoyed, sat up with a disgruntled acceptance, and chose the Bible over late-night TV. I placed it before me and let it open with a flip. It opened to page one of the book of Daniel. I was clueless as to the implications. I went on to read all about how Daniel and his cohorts demanded vegetables and water as their preferred diet and ended up looking healthier and slimmer than the others who were eating the royal food and wine, which clearly was more akin to my contemporary dietary habits.

I subsequently learned that there was certainly a large industry out there based on the Daniel diet. I had no idea this was true. My Bible has 2,006 pages. The odds of having that Bible open up to page one of the book of Daniel by chance was 2,006 to 1. Even if you believe in coincidences—and I don't—this was a long shot against all odds that I wouldn't deny. God was listening to me, and God responded.

Never believe that your prayers aren't heard by our Lord. All you have to do is give God the reverence He deserves. Let our Lord into your being. Open your hearts and minds to our Lord, king of the universe. You have everything to gain and quite frankly, everything to lose.

Metatron

Not long after my separation from my wife, I became upset over how our three children would handle a pending divorce. As with all challenges in my life, I looked to God for the answers. In combination with lots of prayer and meditation, I often read from the many inspiring books I have at home. The Bible is my number-one go-to book, but I also read countless books on Hinduism, the Koran, and books about Jesus, angels, Krishna, Buddha, and other deities that are here to assist humanity.

When I have sufficiently exhausted the supply of books in my home, I occasionally find myself making a trip to the local bookstore. This particular trip was no different than any other. I knew there would be a book there at the store waiting for me. As I've stated before, when I'm out in a bookstore, the book or books will choose me and will usually end up being in a position where they can pique my interest.

As I perused religious books and the always nearby spiritual/metaphysical section, I must have flipped through dozens of books. None really seemed to catch my interest. As I was about to change directions completely and visit the music section, I saw a smaller book face down on the shelf and not upright as were the others. In my attempt to be a helpful customer, I picked up the book and went to put it back in an appropriate slot. There was no space at all on that shelf for any book. I looked at the cover and saw a man from ancient times wearing a robe and writing on parchment at a podium with a feather in his hand. The title of the book was *Metatron Invoking the Angel of God's Presence*.[31]

This caught my eye and stimulated my interest. I thought that the name Metatron had a ring to it that was incongruous with the picture on the cover. Here was a man from many centuries ago, writing with a feather, but Metatron sounded like a children's Transformer toy from outer space. I knew nothing about Metatron.

I took it over to a couch and began to read. As I flipped from section to section, I read a paragraph that said Metatron was not only an archangel but also a seraph, an angelic being of the highest order and one that is found in the inner most circle closest to God. It then went on to say that Archangel Metatron petitioned God to incarnate as a human to gain a more intimate sense of what it meant to be human. God permitted this unusual request. Thus, Metatron incarnated as Enoch.

I had already read two versions of the book of Enoch. Apparently, there are three books out there on the life of Enoch. When I read the books of Enoch, I learned that Enoch did not die as mortals do, but he was taken up into the heavens after living 365 years on earth. It explained in this book that he indeed did not pass and lay subject to decay because he was already Metatron, the archangel. He ascended and was assumed into heaven as the Virgin Mary would also be many centuries later.

Several years had passed since I read this book on Metatron. I hadn't thought of him at all, in fact. There seemed to be an abundance of stress regarding my children, and this is no surprise for most parents. This was one of those nights where I was completely spent from the challenges of the day and should have fallen asleep immediately after my meditations, but worry over my kids was blocking my sleep. Hours were passing, so I sat up and went through a litany of prayer.

As I finished my prayers and discourse, I saw a golden flash from the corner of my eye to the right of my bed. It actually startled me, but then I was filled with the essence of Archangel Metatron. I wasn't even thinking about archangels. I was speaking with God and needed to get to sleep very badly. As the thoughts came flooding into my head, I heard the words, "God's river of love and light will carry your children." As I heard these words very clearly, I leaned forward in my bed and got a hold of myself. Then I pondered what I had just heard and seen. As I sat there trying to hold on to that voice in my head, a very clear vision appeared before me.

I was walking up a hillside covered with dry grass. I came upon a dry riverbed that stretched from the far left of me across my path and far off to my right. I looked down into this dry river that was about one hundred feet across and approximately ten to twelve feet deep. I wondered why I was seeing this, but I knew it was intentional.

Then out of nowhere, my three children appeared on the opposite riverbank. The symbolism of me being on one bank and they on the other was clear. There was a chasm between us, and with that, I felt very strong emotions welling up in me. I wanted to burst into tears as I had no idea why there should be any actual or symbolic impasse between my beloved children and me at all. There wasn't any ongoing feud or angst between us that I knew of.

Just as my emotions were about to get the best of me, a very large but slow lava flow came down this dry riverbed from my left. It took a slow, meandering, serpiginous path as it moved. As I became mesmerized at this amazing scene, I saw that the lava flow was at its core the most intense and pure electric white light. It was so intense that it was difficult to look at. The outside of the flow was encrusted with pure sparkling gold and silver, unlike a real lava flow that would be encrusted with dark cooling pumice. Between the cracks of the encrusted gold and silver came the intense rays of this super brilliant white light.

My children were standing too close to the edge, and I became apprehensive and worried that they could fall into this flow that appeared to be so intense in its energy that nobody would survive it. As the flow neared my children, they all started to happily wave at me with loving smiles on their faces. They were about to demonstrate something to me. They knew what this vision was all about. I apparently did not. As the flow reached them, they purposely allowed themselves to be caught up in it. In fact, they were riding this intense flowing river of brilliance.

Then I heard a voice in my head. It was the voice of Archangel Metatron, a strong, calm, and completely reassuring voice. It revealed to me that this was in fact God's river of love and light. I was being shown an incredible vision that assured me that my three children are not to be worried about and that they are indeed being carried in the flow of God's river of love and light!

As I stood there with a lump in my throat, watching all three of my children being happily and purposefully carried along, I saw them wave to me with beaming faces. It was at that very moment I was given yet another message, but this one was clearly from the perspective of our Creator. He said, "You and their mother have done the job you had been given. You have given all three of my children the life they were meant to have, and now the rest is in My hands."

Psalm 23

My sister Fran is often around me. She passed in 1993. I know she watches from afar, but there are times when she is near and I can feel her sending me love. I say it that way instead of her sending me a message. When I feel her around me, I can feel that the message itself is love. She loves me and is encouraging me. She more often gets close to me when I've been sad, overworked, or discouraged. Hey, it happens to all of us now and then.

There was a rough stretch of time back in 2012 around my divorce when I was just stressed and overwhelmed with all the challenges in my life. The divorce proceedings were coming to a head, so there were many meetings and long discussions with my attorney and all the big bills that came with it. At the same time, there were far too many deathly ill children to be taken care of at the hospital, and at this very same time, my work associate became extremely ill, requiring emergency lifesaving surgery.

Thank God he made it through that ordeal, but it left me on call 24-7 for more than four and a half months in a row. I was nearly at my breaking point. I did healing meditations every night for many people, but somehow I all too often seemed to skip over myself. I was in need of healing emotionally, physically, and spiritually as much as anyone else.

Taking on everyone else's burdens can truly drain the life energy out of you. It affects your chakras and will ultimately affect you physically as well. In being a good healer, you can't forget to heal yourself. It was a Wednesday night, and I really needed to get to sleep. I had a full OR schedule the next day, and I was the only one taking calls for the foreseeable future anyway.

This meant that on top of my five scheduled surgeries, I could end up with another two or three cases added to the list via the ER or transfer service. I went to bed after my meditations, and I was so exhausted that I could feel my whole body pulsing. It was one of those nights when I couldn't get to sleep. An hour went by, and now I was wide awake. I could feel the frustration welling up in me. It was never a good thing when I'd get a glimpse of the digital clock every thirty minutes, and now two hours had passed.

I sat upright in my bed and let out a huff because of my predicament. I could think of how sickeningly exhausted I would be the next day with all that work I had to do. I grabbed my cell phone and read through my emails. Then I grabbed my Bible and tossed it onto the bedspread between my two knees. The rebound of the book off the mattress made it open by itself. I was actually trembling with angst, frustration, and even some panic.

When I looked at the Bible, I saw it had opened to page 880, which in my Bible was Psalm 23, a psalm of David. Psalm 23 was my sister Fran's favorite psalm. She read it and recited it often. When she suspected she was going to pass from her brain tumor, she requested Psalm 23 be on her memorial card. I sat there, my eyes filling with tears. There was no doubt in my heart and mind that this was happening for a reason. Tonight my sister had a message for me. She gave her love to me, but she also was telling me that everything would be okay. The divorce, my children, the operating room, the sick kids, and my associate—all would be okay. Trust in God, Johnny. Trust in Jesus!

Psalm 23 (NIV): A Psalm of David

The Lord is my shepherd, I shall not want.

He makes me lie down in green pastures,

He leads me beside quiet waters,

He refreshes my soul.

He guides me along the right paths for His name's sake.

Even though I walk through the valley of the shadow of death,

I will fear no evil, for you are with me;

Your rod and your staff, they comfort me.

You prepare a table for me in the presence of my enemies.

You anoint my head with oil;

My cup overflows.

Surely your goodness and love will follow me

All the days of my life.

And I will dwell in the house of the Lord forever.

Light Language, Ancient Scrolls

Four times in the last two and a half years, I received what I believed was a light language transmission. In each instance, I should have been fast asleep, but I couldn't sleep. The episodes would occur while I was wide awake. I would be tossing and turning for an hour or so after about an hour of meditation and prayer.

I would be on my back, and a parchment scroll surrounded by backlighting would appear. I could see the upper and lower rolls and tan fabric or the ancient paper stretched between the two rolls.

As I stared at this phenomenon, the scroll would begin to roll up from the bottom to the top. On the scroll would appear symbols in black. The symbols seemed to not have any curved lines. Nearly all the symbols were straight lines forming angles, Ys, triangles with or without stems, parallel lines, and some zigzags. It was clear to me that this meant something and that it was apparently meant for me and me alone to discern. There was no punctuation associated with the symbols. They would merely slowly scroll from bottom to the top in an uninterrupted fashion until it ended. Each occurrence would last about forty-five seconds to a minute.

My research in identifying the symbols indicate a combination of Inuit and Cree Indian symbols, but as I match up symbol for symbol, I find that it really isn't either language at all. The symbols are *similar* to Cree and Inuit. Interestingly, I worked directly with the Cree and Inuit people as a pediatric surgery fellow in Montreal. I never knew of or experienced their symbols. I didn't know if they had any written symbols as many indigenous people do not have written history and it's all verbally told through the centuries. I only learned of their written symbols when I researched them.

Some experts in light language believe these episodes are transmission of information or affirmation from higher realms to light workers on earth. Truly, I tell you I do not know what they are. I always feel good about it, and I'm never left upset or disturbed.

I always get to sleep after one of these episodes. I don't understand why this occurred four times and has not occurred in more than a year. I do know this: When I can't sleep and I'm sufficiently exhausted and should be asleep, I can be receptive to communication from what I believe is God, His angels, or His saints. I welcome the next sleepless night and the beautiful communication it may hold for me.

Improbable Connections

Now and then I will think of a question that keeps nagging me or actually burns in me that I want answered. Sometimes the answer to these questions should be something that I could or should have figured out on my own, such as things that are nearer to my area of professional expertise. Other times, not so much.

There are times when someone will provoke an awakening in you, and *bingo*, you will have the answer to the question that you've been asking for a long time. The answer you sought so diligently can come out of nowhere and blindside you.

Recently, I woke up much earlier than I needed to. I had been sleeping poorly because of horrific acute calcific shoulder tendonitis. I apparently strained both my shoulders months earlier and really didn't understand exactly how bad it would get. I thought it was the result of a difficult surgery where I was holding a laparoscope scope and operating a trocar for my chief resident in the same position for five hours. Two days after that surgery, I couldn't move my shoulders. They only got worse and worse as the days, weeks, and months passed.

I received several orthopedic injections in each shoulder and was doing physical therapy for four months. Every time I tried to roll over in bed, it felt like I was having a sixteen-penny nail driven into each shoulder. I had also gone through this type of scenario several years prior with my hips when I was lifting weights and still playing men's league ice hockey. I had developed acute and chronic calcific tendonitis that would come and go.

Now I was fully awake, in tremendous pain, and very frustrated. This time instead of me grabbing my Bible as I usually did, I logged on to social media. I almost always read my Bible when I can't sleep. This night I was Bible-resistant and "social media-ready. I went with it.

I saw that a friend had sent me a cute video about animals playing and experiencing joy. I really enjoyed this video and realized the timing was perfect. So I figured I would pass it on. I would pay it forward to those whom I thought could use the same feel-good gesture. I sent it out to about forty people.

Immediately, I got a reply from an old high school friend named Joseph Pantel. I wasn't looking for replies at four in the morning, but I read it. I engaged him, and he asked if I had sent this to him by mistake. I explained that I sent it to those I thought might appreciate it. He did appreciate it, and then we got into a brief conversation about other things.

He sent me a photograph of his foot that surgeons had recently operated on for nerve decompression. As we engaged in a question-and-answer session about his surgery, he went on to tell me about his health issues. As he did, he explained to me that he had fairly severe Crohn's disease. The foot surgery was all about his extraintestinal manifestations of Crohn's disease. As a result of the Crohn's, he had developed arthritis and fairly chronic and debilitating tendonitis too.

As he expressed this to me, the lightning bolt hit me. I was stunned that I hadn't figured it all out. Well, two primary care physicians, two orthopedic surgeon, two physical therapist, and a gastroenterologist hadn't put everything together either.

I had recently been diagnosed with Crohn's disease myself. It had been about eighteen months. I was sure I'd had it for many years too. I also had acute on chronic arthritis and tendonitis that had really sidelined me from working out and staying in shape. Over the last year or so, my tendonitis had been a big issue for me regarding working out, but thank God it hasn't been a problem for me to still work or operate.

In this brief exchange on social media so early in the morning that started with a cute animal video from a friend, an old high school friend gave me the answer that I—and a handful of very good physicians— couldn't find for many years.

My severe chronic tendonitis was indeed related to Crohn's. Now I had the answer I had been seeking for a very long time. Thank you, Joseph.

We are all connected by God's river of love and light. There are times when the current flows and you are the clear beneficiary. Other times you may be the benefactor and have no idea that you were indeed playing that role. I now have direction and resolve regarding how best to address my Crohn's-related arthritis and tendonitis.

Just allow yourself to be aware that God works through us and in us for the good of all humanity. Deny this truth is like putting yourself into solitary confinement.

"Then He will send out the angels and gather his elect from the four winds, from the ends of the earth, to the ends of Heaven" (Mark 13:27 ESV).

"And so it will be at the end of the age. The angels will come out and separate the evil from the righteous" (Matthew 13:49 ESV).

The following chapter shows us how seemingly unimportant and often cavalier thoughts, attitudes, and behaviors can lead us astray and add up to a boatload of negativity that can lead to us living lives on lower energy levels. Living our lives at low energy levels leaves us prone to spiritual attack from entities from the lower realms. This, my friends, is no joke. Live at a higher energy level, and leave the lower energies behind. The energy of love cannot be touched by low spiritual energies. Sickness and disease also come from the lower energy realms. Rise above! Be the best you can be!

Chapter 35

The Seven Deadly Sins

When the Holy Spirit is upon you, you will find yourself in a state of constant prayer. Every thought you have is a conversation with God and no longer a talk with your ego-driven mind. When this happens, you are much more likely to be in line with the will of God and much less likely to be led by the world and your ego.

After all, our life task has everything to do with killing off the control our egos have over us. Killing off the ego is what is meant by dying to yourself. Jesus challenged His disciples to follow Him. "Follow in My footsteps," He said. To do so, you must die to yourself. That doesn't mean that you must physically die. That would defeat the whole issue of transcending this world and the ego while still alive. An ego-driven life is subject to the seven deadly sins, which include lust, gluttony, greed, sloth, wrath, envy, and pride.

Let's take a look at these seven deadly sins. They are not found in a list as such in the Bible, but they are certainly referenced individually. Are they so bad? What's the big deal? Why are they deadly?

"For whoever would save his life will lose it, but whoever loses his life for my sake will find it" (Matthew 16:25 NIV).

This verse explains that saving your ego-driven worldly life and all it brings will cause the loss of eternal life. One life is under our noses and is temporary (like a baited trap) while the other is harder to grasp but eternal.

"Enter by the narrow gate. For the gate is wide and the way is easy that leads to destruction, and those who enter by it are many" (Matthew 7:13 NIV).

The Seven Deadly Sins as Written of in the Bible

Lust

Lust is a strong craving or desire that's usually of a sexual nature. Lust is basically the state of intense desire for someone or something. The Bible tells us that lust is just the thought or emotional desiring of something and not the actual acquisition of the physical act.

"Anyone who looks at another *lustfully* has already committed adultery in his heart" (Matthew 5:28 ESV).

"For everything in the world—the *lust* of the flesh, the lust of the eyes, and the pride of life—comes not from the Father but from the world" (1 John 2:16 HCSB).

"Put to death therefore, whatever belongs to your earthly nature: sexual immorality, impurity, *lust*, evil desires and greed, which is idolatry" (Colossian 3:5 HCSB).

"Do not *lust* in your heart after her beauty or let her captivate you with her eyes" (Proverbs 6:25 HCSB).

"Therefore say to the Israelites: This is what the sovereign LORD says: will you defile yourselves the way your ancestors did and *lust* after their vile images?" (Ezekiel 16:36 ESV).

"Having lost all sensitivity, they have given themselves over to sensuality so as to indulge in every kind of impurity, with a continual lust for more" (Ephesians 4:19 ESV).

Gluttony

Gluttony is excessive eating or drinking. Don't we all know this one intimately, especially here in the West? Everywhere we look, we are bombarded with advertisements coaxing us to overeat and drink too much. We have all seen commercials on television where a man wants to eat a third chili dog, but he has indigestion. His friend says, "Try one of my antacid pills," and in the next scene, the man is having another hot dog. What kind of lesson is this? "Take our drug so you can be a glutton!" Is it any wonder why adult and child obesity is endemic and rising just as diabetes and pancreatic cancer is?

"Drunkards and *gluttons* become poor and drowsiness clothes them in rags" (Proverbs 23:21 NAV).

"And put a knife to your throat if you are given to *gluttony*" (Proverbs 23:2 ESV).

Greed

Greed is an inordinate or insatiable longing for wealth, status, and power.

"Woe to you teachers of the law and Pharisees, you hypocrites! You clean the outside of the cup and dish, but inside you are full of *greed* and wickedness" (Matthew 23:25 ESV).

"Watch out! Be on your guard against all kinds of *greed*; life does not consist of an abundance of possessions" (Luke 12:15 ESV).

"I was enraged by their sinful *greed*: I punished them and hid my face in anger, yet they kept on in their willful ways" (Isaiah 57:17 ESV).

Sloth

Sloth is generally taken as laziness, a disinclination to action or labor. It is also spiritual apathy. Laziness basically gets us nowhere, and we become a burden on others. Apparently, some may even see life as a burden upon themselves, especially in a spiritual sense.

"Diligent hands will rule, but *laziness* ends in forced labor" (Proverbs 12:24 HCSB).

"*Laziness* brings on deep sleep and the shiftless go hungry" (Proverbs 19:15 ESV).

"Through *laziness*, the rafters sag: because of idle hands, the house leaks" (Ecclesiastes 10:18 ESV).

Wrath

Wrath is taken as anger.

"At Horeb you aroused the LORD's *wrath* so that he was angry enough to destroy you" (Deuteronomy 9:8 ESV).

"In furious anger and in great *wrath* the LORD uprooted them from their land and thrust them into another land, as it is now" (Deuteronomy 29:28 ESV).

"Because of your *wrath* there is no health in my body; there is no soundness in my bones because of my sin" (Psalm 38:3 ESV).

"Then Moses said to Aaron, take your censer and put incense in it along with burning coals from the altar and hurry to the assembly to make atonements for them. *Wrath* has come out from the LORD; the plague has started" (Numbers 16:46 ESV).

Envy

Envy is the coveting of the possession of another, be it a quality or an object. Envy and jealousy are very close in meaning.

"Love is patient. Love is kind, it does not *envy*, it does not boast, it is not proud" (1 Colossian 13:4 ESV).

"*Envy*; drunkenness, orgies and the like, I warn you, as I did before, that those who live like this will not inherit the Kingdom of God" (Galatians 5:21 ESV).

"And I saw that all toil and all achievement spring from one person's ENVY of another. This too is meaningless, a chasing after the wind" (Ecclesiastes 4:4 ESV).

"Do not *envy* the wicked, do not desire their company" (Proverbs 24:1 ESV).

"A heart at peace gives life to the body but *envy* rots the bones" (Proverbs 14:30 ESV).

"They have become filled with every kind of wickedness, evil, greed and depravity. They are full of *envy*, murder, strife, deceit and malice. They are gossips" (Romans 1:29 ESV).

Pride

Pride is boastfulness, conceit, egotism, and vanity.

"I will break down your stubborn *pride* and make the sky above you like iron and the ground beneath you like bronze" (Leviticus 26:19 ESV).

"In his *pride* the wicked man does not seek him; in all his thoughts there is no room for God" (Psalm 10:4 ESV).

"When *pride* comes, then comes disgrace, but with humility comes wisdom" (Proverbs 11:2 ESV).

"The arrogance of man will be brought low and human *pride* humbled; the LORD alone will be exalted in that day" (Isaiah 2:17 ESV).

"If you do not listen, I will weep in secret because of your *pride*; my eyes will weep bitterly, overflowing with tears, because the LORD's flock will be taken captive" (Jeremiah 13:17 ESV).

"But when his heart became arrogant and hardened with *pride*, he was deposed from his royal throne and stripped of his glory" (Daniel 5:20 ESV).

So you see, the seven deadly sins are absolutely found in the Bible here and there, although not labeled as such. They certainly tell us that the ego-driven life lays us prone to these sins. In living this kind of life, you will certainly forfeit your eternal spirit life. So if you see God in everyone you meet and in everything you do, you can't help but live a Spirit-driven life. If you do, the kingdom of God is yours.

Peace to you.

The next chapter reveals excerpts from the book of Ecclesiastes and the gospel. The chapter speaks to us and tells us to be on guard. We should know the difference between true meaningful spiritual endeavor and that which is a chasing of the wind. King Solomon and Jesus hand us pearls of wisdom that should last for all eternity. Do you understand the difference?

Chapter 36

The Emptiness of Possessions

King Solomon, circa 935 BC

Ecclesiastes 2:4–11 (NIV) says,

> I increased my achievements. I built houses and planted vineyards for myself. I made gardens and parks for myself and planted every kind of fruit tree in them. I constructed reservoirs of water for myself from which to irrigate a grove of flourishing trees. I acquired male and female servants and had slaves who were born in my house. I also owned many herds of cattle and flocks, more than all who were before me in Jerusalem. I also amassed silver and gold for myself, and the treasure of Kings and provinces. I gathered male and female singers for myself, and many concubines, the delights of men. So, I became great and surpassed all who were before me in Jerusalem; my wisdom also remained with me. All that my eyes desired I did not deny them. I did not refuse myself any pleasure, for I took pleasure in all

my struggles. This was my reward for all my struggles. When I considered all that I had accomplished and what I had labored to achieve, I found everything to be futile and a pursuit of the wind. There was nothing to be gained under the sun.

No matter who you are—rich man, poor man, beggar man, thief—the only thing you take from this world when you leave is your legacy of love. How did you love your brothers and sisters? Did you produce good fruit or bad? Did you allow yourself the eyes to see and the ears to hear? What legacy do you leave this world? The old expression "You can't take it with you" is very true except for your spiritual legacy.

What you acquire in this world regarding money, power, position, or fame is of this world and only this world. Open your eyes to what is real and everlasting. Understand what constitutes pursuits of the wind as opposed to what yields a heavenly storehouse for you in God's kingdom. Love God above all else, and love your neighbors as yourself. Wake up and understand that you are being given countless opportunities each day to express your love for God and for your brothers and sisters. It's the little things that mean so much. Shine your light and love for all the world to see.

The solution for the yearnings of man is an understanding of life's trap and trappings. As Jesus started on His way, a man ran up to Him and fell on his knees before Him. "Good teacher, what must I do to inherit eternal life?" (Mark 10:17 NIV).

"Why do you call me good?" Jesus answered. "No one is good—except God alone." You know the commandments. *Do not murder. Do not commit adultery. Do not steal. Do not give false testimony. Do not defraud. Honor your father and mother.* The man declared, "Teacher, all these I have kept since I was a boy." Jesus looked at him and loved him. "One thing you lack," He said. "Go sell everything you have and give to the poor, and you will have treasure in Heaven. Then, come follow me." At this, the man's face fell. He went away sad because he had great wealth (Mark 10:18–22 NIV). Jesus told this spiritual seeker something that He couldn't accept. As the man walked away, Jesus looked around and said to His disciples, "How hard it is for the rich to enter the Kingdom of God!" The disciples were amazed at His words. But Jesus said again, "Children, how hard it is to enter the Kingdom of God! It is easier for a camel to go through the eye of a needle than for a rich man to enter the Kingdom of God" (Mark 10:23–25).[32] And the disciples were exceedingly astonished and said to him, "Then who can be saved?" Jesus looked at them and said, "With man it is impossible, but not with God, for all things are possible with God" (Mark 10:27–28).

A teacher of the Law was impressed with Jesus's wisdom. So like the rich man, he asked Jesus a question. One of the teachers of the Law came and heard them debating. Noticing that Jesus had given them a good answer, he asked Him, "Of all the commandments, which is the most important?" (Mark 12:28 NIV). Jesus answered, "The most important one is this: 'Hear O Israel the Lord our God, the Lord is one. Love the Lord your God with all your heart and with all your soul and with all your mind and with all your strength.' The second is this: 'Love your neighbor as yourself.' There is no commandment greater than these" (Mark 12:29–31 NIV).

Jesus answered with two commands from the Hebrew Scriptures. The first is from Deuteronomy 6:4–5. This passage includes the Shema, which pious Jews recited morning and evening, as well as the command to love God with all our being. The second He takes from Leviticus 19:18—to love our neighbor as much as we love ourselves. Thus, Jesus boils down all the law of God into one principle—love directed to God and to others. Here Jesus is going to the very heart of the core dilemma of ethics. Human thinkers have for centuries felt there was a tension between the Law and love. *Should I do the legal thing or the loving thing?* Jesus is not so much picking one or two rules over the others. Nor is He choosing love over law, but rather He is showing that love is what fulfills the Law. The Law is not being fulfilled unless it is obeyed as a way of giving and showing love to God or others.[33]

"For whoever would save his life will lose it, but whoever loses his life for my sake will find it" (Matthew 16:25 NIV).

"But lay up for yourselves treasures in Heaven, where neither moth nor rust destroys and where thieves do not break in and steal" (Matthew 6:20 NIV).

Chase not the wind!

The following discussion is designed to provoke deep thought in you so that you may put the pieces of this spiritual puzzle we call life together. It will also inspire you to go on your own spirit quest. Fear not! Take God with you on your journey! You can't lose!

Chapter 37

Discussion

For as long as man has walked the earth, there have been questions that persistently beguile all humanity. *Why do we exist? What is the purpose of human life?* These questions have provoked deep soul-searching and have been the nidus of institutional discourse and treatise.

Other multifaceted questions that have also weighed heavily upon humanity include the following: *Who made the heavens and earth? Is anyone in control? Does God exist? If so, what or whom is God, and what is God's role in our lives? If there is a supernatural force that created what we are and where we are, then how do we better understand this Creator and potentially make life better for ourselves in a world that is so harsh, unforgiving, cruel, and always lethal?*

Another infamous question I hear often is as follows: *If God exists, then why would He allow such horrible things to happen?* Questions of God have always existed and always will until the heavens and earth pass away. "Heaven and earth will pass away, but my words will not pass away" (Matthew 24:35 NIV).

God doesn't make terrible things happen in this world. We do! I will explain this now, follow it.

God is love. The very essence of pure love is God. "Anyone who does not *love* does not know God, because God is love" (1 John 4:8 NIV). "In the beginning God created the Heavens and the earth" (Genesis 1:1 NAB). After God created the earth and then the creatures of the earth, He created man. Most of us have heard the Bible verse "Then God said, Let Us make man in our image, according to our likeness" (Genesis 1:26 HCSB).

God created man in His own image, but that doesn't mean that God looks like the men or women we see in the mirror (i.e., our temporary, earthly, fleshy vehicles). "Or do you not know that your body is a temple of the Holy Spirit within you, whom you have from God? You are not your own" (1 Corinthians 6:19 ESV). We hold in us all a spark of God. That's how we were made in the image and likeness of God, not by our physical attributes.

God is loving and forgiving and has challenged His creation of man with the task of acquiring spiritual evolution and growth. Why spiritual evolution? We all emanate from the eternal spirit world where souls come from God. Therefore, souls are perfect and do not need growth. However, humanity certainly does. "For the mind set on the flesh is death, but the mind set on the Spirit is life and peace, because the mind set on the flesh is hostile toward God; for it does not subject itself to the law of God, for it is not even able to do so, and those who are in the flesh cannot please God" (Romans 8:6–8 NASB).

We accept gladly the opportunity to incarnate into the flesh and are given free will as humans. *Free will* is the key to tremendous spiritual growth while in the flesh. Remember, our souls are from God and therefore perfect. *Soul* doesn't require advancement; the spirit of man does.

As stated in the introduction, our ultimate challenge is to align the lowest expression of who we are, our corporeal physical selves, as closely as possible with our highest selves or our God centers. When this is achieved, humanity will communicate directly with God. Therefore, no further need for metaphor or inference will remain in our path to know truth or to understand God's ways and wisdom. The veil will be lifted, and humanity will break all bonds and limitations. Wisdom, talent, and holiness will ring true and free. The kingdom of God will be here on earth as it is in heaven.

When we return to the spirit world from which we came, we do so with evolution and spiritual growth as everlasting accomplishments for humanity. Simon Peter said to Him, "Lord where are you going?" Jesus answered Him, "Where I am going you cannot follow me now, but you will follow afterward" (John 13:36 ESV).

If humanity did not have free will inborn in us, we would only be a species programmed and animated by virtue of our genetic code. Free will is all about challenge, choice, action, outcome, and the consequences that result thereof. Without our free will to interpret and decipher the interplay of challenge, choice, action, outcome, and consequence, spiritual evolution is nil. Free will is a gift from God, but unless subdued and controlled, free will can certainly lead you astray.

Along with being born of free will comes the challenge of hedging your spiritual evolution and growth against the consequences of your actions, thus potentially generating negative karma for yourself. Karma literally means *works* or *actions*. Since most of our actions in life have either positive or negative effects on ourselves and others, we can speak of accruing both good and bad karma during each lifetime.

In theory, if our good karma outweighs our bad karma, our next birth will find us in circumstances that are more conducive to spiritual growth. If the opposite is the case … well, we don't even want to think about that.[34] Many in this world accept the karmic construct as truth, yet many do not. I believe it to be true, but I also believe it may be changing. Humanity as a whole may or may not have passed a karmic marker whereby the chains of karma may no longer be necessary. That topic in and of itself is fascinating but beyond the scope of this writing.

To further elucidate the relationship between free will and karma, we must understand that our free will is also subject to that part of us called the ego. You can think of the ego as a karma generator. Ego is the Latin word for I, that portion of one's self that distinguishes it from the selves of others. Every one of us is born with a fully intact ego. *The ego is the seat of our human will.* Let me repeat that. *The ego is the seat of our human will.*

The ego is apparently also our inborn *human navigation system.* It's like a GPS. It guides us in our quest for earthly and physical success. Chances are that you drive a car equipped with a navigation system (commonly called GPS), or you have a handheld GPS device or a smart phone that comes with GPS. The GPS navigation system serves as a good location finder when you are lost or trying to make your way through busy streets.[35] So the ego is a necessary component to the human experience. If you had no ego, you would not have free will or free choice, which is so important to the spiritual progression of each soul.[36] I take this to mean the human spiritual evolution through the soul's effort and intent. *Remember the soul does not need growth or advancement. The spirit of humanity does!*

You may say, "Okay, what's the big deal? We have an ego that looks out for us and helps us navigate this dog-eat-dog world. Shouldn't we have such a guidance system?" Yes. Ego is not entirely a detriment; it keeps you focused on important matters such as survival and commitment to work.[37]

It sounds logical and straight forward until you consider that, among other things, *the ego is also the father of fear.* When asked the question, "What is the opposite of love?" most people will answer, "Hate." That is a very understandable answer. The correct answer, however, is fear. *The opposite of love is fear.*

If God is love (and God is) and if the ego is the father of fear (and it is), then the ego plays a role that opposes God, thus creating deep inner conflict and challenge within us based upon our inborn spiritual duality of God v. ego, love v. fear, and light v. dark.

You see, we are born into a physical world of duality. Everything seems to have an opposite. If there is a left, there is a right—cold v. hot, up v. down, male v. female, etc. However, we are also born into spiritual duality with a core that is love or, the child of God (our God center). We are also born with an intact and functioning ego that is the father of fear. Remember the opposite of love is fear. How do two major but opposite influences live within the same individual? In the great quest for human spiritual advancement and enlightenment, this is where the rubber meets the road.

Examples of duality within the minds and hearts of man are as follows: love and fear, God and ego, spiritual will and human will. As the opposite of love, fear gives rise to all things negative. *Fear does not exist in the eternal spirit world of our Creator.* The world we know we come from and will return to is eternal, devoid of fear and all that is born of fear. Thus, there is no struggle. No struggle means no growth. Humanity requires growth. Thus, we have our struggles, and they are actually gifts.

Fear gives birth to anger, hate, deception, lies, envy, infidelity, aggression, attack, violence, war, scarcity, greed, starvation, trauma, disease, etc. Pretty much everything you see on any international news program is the derivation of a fear-based world, created by individuals and also by the collective ego of man (i.e., the will of man), not God.

In each and every one of us, we have a battle raging on and on. We have the great battle of the light and the dark going on inside us. There are some who recognize the ego as Satan, the father of fear and lies. You are of your father, the devil, and your will is to do your father's desires. He was a murderer from the beginning, and he does not stand in the truth because there is no truth in him. When he lies, he speaks out of his own character, for he is a liar and the father of all lies (John 8:44 ESV). People lie to us every day on TV through advertising, politics, the news, and in every other aspect of our lives. The lies and deceptions come from the all too pervasive ego-driven mentality.

The child of God within us is battling the ego and its fear-driven mentality. The ego knows that it's child of fear cannot survive in a world of God's love because it is inherently the opposite of and ultimately subject to God's love. Therefore, the ego strives to create a world devoid of God and God's love, thus assuring its own importance and survival. If you deny God's existence and deny the fact that you are a child of God, then there is nothing left but ego and the world that results thereof!

Remember, the light always annihilates the dark. Darkness never obliterates the light. Shine a light into the darkness, and the darkness flees. Take away the light, and you will have darkness but only when the light chooses to not be present. You can't add darkness to a brightly lit room and have it become dark.

So the ego wants to control you. Thus, you end up subject to the ways of this physical plane and all its tendencies and pitfalls. You can think of this internal spiritual battle like a soccer match—the child of God v. the father of fear. The ball being kicked around is your free will. The battle is all about winning your free will and ultimately, your loyalty. Do you choose the ascension and spiritual growth of humanity via God's will or the dark ego-driven world of fear that creates all you see that is negative in this world? Which side are you on?

This great battle between the light and the dark is also known as spiritual warfare. This spiritual warfare is raging on at a universal level, a global level, and within each and every one of us. Because we truly are all connected by God's river of love and light, each one of us by virtue of our overall energy will contribute to the collective net energy of the planet and humanity itself. Believe it.

Many will ask why there is no peace in the world. There will never be peace until all humanity can stop putting ego first and start putting God first instead.[38] Repeat that line to yourself over and over again!

Consider the following: We are all subject to this inner spiritual conflict of the light and the dark. The individuals who are chosen, elected, or born into positions of control and power over us are ultimately a manifestation of the collective free will of the people who put them there. Our minds are constantly bombarded with propaganda to keep you subject to a world driven by fear. Thus, our choices are controlled. Maybe you don't believe this. Just turn on the news. There's a reason that news programming is intentionally one negative story after the next designed to enshroud us in fear and negativity.

If you allow this process to affect you—and we all do to differing degrees—then you make choices based on fear and not God's will. Depending on how susceptible you are as an individual and as a people or nation, this can go either way as most of us know. There is an immense, sustained pressure for the control of our thoughts and will through the educational systems, corporations, banking, consumerism, governments, media, militaries, and/or religious orders for that matter. My brothers and sisters, the stakes couldn't be any higher!

Therefore, how can any nation or people on earth possibly live in peace or with the love of God if the battle hasn't been won over on an individual level? Charity begins at home. Thus, individuals who have yet to put the love of God before their egos will be subject to the ego's child of fear and therefore live in a fear-based world that they have created! However, the child of God within us all will urge us toward unconditional love, compassion, and empathy without the thought of the ego and its influence.

Remember God is love, but the ego is the seat of the will of man and the father of fear. The ego's fear gives rise to all that opposes the love of God. Thus, God doesn't cause terrible things to happen on earth. By our inability to choose love over fear, we do!

By baptism, the Holy Spirit takes up His abode in us, and St. Paul tells us in the epistle to the Romans, "If the Spirit of Him who raised Jesus from the dead is living in you, then He who raised Jesus from the dead will give life to your own mortal bodies through his Spirit living in you" (Romans 8:11). "We must give our most prized possession—our Will—unite it to His, and through the power of His Holy Spirit, be transformed into Jesus. To be called to such a dignity is a greater act of His Goodness than all creation."[39]

Jesus came to us to be the Lamb of God, paying for the sins of humanity, and to lead an exemplary life. That life is to be emulated thus—whether by baptism as infants or by being reborn and baptized in the Holy Spirit as adults. We must strive to be like Jesus. The lamb is a symbol of sacrifice. In ancient times some used a pure heifer or a goat. The term *scapegoat* is an ancient biblical term used for one who was innocent but paid for the sins or indiscretion of others.

Keep watching and praying so that you may not come into temptation. The spirit is willing, but the flesh is weak (Mark 14:38 NASB). In this famous Bible verse, the *spirit* is our God center or highest self, and the flesh represents our bodies with their egos, our lowest self. This Bible verse depicts why we have a great challenge in upholding our godly spiritual nature. Our flesh is weak, and we are subject to our egos and all their tendencies. The potential for great spiritual growth and advancement occurs while in our earthly temples of flesh because it's a great spiritual challenge to subdue the unholy flesh and its ego. What is a temple but a place for learning and spiritual growth?

If you begin to mull over a tempting thought in your mind, your emotions will be affected, and the likelihood of yielding to that temptation is increased. The fact that our emotions are a product of our thought lives is the general opinion of mental health workers. We can't directly control our feelings, but we can control what we think.[40] Stay focused upon Jesus, and live as He lived. The next day he saw Jesus coming to him and said, "Behold, the Lamb of God who takes away the sins of the world" (John 1:29 NASB).

If you recognize certain themes or challenges recurring in your life, then it's a good bet that there's something you haven't mastered, so dig deep and look within! As we evolve, we will eventually recognize that we must put our egos aside and use them as we may and not be used by them. When we have mastered what we were meant to master from the human experience, then we have won the right to stay in the presence of God in a heavenly world of love and light where the tribulations of this world cannot touch us. The cycle of death and rebirth will be broken. However, if you then choose to reincarnate to assist humanity, it's of your doing and a blessing, not a sentence that is inescapable by karmic law.

Many indigenous societies hold a deep belief in reincarnation and in the migration of the departed soul into another person, animal, tree, or other life form.[41] Recall my experience with Indian spirit sage Sliver Birch in the forest of Elm Ridge, New York. Although I do not know (and doubt) if humans become animals and vice versa, I often think about my encounters with my animal spirit guides and the many visions that clearly guided me. God's creatures are as close to us as they can be. Honor them and you honor God.

This is my life. These spiritual and metaphysical things have happened to me all my life, and I am absolutely God's child and servant. Therefore, I titled this book *My Life with God*. God encompasses *all* the things I have spoken of in this book. This book is not about religion. It's about God and *our* relationship with God, no matter who you are.

Although we are here striving for spiritual growth, we are also attempting to regain the Garden of Eden and bringing about the kingdom of God here on earth as it is in heaven. When we reach spiritual enlightenment as a species, the kingdom will be won! "Truly, truly, I say to you, if anyone keeps my words, he will never see death" (John 8:51 ESV).

Ultimately, we will learn to live by the love of God, which was given to us as a gift. Then and only then will we individually live as true children of God who are made in the image and likeness of the Lord. That which is born of the flesh is flesh, and that which is born of the spirit is spirit (John 3:6 NIV).

"For the Kingdom of God is not eating and drinking, but righteousness and peace and joy in the Holy Spirit" (Romans 14:17 NIV).

I believe that each story in this book shows what can be achieved when we live by God's love and light and let our hearts lead the way as we walk! Whether you turn to the right or to the left, your ears will hear a voice saying, "This is the way; walk in it" (Isaiah 30:21).[42]

Therefore, let God's love take over as your willful navigation system. Open your hearts and minds to God's river of love and light, and share it with your brothers and sisters. When enough of us choose to live lives with love, then we truly find our lives with God. When enough of us choose our lives with God, we then bring the kingdom of God here on earth as it is in heaven.

"Again, I tell you, it is easier for a camel to pass through the eye of a needle than for a rich person to enter the Kingdom of God" (Matthew 19:24 ESV).

"Enter by the narrow gate. For the gate is wide and the way is easy that leads to destruction, and those who enter it are many" (Matthew 7:13 ESV).

"For the gate is narrow and the way is hard that leads to life, and those who find it are few" (Matthew 7:14 ESV).

"And Jesus spoke to them saying; I am the light of the world. Whoever follows me will not walk in darkness, but will have the light of life" (John 8:12 ESV).

"Jesus said to him, I am the way, and the truth and the life. No one comes to the father except through me" (John 14:6 ESV).

"Neither shall they say, Lo here! Or, Lo there! For behold, the Kingdom of God is within you" (Luke 17:21 KJV).

The conclusion that follows should entice you to seek God in all that you may do. Remember this physical life is brief and can be thought of as a spiritual test. Why would you leave your best effort at the door? Open your hearts now, and choose to enter the kingdom of God!

Chapter 38

Conclusion

"In the beginning was the Word, and the Word was with God, and the word was God. He was with God in the beginning" (John 1:1 ESV). "Life was in Him, and that life was the light of men. That light shines in the darkness, yet the darkness did not overcome it: (John 1:4–5 ESV). "But to all who did receive Him, He gave them the right to be children of God, to those who believe in His name, who were born, not of blood, or of the will of the flesh, or of the will of man, but of God" (John 1:12–13 ESV). So, Jesus said to them, "The light is among you for a little while longer. Walk while you have the light, lest darkness overtake you. The one who walks in the darkness does not know where he is going" (John 12:35 ESV).

The world has fallen into accelerated darkness over the last two hundred years or so. It isn't that darkness and out-of-control egos didn't exist in ancient times. We know they did and in a very big way. Although modern progress and industrialization are good things, they have also been unfortunately manipulated and misused to bring about a displacement or an un-grounding of man. Along with displacement comes an uncoupling from God, our very life source.

346

After the agricultural age was supplanted by the industrial era (circa 1760–1840), families, which are the sovereign building blocks of any society, have been methodically undermined and intentionally attacked by dark forces driven by greed and the lust for power and control. "Bless those who curse you, pray for those who abuse you" (LUKE 6:28 ESV).

Industrialization has made it easy for a relatively few powerful people who are apparently estranged from God's love and light to systematically control and enslave the world. The out-of-control egos of these people and principalities (bloodlines) that believe themselves the rulers of the world have perpetrated intentional chaos to control humanity and make it appear as though God doesn't exist. Thus, we might place our only hope in them! *These perpetrators of darkness are* not *the solution to the chaos that they themselves have intentionally created in the world. God is!*

People everywhere now place their thoughts and energies into protecting themselves and their families from the fear and horrors of corrupt and deceitful political systems, war, terrorism, homelessness, forced displacement, out-of-control immigration, violence, disease, a deceptive and corrupt global pharmaceutical industry, starvation, malnutrition, poverty, a corrupt world banking system, and the corrupt global business cartels including the politicians manipulated by their power, etc. People are in a contrived survival mode, and the emotional trauma put upon them is horrific and has never been worse.

As long as the fear mentality is fed and nurtured by a very capable and powerful media system—and it is. It really doesn't matter if the threat is real or just perceived. Perception *is* reality, and the perception of fear absolutely drives a consciousness of sickness and disease. The news media keeps your consciousness tuned to the channel of fear. Fear also effectively and convincingly drives a wedge between individuals within any given country and also between nations.

Consider this profound concept: "Your consciousness affects every single cell in your body." Look up *The Biology of Belief* by Dr. Bruce Lipton.[43] Dr. Lipton was one of my former medical school professors. If your manipulated, ego-driven consciousness tells you to be concerned with only yourself, then you won't go the extra mile for your brothers and sisters. However, when you hold God's love and light or the Christ consciousness, you will foster health and well-being, and you will surround yourself and others with God's love. When you hold the Christ consciousness, you will no longer be subject to fear and the manipulation being perpetrated upon people all over the world. The dark, fear-based, ego-driven system of a lower energy can't reach you because you will literally live at a higher energy level.

Who benefits from a sick society? The very same people who create it and control it benefit from it. Just observe how fear, negativity, and sadness is pumped into your brains by the news or other television programming, which is then followed quickly by a commercial for pharmaceuticals. Do you think that's a coincidence? Television "programming" absolutely refers to what is being fed to you so as to "program" your brains therefore your consciousness.

The very people who are guilty of throwing the world into intentional chaos are, in fact, our brothers and sisters that unfortunately walk in darkness. They have either lost their way or have never known the right path. They may be victims themselves of generational darkness. And Jesus said, "Father forgive them, for they know not what they do" (Luke 23:34 ESV). "They truly do walk in darkness and can't comprehend the light. But whoever hates his brother is in the darkness and walks in the darkness, and does not know where he is going, because the darkness has blinded his eyes" (1 John 2:11 ESV).

Understand that the deep, persistent feeling of emptiness and longing that so many in this world experience is really their deepest inner desire to reconnect with their Creator and no longer be subject to a fear-based world. For some, those feelings are all-consuming, but unfortunately for others, not so much. Those feelings are a sure sign that you know you've been distracted from the truth and that you have been engaged in a chasing of the wind, thus missing out on a far better, much more glorious way to live. You are waking up to realize that what you thirst for is truly the love and the light of God. This is exactly what is supposed to happen to all of us. "For at one time you were darkness, but now you are light in the Lord. Walk as children of light" (Ephesians 5:8 ESV).

If you have been affected by the darkness and the trials and tribulations of this world as most have, then it's your time to take action! It is the time for the billions of people on this planet to respond to the spiritual call to arms. It is time to stop the madness of a manipulated, out-of-control, fear-based world and shine God's light brightly to drive the darkness away. There is an appointed time for everything and a time for every purpose under the heavens (Ecclesiastes 3:1–8 NAB).

The spiritual call to arms means learning how to pray, meditate, and acknowledge that you are a child of God! It means remembering who you are, a child of the creator of heaven and earth! You will start living a glorious life filled with God's love and kindness every day of the rest of your life when you love God above all and love your neighbor as yourself. Connect with God, your heart's true desire. As you become joyous in your connection to God, you will fall in love with God like a bride has fallen in love with the bridegroom.

As you allow God's presence to grow in you, there will be a moment when you reach a state of constant prayer. This means that you have now accepted God as your inner navigator and subdued your ego. Every inner thought will no longer be between you and your ego but will be a conversation between you and God!

This book isn't just about John Gerard Gallucci. This book is about you, the reader. Understand that you are never alone. Invite the Holy Spirit into your life. This is the way you will change the world—one person and one thought at a time.

"For as a young man marrieth a virgin, so shall thy sons marry thee: and as the bridegroom rejoiceth over the bride, so shall thy God rejoice over thee" (Isaiah 62:5 KJV).

God bless you, my brothers and sisters. May our Lord's love, peace, and wisdom be within you all the days of your life.

Remember who you are!

Notes

1   Evan T. Pritchard, *Bird Medicine: The Sacred Power of Bird Shamanism.* (Rochester, VT: Bear & Company, 2013), 31.

2   Mike Williams, *The Shaman Spirit: Discovering the Wisdom of Nature, Power Animals, Sacred Places and Rituals* (London: Watkins Publishing, 2013).

3   Pritchard, *Bird Medicine*, 102.

4   Pritchard, *Bird Medicine*, 100.

5   Ted Andrews, *Animal Speak: The Spiritual and Magical Powers of Creatures Great and Small* (Woodbury, MN: Llewellyn Publications, 1993).

6   Manley P. Hall, *The Secret Teachings of All Ages* (Los Angeles: Philosophical Research Society, 1977), LXXV.

7   Andrews, *Animal Speak*, 2.

8   Andrews, *Animal Speak*, 16.

9   I. William Lane and Linda Comac, *Sharks Don't Get Cancer: How Shark Cartilage Can Save Your Life* (New York: Avery Publishing, 1992).

10   Pritchard, *Bird Medicine*. 2.

11   Ron Rhodes, *1001 Unforgettable Quotes about God, Faith and the Bible* (Eugene, OR: Harvest House Publishers, 2001), 63.

12   Rhodes, *1001 Unforgettable Quotes about God, Faith and the Bible*, 234.

13   Rhodes, *1001 Unforgettable Quotes about God, Faith and the Bible*, 232.

14   Rhodes, *1001 Unforgettable Quotes about God, Faith and the Bible*, 185.

15   Jacqueline Mros, "Saving Olivia," *New Jersey Monthly Magazine*, November 2008, 43–44.

16   Anthony Stern, *Everything Starts from Prayer, Second Edition* (Ashland, OR: White Cloud Press, 2009), 142.

17   "Our Catholic Prayers," 2016, www.ewtn.com/faith/teachings/purgb3.htm.

18   Ray T. Malbrough, *The Magical Power of the Saints, Evocations and Candle Rituals* (Woodbury, MN: Llewellyn Publications, 2010), 68.

19   Malbrough, *The Magical Power of the Saints, Evocations and Candle Rituals*, 68.

20   Stern, *Everything Starts from Prayer*, 1.

21 Charles Hunter and Frances Hunter, *How to Heal the Sick* (New Kensington, PA.: Whitaker House, 1971), 50.

22 Rhodes, *1001 Unforgettable Quotes about God, Faith and the Bible*, 10.

23 Rhodes, *1001 Unforgettable Quotes about God, Faith and the Bible*, 11.

24 Hunter and Hunter, *How to Heal the Sick*, 184.

25 Vassula Ryden, *Heaven Is Real but So Is Hell* (New York: Alexian Publishers, 2013).

26 Vassula Ryden, *True Life In God* (New York: Alexian Limited, 2013).

27 Mark Virkler and Patti Virkler, *Rivers of Grace: Raising Children by the Spirit Rather than the Law* (Kent, England: Sovereign World Publishers, 2002), 107.

28 John Eckhardt, *Prayers that Bring Healing and Activate Blessings* (Lake Nary, FL: Charisma House, 2011), 28.

29 Sylvia Barbanell, *When a Child Dies* (Norwich, England: Pilgrim Books, 1942), Foreword.

30 Paula A. Price, *The Prophet's Dictionary: The Ultimate Guide to Supernatural Wisdom* (Kensington, PA: Whitaker House, 2006), 409.

31 Rose Vanden Eynden, *Metatron: Invoking the Angel of God's Presence* (Woodbury, MN: Llewellyn Publications, 2008).

32 Timothy Keller, *Jesus the King: Understanding the Life and Death of the Son of God.* (New York: Riverhead Books, 2011), 136–37.

33 Keller, *Jesus the King*, 145–46.

34 Richard Harper, *Jesus, Buddha Krishna and Lao Tzu: The Parallel Sayings* (Charlottesville, VA: Hampton Roads Publishing, 2007), 135.

35 Jide Lawore, *GPS: God's Positioning System: Locating God's Plan and Purpose for Your Life* (Maitland, FL: Xulon Press, 2012), 25.

36 Eynden, *Metatron*, 159.

37 Eynden, *Metatron*, 131.

38 Eynden, *Metatron*, 132.

39 Mother M. Angelica, *Inside the Kingdom* (Irondale, AL: EWTN Catholic Publishers, 1977), 37–38.

40 Neil T. Anderson, *Victory Over the Darkness: Realize the Power of Your Identity in Christ* (Minneapolis, MN: Bethany House Publishers, 2013), 155–56.

41 Itzhak Beery, *The Gift of Shamanism* (Tortonto: Destiny Books, 2015), 44.

42 Lawore, *GPS: God's Positioning System*, 25.

43 Bruce Lipton, *Biology of Belief*, www.youtube.com/watch?V=jjj0xVM4x1I

Bibliography

Anderson, Neil T. *Victory Over the Darkness: Realize the Power of Your Identity in Christ.* Minneapolis, MN: Bethany House Publishers, 2013.

Andrews, Ted. *Animal Speak: The Spiritual and Magical Powers of Creatures Great and Small* Woodbury, MN: Llewellyn Publications, 1993.

Angelica, Mother M. *Inside the Kingdom.* Irondale, AL: EWTN Catholic Publishers, 1977.

Barbanell, Sylvia. *When a Child Dies.* Norwich, England: Pilgrim Books, 1942.

Beery, Itzhak Beery. *The Gift of Shamanism.* Toronto: Destiny Books, 2015.

Eckhardt, John. *Prayers that Bring Healing and Activate Blessings.* Lake Nary, FL: Charisma House, 2011.

Eynden, Rose Vanden. *Metatron: Invoking the Angel of God's Presence.* Woodbury, MN: Llewellyn Publications, 2008.

Hall, Manley P. *The Secret Teachings of All Ages.* Los Angeles: Philosophical Research Society, 1977.

Harper, Richard Harper. *Jesus, Buddha Krishna and Lao Tzu: The Parallel Sayings.* Charlottesville, VA: Hampton Roads Publishing, 2007.

Hunter, Charles, and Frances Hunter. *How to Heal the Sick.* New Kensington, PA: Whitaker House, 1971.

Keller, Timothy. *Jesus the King: Understanding the Life and Death of the Son of God.* New York: Riverhead Books, 2011.

Lane, William I., and Linda Comac. *Sharks Don't Get Cancer: How Shark Cartilage Can Save Your Life.* New York: Avery Publishing, 1992.

Lawore, Jide. *GPS: God's Positioning System: Locating God's Plan and Purpose for Your Life.* Maitland, FL: Xulon Press, 2012.

Lipton, Bruce. *Biology of Belief.* www.youtube.com/watch?V=jjj0xVM4x1I.

Malbrough, Ray T. *The Magical Power of the Saints, Evocations and Candle Rituals.* Woodbury, MN: Llewellyn Publications, 2010.

Mros, Jacqueline. "Saving Olivia." *New Jersey Monthly Magazine*, November 2008.

"Our Catholic Prayers," 2016, www.ewtn.com/faith/teachings/purgb3.htm.

Price, Paula A. *The Prophet's Dictionary: The Ultimate Guide to Supernatural Wisdom.* Kensington, PA: Whitaker House, 2006.

Pritchard, Evan T. *Bird Medicine: The Sacred Power of Bird Shamanism.* Rochester, VT: Bear & Company, 2013.

Rhodes, Ron. *1001 Unforgettable Quotes about God, Faith and the Bible.* Eugene, OR: Harvest House Publishers, 2001.

Ryden, Vassula. *Heaven Is Real but So Is Hell.* New York: Alexian Publishers, 2013.

Ryden, Vassula. *True Life In God.* New York: Alexian Limited, 2013.

Stern, Anthony. *Everything Starts from Prayer, Second Edition.* Ashland, OR: White Cloud Press, 2009.

Virkler, Mark, and Patti Virkler. *Rivers of Grace: Raising Children by the Spirit Rather than the Law.* Kent, England: Sovereign World Publishers, 2002.

Williams, Mike. *The Shaman Spirit: Discovering the Wisdom of Nature, Power Animals, Sacred Places and Rituals.* London: Watkins Publishing, 2013.

John Gerard Gallucci, MD, is a board certified, award-winning pediatric and neonatal general and thoracic surgeon who has held the designation of "Top Doctor" in his home state of New Jersey for many years. He is also a reiki master, energy healer, and prayer warrior who genuinely uses the energy of the Holy Spirit to heal families' hearts, minds, bodies, and souls.

CPSIA information can be obtained
at www.ICGtesting.com
Printed in the USA
BVHW041910260619
552045BV00001B/12/P

9 781982 222093